S0-BDL-286

DON'T LOOK
ROUND

"One is never cured of his childhood. Too happy, as in my case, it exhaled an aroma with which the present cannot compete; too unhappy, it poisons life at its source. In either case, it is wiser *not to look round.*"

VIOLET TREFUSIS

DON'T LOOK
ROUND

with an introduction by
PETER QUENNELL

VIKING

To the memory of my beloved mother

VIKING
Published by the Penguin Group
Viking Penguin, a division of Penguin Books USA Inc.,
375 Hudson Street, New York, New York 10014, U.S.A.
Penguin Books Ltd, 27 Wrights Lane, London W8 5TZ, England
Penguin Books Australia Ltd, Ringwood, Victoria, Australia
Penguin Books Canada Ltd, 10 Alcorn Avenue, Suite 300,
Toronto, Ontario, Canada M4V 3B2
Penguin Books (N.Z.) Ltd, 182–190 Wairau Road,
Auckland 10, New Zealand

Penguin Books Ltd, Registered Offices:
Harmondsworth, Middlesex, England

First American Edition
Published in 1992 by Viking Penguin,
a division of Penguin Books USA Inc.

1   3   5   7   9   10   8   6   4   2

Copyright in all countries of the International Copyright Union
All rights reserved

LIBRARY OF CONGRESS CATALOGING IN PUBLICATION DATA
Trefusis, Violet Keppel, 1894–1972.
Don't look around : her reminiscences/Violet Trefusis ; with
decorations by Philippe Jullian.
p.   cm.
Originally published: London : Hutchinson, 1952.
ISBN 0-670-84067-X
1. Trefusis, Violet Keppel, 1894–1972—Biography.   2. Novelists,
English—20th century—Biography.   3. Paris (France)—Intellectual
life—20th century.   I. Title.
PR6039.R39Z465   1992
823'.912—dc20   91–40790

Printed in the United States of America

Without limiting the rights under copyright reserved above,
no part of this publication may be reproduced,
stored in or introduced into a retrieval system, or transmitted, in any form
or by any means (electronic, mechanical, photocopying, recording or otherwise),
without the prior written permission of both the copyright
owner and the above publisher of this book.

CONTENTS

INTRODUCTION BY PETER QUENNELL

VIOLET TREFUSIS, who died on February 29th 1972 after a crippling accident and a long exhausting illness, both borne, I am told, with great courage, was a survivor of two interesting periods of recent European history—the Edwardian Age, when she had emerged as the attractive first child of her celebrated mother Mrs. George Keppel, and the busy, crowded years that preceded and followed World War II, during which, both at home and abroad, she had displayed her adult gifts.

On her contemporaries, even in her childhood, she evidently made a deep impression. Osbert Sitwell, at the time still a young officer, remembered meeting her some while before 1914 in Mrs. Keppel's London drawing-room—a highly precocious girl, already "cosmopolitan and exotic . . . with a vivid intelligence, a quick eye for character . . . an irresistible gift of mimicry and the ability to gather unexpected pieces of information . . . which she was wont to impart in a voice, eager but pitched in so low a key as sometimes to be inaudible. . . ." Similarly, again before 1914, she had gained the friendship of Victoria Sackville-West, the future poetess and novelist, who found her "Brilliant . . . extraordinary . . . almost unearthly", and rewarded her with a grown-up kiss at the conclusion of their earliest meeting.

The autobiography Violet Trefusis published in 1952 and dedicated "to the memory of my Beloved Mother" is a fascinating work from several different points of view—not only for what she tells us in her gaily cursive style, but also for what she deliberately omits; and her omissions include some of the most important details of her background and her personal career. Thus in the chapters that describe her Edwardian upbringing she makes no reference to the fact that Mrs. Keppel owed her place in Edwardian High Society to the position she long occupied, always with the greatest charm and discreet reserve, as the mistress of the King. Violet's new friend Victoria Sackville-West, on the other hand, was well acquainted with this open secret; and in her own autobiography (which her son Nigel Nicolson discovered after her death, and bravely and rightly published in 1973) she describes the visits she paid to the Keppels' house, and how she would often see an unobtrusive little one-horse brougham waiting at the door, and the butler would slip her into a dark corner of the hall, while a mysterious caller walked downstairs.

Certain episodes of Violet's later life are themselves given a slightly fictionalised shape. As a middle-aged war-time exile, she would talk frankly and amusingly about her engagement to Osbert Sitwell, and connect its breakdown with Osbert's disappointing insistence that, if they presently married, they would sleep at opposite ends of his father's gigantic medieval house, divided by many historic state-apartments and various alarming haunted rooms. But in her narrative Osbert has become an elusive Italian nobleman named Guido, whose strangely escapist tendencies she found it no less difficult to understand.

Finally, of course, her readers are told nothing of her stormy relationship, which blazed up between 1918 and 1921, and while it lasted nearly wrecked two marriages and enraged her extremely tolerant father, with Victoria Sackville-West, now the wife of Harold Nicolson. Nor does she seem quite fair to Denys Trefusis, her ill-fated but good-humoured husband, whose rôle in her life is rather summarily dealt with. That, while the crisis was at its worst, he must have suffered intolerable anxiety and strain is an aspect of the situation that she does not even cursorily admit, but she writes at some length of his 'nocturnal peregrinations' and his passion for Parisian night-clubs to which she vehemently objected.

Don't Look Round then is an assemblage of revelatory sketches —as she says in her preface, an anthology of 'selected moments, hand-picked'—rather than a conscientious self-portrait. But, as such, it continues to deserve our notice. Though it may not tell the whole truth, occasionally suppresses facts or refurbishes and improves on them, it still provides a 'speaking likeness' of the writer's many-sided personality.

Violet Trefusis, if we are to be completely candid, was a natural mythomaniac; and in England, during the Second World War, one soon grew accustomed to her habit of telling odd romantic tales. A country clergyman, whose church she sometimes attended when she inhabited a neighbouring manor house, was so enamoured of her, she said, that, once she had appeared, he could hardly get through the service; while, in London, an elderly retired diplomatist, a small nervous-looking man who bore some resemblance to Lewis Carroll's White Rabbit, pursued her with the ardour and assiduity of a Restoration rake.

All her stories, however, were told with a redeeming imaginative gusto; and in *Don't Look Round*, whether one suspects that she is blending fact and fancy, or deliberately by-passing a fact that now struck her as 'unpalatable', there is the same vivacious mind at work. It was not her fault, she must clearly have assumed, if the real everyday world were not always so picturesque and romantic as she felt it ought to be. Some additional flying touches, a few strokes of colour here and there, would give her recollections point and brio.

Latterly, after she had bought herself a delightful ancient house near Paris, she was more at her ease with French notabilities than in English social life; and a particularly rewarding section of the present book is devoted to the writers and artists she encountered while she lived and held her court at St. Loup. Besides Cocteau, whom she admired but did not altogether approve of, we meet the great poet Paul Valéry, "mumbling almost unintelligible epigrams beneath his chewed moustache", and the Franco-Roumanian poetess, Madame de Noailles, "tiny, brilliant, restless . . . always to be found at any hour of the day in precisely the same room . . . in precisely the same state of combative inanition . . .". The splendid Colette, too (who nicknamed Violet *Madame Géranium*, as her complexion grew slightly florid with the years), she captures in a line or two:

> I expressed surprise at seeing no animals hovering about her chair. "What," I enquired, "has become of the *chat si caressant* described in your last book?" "*Erreur*," rumbled the rich Burgundian voice, "*un chat n'est jamais caressant, il se caresse à vous.*"

Thus, despite its obvious limitations as a piece of searching self-analysis and an accurate record of her past, *Don't Look Round* remains a remarkably readable book, which its writer must surely have enjoyed composing. Her spirited narrative bounds along self-confidently from page to page. Biassed and partial it may be: pedestrian it never is.

PREFACE

I OWE an apology to those who expect, and are entitled to expect, accuracy, coherence, chronological order. This is not so much a narrative as an anthology: selected moments, hand-picked. Why burden the book with the 'long littleness of life', which the reader would only skip, and which I have skipped for him? On the other hand, may I remind him that *toute vérité n'est pas bonne à dire*. I have not lied, I have merely omitted, by-passed the truth, whenever unpalatable.

Violet Trefusis.

ITHAKA

Setting out on the voyage to Ithaka
You must pray that the way be long,
Full of adventures and experiences.
The Laistrygonians, and the Kyklopes,
Angry Poseidon,—don't be afraid of them:
You will never find such things on your way,
If only your thoughts be high, and a select
Emotion touch your spirit and your body.
The Laistrygonians, the Kyklopes,
Poseidon raging—you will never meet them,
Unless you carry them with you in your soul,
If your soul does not raise them up before you.

You must pray that the way be long:
Many be the summer mornings
When with what pleasure, with what delight
You enter harbours never seen before:
At Phoenician trading stations you must stop,
And must acquire good merchandize,
Mother of pearl and coral, amber and ebony,
And sensuous perfumes of every kind:
As much as you can get of sensuous perfumes:
You must go to many cities of Egypt,
To learn and still to learn from those who know.

You must always have Ithaka in your mind,
Arrival there is your predestination.
But do not hurry the journey at all.
Better that it should last many years:
Be quite old when you anchor at the island,
Rich with all you have gained on the way,
Not expecting Ithaka to give you riches.

Ithaka has given you your lovely journey.
Without Ithaka you would not have set out.
Ithaka has no more to give you now.

Poor though you find it, Ithaka has not cheated you.
Wise as you have become, with all your experience,
You will have understood the meaning of an Ithaka.

Translated from the Greek of G. P. Cavafy.

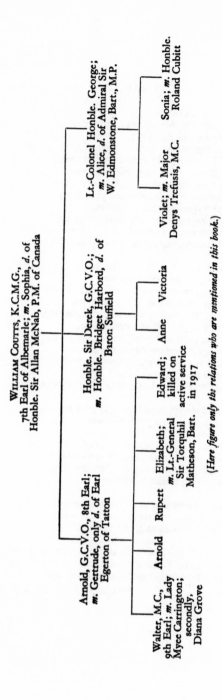

WILLIAM COUTTS, K.C.M.G.,
7th Earl of Albemarle; *m.* Sophia, *d.* of
Honble. Sir Allan McNab, P.M. of Canada

Arnold, G.C.V.O., 8th Earl;
m. Gertrude, only *d.* of Earl
Egerton of Tatton

Honble. Sir Derek, G.C.V.O.;
m. Honble. Bridget Harbord, *d.* of
Baron Suffield

Lt.-Colonel Honble. George;
m. Alice, *d.* of Admiral Sir
W. Edmonstone, Bart., M.P.

Arnold   Rupert   Elizabeth;   Edward;
m. Lt.-General   killed on
Sir Torquhil   active service
Matheson, Bart.   in 1917

Anne   Victoria

Violet; *m.* Major
Denys Trefusis, M.C.

Sonia; *m.* Honble.
Roland Cubitt

Walter, M.C.,
9th Earl; *m.* Lady
Myee Carrington;
secondly,
Diana Grove

(Here figure only the relations who are mentioned in this book.)

Part One

CHILDHOOD

CHAPTER ONE

WHAT, I ask myself conscientiously, is the first thing I remember?

Not one, I fear, that throws a very becoming light on the saturnine brat who trotted beside her aunt one dusty summer afternoon some fifty years ago. "Your hair," observed the brat, "is grey, but you think it is brown."

It must have been almost the first sentence I uttered. A child backward to the point of her mother's tapping her forehead and saying, "I detest precocious children, *but . . .*" I only translated my thoughts into speech when I was more or less certain of the pronunciation of the words I was about to utter. I remember feeling at a very early age a profound disgust for those contemporaries who traded on their baby ways to melt the hearts of grown-ups.

Of course, there were setbacks. One morning, upon being deposited on my mother's bed, she inquired what I had had for breakfast.

[15]

"Don't ask questions, fiss," was the reply—clearly a most unpleasant child.

Be it said in extenuation that I was very anxious not to be made a fool of. One of the things I most resented was that relations were in the habit of spelling words that they did not want me to understand. One day I remember deliberately laying a trap for them. I contrived to look so careworn that they bent over me solicitously. "What's the matter? Have you got a pain?"

"No. I am feeling very C I T."

"And what does that mean?"

"Cross."

My parents spoiled me disgracefully. My mother began as an atmosphere, a climate, luminous, resplendent, joyously embattled like golden armour; it was only later that I became conscious of her as an individual.

I basked in the climate of her love without asking myself any questions, until I was about five. Very soon she hit upon the right technique in dealing with me. Once, when I was very small, and of the opinion that I was not getting enough attention, I announced that I was going to run away. "Very well, run then," came the bland reply.

I started on a singularly flat fugue, pushing my little wheel-barrow in front of me. Nobody called. Nobody came. It was a complete fiasco. (In later life, other fugues were to be nipped in the bud by the same method.)

My mother never lost her temper. When roused to anger, which was seldom, she would let fall a few icy sentences. She never bore malice; was always the first to say she was sorry. She not only had a gift of happiness, but she excelled in making others happy. She resembled a Christmas-tree laden with presents for everyone. There was no limit to her largesse. In her many-chambered heart, the humblest had his niche. Old bores, old governesses, poor relations, were welcomed as though they were the cat's whiskers. Under her manipulation, the outcast blossomed as the rose.

The other person who, together with my mother, first impinged on my consciousness was my maternal grandmother, Lady Edmonstone.

A daughter of a Governor of the Ionian Isles, she was born in

Ithaca, where she lived a bare-footed and idyllic existence playing with her sisters among the bone-white rocks, tufted with thyme and rosemary.

As most children are regaled with fairy tales, she was regaled with stories from the *Odyssey*. Had not Odysseus and his companions set sail from this self-same island? When she was barely sixteen, a dashing young Scots naval officer appeared on the scene. Like young Lochinvar, he came out of the West. My grandmother was wooed and won, and taken to live in Glasgow. From Ithaca to Kelvinside! What an odyssey. How she must have loathed and resented the indefatigable rain, the sulphurous fogs, the grim bewhiskered elders!

Apparently, she bore it all with stoicism and philosophy. Year after year she gave birth to daughters; the long-awaited heir died in his infancy. At last, in 1868, she was rewarded. My uncle Archie was born, to join a plethora of sisters. Meanwhile, my grandfather had succeeded to the title and estate. Duntreath had been in the family ever since 1445, when Mary, daughter of Robert III of Scotland, married Sir William Edmonstone of Culloden; to her and her husband the lands of Duntreath were granted.

Extreme fastidiousness was the keynote of my grandmother's personality; she had the gift of making everything she touched seem precious—a cake, a book, a box of matches. She would make other people seem gross, earth-bound, as other countries appear fleshy and redundant compared to Greece. She enjoyed drawing birds with long, comet-like tails, like the birds in Coromandel screens. Once, when she was thus engaged, the house caught fire, and gusts of smoke invaded the room in which she was sitting; engrossed in her birds, she did not immediately notice.

Happily, in Grandmama's background hovered two blackish figures, her maid, Mrs. Wells, and Aunt Jessie Winnington-Ingram. They watched over her as guardian crows might watch over a bird of paradise.

Bewitched by Grandmama, I did not immediately appreciate the more sober charms of Aunt Jessie, whom I was to love so devotedly later on. If Gabbata (this was my nick-name for my grandmother) was her 'folly', she was Gabbata's 'reason'. I think that, in course of time, I may, to some extent, have become a reincarnation of that 'folly', as she forgave me everything unquestioningly.

[17]

My mother would remark, with legitimate disgust: "If Violet strangled a baby, Jessie would merely say: 'Why not indeed! There are far too many mouths to feed in the world already!'"

Aerial, ethereal, wise and innocent, my grandmother bore the same affinity to spring as winter branches, framed in frost, recall spring branches framed in blossom.

In the prim, conventional, L-shaped Wilton Terrace drawing-room she was indeed an incongruous, fairy-like figure. I always remember her in white.

★   ★   ★   ★   ★

As a child I was extremely fond of shopping, though I secretly resented the fact that I was never allowed to shop on my own. I once accompanied my mother to Bumpus's, the booksellers. Bumpus's was nearly always a prelude to a visit to Grandmama's. On this occasion, when we arrived to tea, I sidled up to the latter, dived into my diminutive muff, and produced a small, beautifully bound volume. "I stealed it for you," I announced with pride, and could not understand why, by no means convinced of wrong-doing, I was subsequently compelled not only to return the book, but to apologise to the bookseller.

I fear I must confess to recurrent thefts, chiefly of a hygienic nature (sponges, toothbrushes, etc.). I don't recollect how soon I gave up thieving as a profession. I think as soon as I realized it really upset my grandmother, and not, characteristically, because I realized it was in any way reprehensible.

Antique dealers ranked immediately after booksellers in my estimation. Little did my poor mother guess what seeds of future extravagance she was sowing in my all too receptive mind!

I remember being taken on one occasion to Duveen's in Bond Street. Sir Joseph was a friend of Mama's, and he had previously told her that he had just bought a charming old Victorian doll's house, with a lot of contemporary dolls 'for fun'. "Just the thing for your little girl! She can choose whatever doll she likes!" It sounded safe enough. It should not be difficult to orientate me on the doll's house. Off we went.

"There!" beamed Sir Joseph, opening the doll's house. "She can have her pick. She's not going to leave these premises without a present!"

"May I choose what I like?"

"Of course, of course! Now come, Mrs. Keppel, we will leave your little girl to play with the dolls. I want to show you some very fine pictures . . ."

I could scarcely prevent my lip from curling. I secretly despised dolls and all their ways. The moment their backs were turned, I started prowling round the shop. There were dozens of things which appealed to my fancy. What about the clock with the two little figures which looked as if they were playing hide-and-seek? What about the kneeling nigger holding a gilt shell, and the slippery red cabinet upheld by mermaids, and what about the ring that looked like a large blob of sealing-wax with a tiny person in the middle? Surely this was just the thing for me? Greatly daring, I took it out of its case. It would almost go round my wrist.

Taking everything into consideration, it could not fail to be the right choice. The other things would, no doubt, be thought too big. Twirling the ring round my thumb, I flew in search of my mother, and kind Sir Joseph.

"Hullo, hullo! What have we here!" exclaimed Sir Joseph with false joviality. "The Doge's ring! Now, what a clever little girl it is to have nosed that out!"

"Go and put it back at once, darling," my mother commanded.

"But it's my present!" I protested, clutching the ring with both hands. "Sir Joseph said I might choose what I liked!"

"He meant a doll, dear, not a ring. Go and put it back this minute!"

The tears welled up in my eyes. My faith in human nature was shaken.

Sir Joseph's eyes wandered distressfully from my mother to me. Would it not be a gesture on his part, so unsemitic, and, yes, lordly, to give a fifteenth-century ring to a little girl of six?

"No, Mrs. Keppel," there were almost tears in *his* eyes now, "she shall keep it, as she chose it. After all, it is only made of lava; it is the historical association which makes it valuable."

"Sir Joseph, you must not dream——"

"But I must, Mrs. Keppel, I must! It will be something for her to remember me by, when she's grown up . . ." His voice trailed away. . . .

★   ★   ★   ★   ★

"Never, as long as I live," scolded my mother, as soon as we got into the electric brougham, "will I take you shopping again!"

★   ★   ★   ★   ★

Because I have not yet mentioned my father, let it not be imagined that he had no place in my heart.

A more detached figure, he was not fraught with the immediate significance of my mother and my grandmother; there were no penalties connected with his personality, no criticism came from his handsome lips. I loved him very much, but quite differently, with coquetry, admiration, and, yes, camaraderie. I neither dreaded, nor idolized.

Kind-hearted, spontaneous, he was easily pleased, easily appeased, willing to believe the best of everyone, the best of life. He was what the French call *bon public*, an optimist.

Though, of necessity, a man of the world, certain things were sacrosanct: his country, family traditions, friendships; no one ever had a loyaller or more disinterested friend. He could be relied upon to see the ethical aspect of every situation in its pristine form, unclouded by fashionable prejudice, uncamouflaged by extenuating circumstances. (There are certain invincible errors which should never be attacked.)

Like most large men, he was methodical, scrupulously tidy, deriving great satisfaction from small neat things, gadgets, labour-saving devices.

Late in life he discovered classical painting. The pictures he had always taken for granted suddenly spoke to him: he was enlightened, transported. No neophyte ever laboured more conscientiously to become acquainted with the tenets of his newly found faith.

Till the end, he retained the faculty of awe and marvelling, a singular freshness of spirit. He never really grew up, that is why he got on so well with children who instinctively felt he was 'on their side'.

Both parents competed in telling me bedtime stories. Papa's were intrepid, if orthodox, in the manner of Sandford and Merton, Mama's, on the other hand, were a startling mixture of fantasy and realism.

'Once upon a time, there was a Manchu princess, who kept a singing cricket the price of a Derby winner'. . . .

My sister, Sonia, was born when I was six. Jealous, no doubt, of my prerogative as an only child, I did not fancy her, and eyed her cradle with distaste.

Later so good-looking, she swiftly developed into a remarkably plain little girl with tow-coloured hair and protruding teeth. Her tastes were rakish, plebeian: she had the impudence of a gutter-snipe. There was no attempt at fraternizing; she went her way, I went mine. Whenever our wills crossed, she had a wonderful retort, an ear-splitting whistle, which she kept up for hours. It is her proud boast that at the age of three she pushed me into the bath-tub fully dressed. I can remember the humiliation to this day. There I stood smug, secretive, stand-offish, tightly buttoned into a party frock; the incentive to push must have been irresistible.

She maintains that I did not speak to her until she was ten; it is quite possible that we exchanged more whistles than words.

What, as far as I can remember, finally broke the ice, was that we knew no one else on the homeward-bound boat to Europe from Ceylon in 1912, but I am anticipating.

*   *   *   *   *

Every year, on the first of August, we travelled North. The journey to Scotland was an excitement which never palled; we got our first taste of Edinburgh rock at Carlisle. After that, the stone walls, like crumbling necklaces framing a more and more lunar landscape, would begin. Sheep, with long melancholy black faces (not unlike Spanish grandees), would peer over them in a munching trance. The names of stations would be shouted out in an accent increasingly guttural: Edinburgh, Glasgow, Perth.

Aunt May lived in Perthshire, Aunt Sophie in Edinburgh, Uncle Archie in Stirlingshire. It would have been difficult to find three places more dissimilar. Stenton, in Perthshire, was the jolliest; Belmont, in Edinburgh, the most sedate; Duntreath, in Stirlingshire, the most beautiful.

Even as a child, I vaguely sensed that Stenton, as a house, was not all it should be, but I could not then, of course, have realized its enthusiastic, wanton, devil-may-care, hideosity. Architecturally non-committal, the interior was stuffed with all the horrors of the period. A period profaned, enlivened, by sport; cluttered up with tennis balls, golf clubs, fishing rods, aquascutums, croquet mallets, waders, gaffs.

True, in the drawing-room, where no one lingered, there was a semblance of decorum, a sop to convention. There were scalloped screens, fluffy lamp-shades, glossy landscapes which looked as though they might have been bought by the yard. There wasn't a single object in the room worth ten pounds. What did it matter? One was so seldom in it. When the inmates of Stenton weren't fishing, they were shooting; when they weren't playing golf, they were playing tennis. Comfort was exterior, rather than interior.

Then there was the Tay. The life of our community centred round the Tay. It was the justification of Stenton, its *raison d'être*. We anxiously studied the river's moods—was it 'muddy', was it 'low', were 'they' rising, were 'they' sulky? Was it to be a Jock Scot or a Silver Doctor? Oh, the thrill of watching the fisherman, a privilege I knew at six!

"Are they rising, Papa?"

"Hush, don't talk so loud."

"Please, may I come a little closer?"

"No, you'll get hooked."

Then the sudden plunge of the rod, the whirl of the reel, the leap to get clear, the bluff, the strategy, the final exhaustion of both fisherman and fish.

* * * * *

There was a pond for beginners. I began on the pond. You stood up to your knees in St. John's Wort, in a haze of midges, which, in venom and initiative, could out-do any mosquito.

You fished with a worm, miserably conscious of your inferiority. A tiny tug. You raised the rod too quickly. A tiny plop. Too small to keep, anyway.

If you were lucky, you returned home with four or five muddy little trout slung by their gills to a twig.

* * *. * *

Stenton was inhabited by a remarkable, an unconventional, family, despite its reassuring sporting activities. My Uncle Graham, at one time Lord Advocate of Scotland,[1] was one of the ablest men of his

[1] Later Viscount Dunedin.

day. His many-faceted mind embraced all kinds of things, from the humanists to the encyclopaedists, from Melanchthon to Diderot; he spoke ten languages, all equally badly, but wrote at least three excellently well. One of his languages was Roumanian—*et pour cause*! He was for years the *cavaliere servante* of the so photogenic Queen Marie of Roumania. Physically, he resembled a pug.

He was unfailingly kind to me, and would, as a treat, take me for rides on his bicycle. My short legs dangled over the handlebars. "Who taught you to bicycle, Uncle Graham?"

"No one, I taught myself."

"The Duke of Connaught taught me!" I lied ecstatically. He had married my mother's sister, Mary, the one with whom she had most in common, who shared her tolerance, verve, enterprise, generosity. Indeed, Aunt Mary's generosity was a by-word, even in a notoriously open-handed family.

At the age of eight, or thereabouts, I became an ornithologist: I collected birds' eggs. Having seen an exhaustive work on the subject—four handsome Morocco-bound tomes at Bumpus's—I brazenly asked Aunt Mary to make me a present of it.

Even Aunt Mary thought this was going a bit too far.

"Surely, darling, you might find something a little cheaper? Ten pounds is a lot to give for books, especially to a little girl of your age."

"But, Aunt Mary, I am a Collector, I collect eggs."

"Yes, darling, I know: you also collect books, preferably first editions: likewise fifteenth-century jewellery. As far as I know you possess at least five eggs: a thrush's, a hedge sparrow's, a robin's, a linnet's and a pheasant's. Do you really consider your collection entitles you to such an important work of reference?"

Temporarily defeated, I let the matter drop, but what I could not have by fair means, I was determined to have by foul. A week later, I innocently inquired how many carriages my uncle and aunt possessed.

"Let me see: there's the brougham, the victoria, the wagonette, the dog cart——"

"Do you mean to say, Aunt Mary, that *with all those carriages* you cannot afford to give me my bird books?"

*   *   *   *   *

Neither were the Dunedins' progeny devoid of interest. First came Ronnie, a handsome, debonair, not very reliable figure; he and his elder sister were the least intelligent members of the family; then came Gladys, who had inherited the lion's share of the paternal brain. There was nothing on which she could not bring her luminous mind to bear: philosophy, philology, astronomy, theosophy: everything was grist to her mill. A genial sense of humour pervaded all her knowledge. Her younger sister, Marjorie, was just as good company; to a pungent wit, she added *cocasserie*, a sense of the ridiculous. They were all years older than I.

★　　★　　★　　★　　★

We usually went from the hurly-burly of Stenton, with its charades, practical jokes, larder-scavenging, salmon weighing, to the slightly etiolated, academic atmosphere of Belmont. Belmont was in the purlieus of Edinburgh, a large, square, Regency house filled with hot-house flowers and fine, rather 'late', Italian pictures.

Aunt Sophie was the antithesis of Aunt Mary, nervous, sensitive, highly emotional, she was continually blown from vapour to vapour, seldom getting through the day without a tiny tornado of tears. She had delightful, if absent-minded, manners.

Her maid, it is told, once burst into her bedroom in a state of panic. . . . "Madam! Madam! I've swallowed a pin!"

"Never mind, my dear, here's another."

Aunt Sophie was also addicted to malapropisms. "I refuse," she once declared, "to be a mere siphon in my own house!"

She was charming, gentle, forgiving, but she belonged to the neurotic, inhibited, *Angst*-conditioned side of the family.

★　　★　　★　　★　　★

Last of the Scottish visits, we come to Duntreath.

A car would meet us in Glasgow; it would drive us out, a matter of some fifteen miles. The mean streets of Glasgow, with its red-haired children playing in the gutter, the grim, shapeless figures rolling out of pubs, held a curious fascination for me. It had none of the civic dignity of Edinburgh, the prestige of Princes Street, with its extraordinary jewellers' shop windows over which, as a rule, a ram's head presided with cairngorms stuck in the tip of each horn. Glasgow, raw, strident, hideous, had a vitality of its own, mostly, it is true, derived from drink, but not without a certain raffish picturesqueness, reminiscent of a drawing by Jacques Callot. It is to Scotland what Chicago is to America, whereas Edinburgh is its Boston.

Once we had shaken off the slums, the suburbs, the hills rose, as it were, to meet us; presently, we would come to a little loch high and lonely, set in the moors like a monocle.

Suddenly, my favourite landmarks would heave in sight. The twin hills above Duntreath, Dumfoyne and Dumgoyne (they might as well have been called Tweedledum and Tweedledee), looked as though a giant had cut a slice out of them. A third and smaller hill, Dumgoyach, covered with curly, tousled trees, soared like an obelisk from the middle of the park. Compared with the austere and purple baldness of Dumfoyne and Dumgoyne, it had all the misplaced luxuriance of a periwig. A highland stream, locally termed 'river', was looped about its base like a fallen girdle. In the pool under the bridge, the most sordid object became a work of art; an old battered tin turned into a pinchbeck snuff-box. It was also the hiding place for baby trout; a discarded boot, with very little imagination, could be mistaken for the profile of a drowned negro. I would hang for hours over the bridge watching the slim brown trout darting from under pebbles, speckled as a kestrel's egg. Roe deer browsed on the slopes of the hill, despite the fact that a small and breathless train, highland bound, panted round it. One had to cross the railway line in order to reach the winding hill path. I used to enjoy treading my way across the cindered track which smelled of tar and was liberally sprinkled with rabbit droppings. The view from the top of the hill was most rewarding. A couple of sparrow hawks nested in a scraggy pine where they appeared to mount guard, like a crest over a coat of arms.

You looked down on a toy castle surrounded by artificial flower beds. If you were unlucky, the courtyard bell would ring, summoning you to a meal you could not fail to be late for.

The ascent of one of the 'twins' was quite another matter. It called for sandwiches, and an accomplice; usually, a very hot, cross cousin, who had all the pushing to do, and was expected to take the blame for grazed knees and torn clothes.

The first thing that struck you on entering the castle was its smell. Duntreath smelled of cedar wood, tuberoses, gunpowder, and *mince*. When I say mince, I mean mince. I refuse to mince mince. The kind of mince you put into the most savoury kind of cottage-pie. The origin of this mince was most extraordinary. It was improbable that mince played more than an occasional part in the Duntreath menus, yet there it was, basic, omnipresent, unforgettable. The other in-gredients were more easily accounted for: the lavatories were panelled in cedar wood, and there seemed to be tuberoses all the year round. The hot-houses were full of them, but they were of secondary im-portance, mere satellites, attendant on mince, which, I must admit, was more pungent in the basement than in the reception rooms. *There* it was quiescent, negative, partly stifled by tuberoses, but if you were a connoisseur you could nose it out, even there. The gunpowder stratum was more noticeable on the ground floor due, no doubt, to the proximity of the gun-room, where the walls were hung with glass cabinets lined in green baize, and full of well-greased guns. Cartridges would be littered about the large circular table. Trout fishing rods, varnished and elegant, tickled the ceiling, salmon rods, more ponderous, protruded from holland covers. Two tawny owls with eyes like cairngorms (one had a baby rabbit in its talons) glared at each other from opposite walls; a mouldy wildcat bared its teeth in a synthetic photographer's landscape. As the gun-room adjoined the billiard-room, it was seldom empty. The billiard-room was full of clicks and snores, and the rustle of newspapers. It was forbidden territory, but we used to peep through the hinge of the gun-room door. So much for the exclusively masculine side of the house, if one must exclude the armoury, which was seldom used, but where one felt a feminine presence would not long be tolerated.

The armoury was small and hunch-backed. One wall was dis-figured by a large tumour which we knew to be a tiny secret room blocked up by the orders of my grandfather. Panoplies, stiff with uncouth weapons on red baize, hung on the walls. They were so well polished that one asked oneself uneasily if they were not still in use? It was lit by the parsimonious light of one small window. The room had all the suggestiveness of a Madame Tussaud's reconstitution of a crime—the sadistic guardian, sequestered child, faked codicil.

The armoury fairly reeked of mince, also mice. (Minced mice?)

It was the thing to dare my cousins to spend the night in it. The inventory of fear-provoking apartments, is, however, by no means exhausted. There was the dungeon with its worm-eaten stocks and rusty thumb-screw, and last, but not least, the Oak Room, which at least had the decency to confess it was haunted. Here, no matter how fine it was outside, an aquarium-like penumbra prevailed. It never seemed empty, one always felt an intruder. The ghost it was accredited with was a particularly unpleasant one, an ancestor known as the Dumb Laird who was supposed to crouch over the fire making inarticulate noises in his throat. I never saw him. I tried so hard not to.

Yet I have completely misled you, if you imagine that Duntreath was a dour Scottish fastness, reeking of Balmorality: it was nothing of the kind. It was romantic, of a standard of luxury without equal in those days; gay with a touch of Frenchness in its *salons en enfilade*, and premeditated perspectives. One fled from terror to enchantment. The atmosphere of the place was complex, half mediaeval, half exotic. The Greek goddess wedded to the Scottish ogre.

* * * * *

My uncle had converted a turret room into a studio. Fascinated, I would watch him paint shepherds and shepherdesses, *fêtes galantes*, saucy harlequins, wistful pierrots. (Nowadays his painting would be deemed escapist.) He was haunted by the French eighteenth century; yet another anachronism in a Scottish castle built for Robert III!

Vulnerable, witty, apprehensive, he belonged to the Aunt Sophie side of the family. He detested sport, winced through the glorious 12th, took little or no interest in fishing. Gardening was his hobby: together with my mother (whom we were later to christen La Nôtre) he planted water garden and herbaceous border.

They were like twins, those two (there was only a year between them), they seemed to complete one another. My mother all dynamism, initiative, and, yes, virility, my uncle all gentleness, acquiescence, sensibility. They adored each other, could not bear to be long parted.

My mother was, in many ways, typically Scots. Intelligent,

downright, devoid of pettiness or prejudice, she loved a good argument, especially a political one. Her impartiality and sound judgement were proverbial.

I should think she was one of the most consulted women in England; she was certainly one of the funniest.

She never seemed more at home than at Duntreath swinging across the moors with her light and buoyant step. "Your mother," someone once observed, "walks like the Victory of Samothrace."

She was adored by the gillies. A keen cricket player in her youth, they would encourage her with cries of: "Rin, Allus, rin!"[1]

Once, when she and Uncle Archie were children, pressing their noses against the window of their Edinburgh home, a funeral passed the house. "Oh, look," wailed wee Archie, clutching his sister's arm, "look at that great black coach, those great black horses, all those black people!"

"Never mind, Archie," came the characteristic reply, "the coachman's alive!"

One of the major attractions of Duntreath, as far as I was concerned, was the lodge-keeper, Mrs. Strachan. Although she had seldom, if ever, left the castle precincts, Mrs. Strachan, like most Scottish peasants, was intelligent and receptive. Her ease and her self-assurance would not have been misplaced in an embassy. Her husband, whom she never referred to as anything but 'the Master', was the house carpenter. He resembled a particularly ferocious Samurai, with his little oblique eyes and drooping moustaches. Cautious, monosyllabic, he was only interested in the Bible, the Edmonstone family, and his dog, which went by the curious name of Do It. Mrs. Strachan he took for granted. He treated us with the respectful familiarity which was the custom in Scotland; had not his little family tree grown up in the shadow of the greater one?

The Lodge was situated at the entrance of the West drive. The principal room was the bed-kitchen, with an immense bed and a tiny oven. On the bed, a patchwork quilt, composed of multi-coloured scraps, looked as though it might have belonged to some indigenous Harlequin. Divorced from fantasy, it was reduced to the distasteful task of cosseting rheumatics.

Conscious of indelicacy, you could not help noticing that the walls

[1] "Run, Alice, run!"

were hung from top to bottom with calendars, calendars dusty obsolete, from which all the leaves had been plucked: only the illustrated cardboard background remained. The theme was usually a romantic one; a cavalier drinking the health of some pretty 'serving wench', or a lady leaning over a gate with a distressingly vacuous expression. 'The Broken Tryst' would be the caption for this one. The collective effect of the calendars was oppressive in the extreme: so many days, they seemed to sigh, so many days, what have you done with so many days? They were as importunate as creditors.

With relief, we turn to the Strachans' parlour, an apartment the Master never set foot in out of respect for the furniture. A huge mahogany chest of drawers occupied practically the whole of one wall: how, one wondered, could it ever have got into the room without lifting the roof? In the middle of each drawer was what appeared to be a mother-of-pearl glove button. A grandfather clock, solemn as a butler, faced the chest of drawers. The rest of the room was entirely given over to frivolity. Swarms of photographs and snapshots of Edmonstones past and present, had settled on all available landing ground, on table, mantelpiece, shelves, bookcase. Was it a fête or a plague, a toy regatta, or a swarm of gigantic moths?

Then there were the knick-knacks, packs of china greyhounds, *couchant*, heraldic; glass paper weights, Staffordshire couples, lumps of quartz, boxes made of shells, *papier mâché*, pebbles. To-day, Mrs. Strachan's bibelots would fetch hundreds of pounds.

Occasionally, we would be invited to tea. I shall never forget those teas: drop-scones, ginger cake, shortbread, oatmeal scones, heather honey, Edinburgh rock and butterscotch! No wonder our schoolroom teas seemed meagre in comparison.

Round about the age of thirteen, when I took myself very seriously as an art student, I suddenly became alive to Mrs. Strachan's pictorial possibilities. The poor old lady, draped in a Paisley shawl, with a lopsided turban, was made to sit as a modern version of Rembrandt's Mother. Unfortunately, the Old Master *had* an old master, whose nerves began to get slightly frayed. He was slow to understand that Rembrandt's Mother could not minister to his material needs in the way to which he was accustomed. Little by little, Mrs. Strachan began to see herself in the part; she was given art magazines, the lives of the Dutch painters; the Master was given scalded porridge and cold comfort. My uncle complained that callers were kept waiting interminably at the lodge gates. Something had to be done. With my puny economies, I managed to bribe a village waif to wait on Rembrandt's Mother. The child opened the gate more often than not. My uncle grew to hear of the demoralization of his lodge-keeper.

The waif and I were sent about our business "and no nonsense, mind, about the Master resembling a piece of Early Ming, because it won't work!"

Abashed, *déclassées*, the artist and her model tried to live down the episode of Rembrandt's Mother as best they could. The servants were forbidden under any circumstances to 'sit' to Miss Violet.

Second only to Mrs. Strachan, was Miss Laurie, who lived not ten miles away in a small prim house most suitably named The Moss. Miss Laurie was an impenitent old maid with a round comely face and neat features. Young, she must have resembled a drawing by Ingres. In more ways than one, she might have been French. She was caustic, well-educated, insatiably interested in her fellow creatures; a realist. She kept house for her tea-cosy-shaped bachelor brother, a retired Civil Servant; their little house was the acme of discomfort. (I have seldom slept on a harder bed.) They both took great pride in a series of etchings by D. Y. Cameron, who was a dear friend, or, maybe a relation? The sayings of 'Louisa' were cherished by my family. I can only recall one. At luncheon one day, she complained, in mock despair: ' I shall neverr taste a rripe peach. When I was young, they were all kept for the old, now that I am old, they are all kept for the young!"

Once a month she would motor to lunch at the 'Castle' in a car which contrived to resemble a toque, a gondola, and a sedan chair. It was extremely high; it boasted curtains; it had a curiously low bonnet, like a lap.

Miss Laurie inspired in her neighbours both admiration and dread; they never knew what she was going to say next. Her great 'fan' was a Mrs. Campbell, who lived in a house half farm, half manor, on the lower slopes of Dumgoyne.

Mrs. Campbell was a giantess who vaguely reminded one of a woman. Unfortunately, she saw herself as a helpless, rather pathetic little creature; her affectations were as frightening as the mannerisms of a mountain, the kittenishness of a skyscraper. She was really interested only in gossip, genealogies, lingerie, and love. She was married to a small diffident man with an excellent brain; they would have made an ideal music-hall turn, with patter to match; 'I sez to me better 'alf—' 'Three-quarters, you mean.' Mr. Campbell was, in point of fact, an extremely successful Glasgow lawyer, and, between them they had reared a cultured, individualistic, humorous family with long upper lips and soft Highland voices. Their home was charming. The small, low-ceilinged rooms invited confidences; they were strewn with objects perhaps more personal than valuable, for instance, a rug with the grandfather's initials, and the date 1827 woven into the pattern; a small map drawn by Stevenson, a series of petit point chairs worked by a great aunt.

All the Campbells were gifted, successful, eloquent. The eldest son was studying for the Bar, one of the daughters spoke admirable French, the other had learnt singing in Munich. It was delightful to listen to her singing from a bench by the open front door. Her voice was so sweet, so intimate, it seemed to be the voice of the place itself, rising from the low, two-storied house. It seemed to mingle with the smoke rising from the chimney. Was the smoke singing or the voice smoking?

Sometimes we had the privilege of inviting the younger members of the Campbell family to schoolroom tea. A word about the schoolroom in passing. One of the windows framed the cone-shaped summit of Ben Lomond, tremulously blue as the eyes of the aged. My mother had climbed Ben Lomond as a girl. I always endeavoured to sit facing this window. Whenever at a loss during my lessons, mine eyes, as in the psalm, would turn unto the hills, whence, however, came no help. When I wasn't staring out of the window, I was gazing at a stubborn little blackish drawing of Duntreath before the restoration; it looked crippled and murderous, very different from its present many-windowed hospitality. There was also a portrait in pastel of Aunt Ida, which looked as though it had run in the wash; no doubt it had been flicked too often by the duster of an over-zealous housemaid?

A meticulous pen-and-ink drawing of my despotic old grandfather hung over the fireplace; characteristically it bore *his* signature, not the artist's. From the south window one obtained a view of the lawns. One knew, without looking out, what was going on. In the morning they were apt to resound with the virile interpellations of lawn tennis, in the afternoon the genteel click of croquet balls informed us that a feminine foursome was in progress.

A perfect rabbit-warren of passages, all smelling richly of mince, led to the boys' playroom which was, as it were, the culmination and apotheosis of the Nursery Wing, the Senate where all problems were thrashed out. I had three male cousins, all rampageous, self-willed, handsome. My favourite was the eldest brother, Willie, who was about my own age. I secretly hoped he would marry me when he was grown up. One year, we were told we were to be nice to a very shy young tutor who had been imported for the boys' holidays.

I did not take to him at once. He was stocky, gauche, with a peninsula of fairish hair, sparsely covering a high and dome-like forehead. He seemed ill at ease, unhappy in the midst of a large, self-centred Edwardian house party. Nobody attempted to make friends with him; the boys bullied him slyly, going as far as they dared. They had been told he was the son of a bishop, and many were the seemingly innocent allusions to 'gaiters'.

One day after luncheon, when the guests had dispersed, and my cousins were momentarily out of hearing, he burst out: "I can't stick it any longer! I loathe all these beastly self-satisfied smart people. How dare they treat me as though I were an outsider, a pariah! Damn it all, I'm every bit as good as they are!"

"Of course, you are," I attempted to soothe; "please don't be so miserable, they don't mean it, they're just like that."

"I've never been in a house like this before," he went on, unhappily. "I might have known! My people are very simple people, they don't hold with this kind of thing."

"What kind of thing?" I was anxious to know.

"Oh, chefs and valets and changing your clothes all day long. I haven't got any clothes to change into, and what the hell am I supposed to do when the boys have gone to bed?"

"Why," I suggested, greatly daring, "don't you come and talk to me?"

"How can I? You're supposed to be in bed, too."

"You could come while Nana is at her supper. Oh do, you can tell me stories. I love being told stories in bed. *Please!*"

"All right. As a matter of fact, that is one of the few things I *can* do!"

This was the beginning of a lifelong friendship with Hugh Walpole.

* * * * *

Duntreath was nearly always full up. Waves of guests succeeded each other up to the end of October. When we were older we were promoted to have luncheon in the dining-room, but at another table, it goes without saying. There were no privileges attached to this promotion. We had the same food, but different admonishment.

"Don't stare so. It's rude. Yes, I know that lady's hair is bright pink, but you must pretend not to notice."

"Why must I? She would notice if it were *my* hair."

"That's different, she's grown up."

"I'd rather not be grown up if my hair's going to get like that!"

"Hush, don't speak with your mouth full."

On one occasion King Edward came to shoot at Duntreath. We were all bundled off to Miss Laurie's as they had need of our bedrooms. We used to come over for the day, however. The King was very kind to us children. He had a rich German accent and smelt deliciously of cigars and *eau de Portugal*. He wore several rings set with small cabochon rubies and a cigarette-case made of ribbed gold, no doubt by Fabergé. A Fabergé cigarette-case was the emblem of Royalty, as symbolical as the bookies' cigar, or the ostler's straw.

★   ★   ★   ★   ★

How I used to dread the return to London on November 1st, dressing by electric light to catch the early train, the breakfast that stuck in one's throat! I have consistently loathed London ever since I can remember. I hated everything about it—streets, climate, smell. As far as I was concerned, there was no redeeming feature; I didn't even care for my home, which was a highish, narrowish house in Portman Square. It seemed singularly lacking in all the things I had lately grown to love—privacy, silence, mystery, the unexpected. It wasn't even pretty, though I should have been incapable of saying why.

In retrospect the most outstanding feature of Portman Square was a boiler, unaccountably situated in the schoolroom cupboard. This was, in its way, a godsend. Many were the amnesia-stricken silences it broke with its gurglings during the lesson hours, many the avowals it cut short. In fact it could be counted on to create a diversion; it was an unfailing topic with newcomers.

"Don't be scared! It's only the boiler."

"Does it always make tummy rumbles?"
"Mmm! Whenever it feels inclined!"
"I must say, it does give one a start!"
"Oh no, you get accustomed to it."

*   *   *   *   *

As soon as February came, I would begin to look forward to Easter, which was always spent at Quidenham, the home of my uncle, Lord Albemarle. No greater contrast to Duntreath can be imagined. Here was no voluptuousness, no paradox, no secrecy. Quidenham, an honest-to-God red brick eighteenth century mansion, was innocent alike of dungeon and bath-salts, tuberose and thumbscrew. True, it boasted a headless coachman, but I preferred the headless coachman to the tongueless laird. Besides, Quidenham had an atmosphere of high spirits and facetiousness which would have put the most intrepid ghost to flight. The inmates were the reverse of pampered. The passages echoed with the feet of scampering boys, and the feet of scampering rats. If Duntreath fluttered a scarf, Quidenham waved a flag.

The salubrious, draughty house was full of wagers, squabbles, dressings-up, dressings-down, declamations, caricatures, limericks.

Uncle Arnold, as handsome as a tiger, was a sculptor of merit, a caricaturist of genius, an amateur builder of yachts. He sailed his *chef d'oeuvre* from the East Coast to Cowes. On this occasion he had had to knock down the workshop in order to get the boat out!

He was accustomed to do everything himself, which included straining and bending his own timbers. Improvising came easily to him, he had the confidence born of true craftsmanship. He was good, too, at design, both of boats and sails, and was a practical yachtsman, so that it could be said of him that he could design, build, and sail a boat.

I can see him now, standing at his tall desk, on which there was always some work, a plan, a map, or perhaps, some water-colour for finishing. He was never idle. His little cardboard personages, about a foot high, were merciless indictments of most of the celebrities of his day. An old-fashioned, joint-carving, lesson-reading, British sportsman, his talents rather took one by surprise; he had had a distinguished career as a soldier during the South African War and, as regards his family, was a stern disciplinarian. Nevertheless, an infallible sense of humour (which he shared with his wife) softened his sentences, turned away his wrath. He was the kind of man I should have married. (Some of his statues filled me with awe; one, of a nymph, in an attitude of nude and narcissistic abandon, intrigued me particularly. "Uncle Arnold," I inquired, in a small hushed voice, "is that Aunt Gertie?")

Quidenham, as I have said, was as spartan as Duntreath was sybaritic. A precocious epicurean, I would lay traps for my aunt.

"Aunt Gertie, have you no cows?"

"No cows? Why, you have only to look out of the window!"

"Well, if you have so many cows, why is there no cream?"

One of the worst wiggings I ever got, and in this case, wigging, I think, was *le mot juste*, was when Aunt Gertie's stepmother, the Duchess of Buckingham and Chandos, came to stay.

" 'Grandmama Lily' has rather a peculiar shade of hair, dear, you must be a good little girl, try not to stare, and above all, do not refer to it in any way."

But the first glimpse of 'Grandmama Lily's' magnificent mahogany edifice was too much for me. "Wiggy!" I piped, "Wiggy! Wiggy!"

Though seldom out of trouble, I adored my Aunt Gertie, the best-educated, the most human of all the aunts, her *fou-rires* were irresistible, she would laugh until she cried.

She was an only child, and was raised in Cheshire. Her father, Lord Egerton of Tatton, was descended from a younger son of the Bridgewater Egertons. Life at Tatton was lived in a sort of semi-state, the atmosphere was almost feudal, the prestige of the Egerton name the ceiling. From her life as an only child, she found herself plunged into a huge family who apparently took her to its large bosom; she won great approval by her powers of mimicry, wholehearted sense of humour, and her incapacity to stifle her *fou-rires*. Thanks to Aunt Gertie's initiative and generosity, the Keppel heirlooms, dispersed by 'Rowdy Dow',[1] were restored to the family. She was the inspiration under which everything worth while was ever accomplished, identifying herself with all her husband's interests, by land or sea. The

[1] The Rowdy Dowager, wife of the fourth Earl. A Hogarthian character, she even gambled away the mahogany doors of Quidenham. A tumbril came to remove the family plate!

magnitude of her influence could be gauged by people's sense of loss at her death.

Like my mother, she was a creature of light, a promoter of happy families of which her own was, perhaps, the happiest. Once Aunt Gertie liked you, you could get away with murder. She would have gone to the stake swearing you were innocent. I once made her a present of a brooch representing a cock, Chanticleer, the emblem of France. The thing was quite worthless, the kind of topical trash you could buy for a few hundred francs in the rue de Rivoli. When the collapse of France came, which most people inevitably looked on as a betrayal, Aunt Gertie, who knew I was heartbroken, gave a small dinner party for me at Claridges. The women were in evening dress with a discreet sprinkling of jewellery. The only jewel Aunt Gertie wore was the trashy little cock.

Each of my cousins specialized in something. Arno drew, Rupert composed, Betty painted. More often than not, she would be draped in a scarlet curtain, with a cottonwool imperial glued to her lower lip, in a life-like impersonation of Cardinal Richelieu who was her hero for the time being. Edward, the Benjamin, was an *enfant terrible*. Irrepressible, fearless, he was the bane of my old nurse's existence. Once, his nanny had gone to Norwich, leaving ours supreme. She lisped to him in the garden, "Time you came in now!" Edward, aged six, holland pinafore, large straw hat, perennially grazed knees, "I'll trouble you to look after your *own* children, Mrs. Eeles, and I'll look after myself!"

He and Willie Edmonstone, both aged nineteen, were killed within a year of one another; they were equally lovable, though very different.

As the Keppels have always been a seafaring family, it is, perhaps, not surprising that there was something spacious, adventurous, about the atmosphere of Quidenham. Portraits of the famous admiral by Reynolds, his *protégé*, showed him, menacing, against a wind-swept sky; great-uncle Harry, Admiral of the Fleet, a dwarf in stature, a giant in achievement, presided, at least in spirit, over many of our imaginary adventures. Uncle Bill[1], also a sailor, added yet another nautical note. There was a tang about the Norfolk air, a latent saltiness, that brought the sea and its piracies very close.

That, and the birds blown in from the coast. We were inveterate

[1] Later Admiral of the Fleet the Earl of Cork and Orrery.

egg collectors. Betty and Edward would sometimes go birdnesting on their ponies; the groom, in cockaded top hat and white breeches, who accompanied them, would be persuaded to stand on his saddle and pole a stick with a spoon lashed to the end of it down a neat round hole in some trunk high out of reach in which they expected to find the nest of one of the wood-pecking tribe, the wretched man grasping the tree, and hoping the horse would not walk off in the meantime! If they drew lucky, he was expected to wrap the egg in his handkerchief and place it under his top hat. I remember disgusting subsequent scenes, blowing the eggs, when sometimes they were addled, or a small bird appeared.

The black-and-white stuffed bird in the nursery was a little auk. Goosander and Canada goose, tufted duck, pochard, teal, shoveller and gadwall were among the species that were shot from time to time or caught during the period my uncle had a duck decoy at the mere; great crested grebe nested there annually.

In Spring, Quidenham was an enchantment, carpeted with daffodils, primroses, bluebells, and nests to be found for the searching every hundred yards or so. To this day, I vaguely pry for nests, but I have lost the knack.

CHAPTER TWO

I WAS, as I have already said, a backward, sultry, child. London made me worse. I would break into a storm of weeping for no reason at all; I was suspicious, introspective, passionately possessive about the people and things I cared for. The most blameless books for the young racked me with sobs. One, notoriously, by L. T. Meade, entitled *The Gay Charmer*, reduced me to such a pulp of despair that my parents made it their business to read the book.

They were completely nonplussed; there was nothing in *The Gay Charmer* that could possibly promote an emotional crisis. Perhaps I lived too much with grown-up people, perhaps I needed a companion of my own age? My sister, it was felt, was too young to be of any use to me—after all, there is a gulf between ten and four. The outcome of it all was that my dim, indifferent English governess who had lost her fiancé in the Boer War, was replaced by a combative little French bantam of a woman only about ten years older than I was.

Hélène Claissac, in those days a small plump blonde, with the accent of the *midi*, was, in every respect, the antithesis of the bereaved Miss Ainslie. She possessed the impudence and ubiquity of the toy trumpet which orders French trains about. A staunch Republican, she did not hold with kings. When, on some public occasion, she was presented to Edward VII, she gave him what she would have termed '*un cordial shakehand*'. He was much amused. She had cheek, spunk, guts, panache; nothing, no-one, could *épater* her. Exempt from any kind of snobbishness, she did not give a fig for riches, rank, renown. It was my first (and salutary) contact with French intellectual integrity, so remote from the breathy beatitudes Miss Ainslie would exhale over some cliché attributed to a member of the Royal Family.

With Hélène, re-christened Moiselle, you began from scratch; divested of all prestige, divorced from past achievement, you had to show what you were made of. Either you were a success, or you weren't. Many of my parents' illustrious guests grew to look upon Moiselle as a test they could not face without flinching.

Moiselle led, prematurely, to Paris. Paris was to be an experiment, in the nature of a 'rouser'. Where London had failed, Paris, it was felt, might succeed. Most girls of my generation were 'finished' in Paris. I was begun there. We accordingly set out, Moiselle, Aunt Jessie and I, one May morning, elastic under chin, tightly buttoned into a hideous tweed ulster, wrinkled lisle stockings, and all. Contrary to the expectations of my elders, I was not sick (any more than I was to be homesick). I declined my aunt's cabin, eyed with revulsion the greenish faces sniffing smelling salts all round me.

My first pleasurable surprise was the onslaught of vehement blue-chinned, blue-bloused porters at Calais. Something stirred in my lethargic bosom. This, I said to myself, is Life. I enjoyed even the vociferating crowds in the Customs House. We had, I remember, a delicious luncheon in the buffet, served on a wringing wet tablecloth. I had to be hoisted up to the high steep step of the Paris-bound train. (Did the English trains of those days, I wonder, indulge in the arch feminine Christian names which the Golden Arrow has so enthusiastically adopted? Three coaches, I noticed recently, had been christened Doris, Pamela and Sappho.) The pale unemotional landscape flowed past. It seemed singularly aerial, singularly empty, after the neat little fields, huddled cottages, I was accustomed to. It didn't attempt to be pretty, it had a certain take-it-or-leave-it quality which impressed, if it did not endear. Puzzled and daunted, I tried to catch the names of the stations, Abbeville, Amiens, Chantilly, which reminded one of the kind of forest you see in tapestry. Where was the wild boar at bay, the gored and writhing hounds?

The outskirts of Paris seemed uncompromising, grim—there was none of that pitiable straining after a garden; not even a flowerpot graced the sooty window ledges. A few dusty cloches were the only concession to horticulture. The Gare du Nord was even more frightening, with trolleys coming at you from every side, voracious porters, and seemingly furious crowds at the barriers.

We crammed ourselves into a *fiacre*, leaving the hotel *chasseur* to deal with the luggage. Up the populous rue Lafayette we drove; the unfamiliar aroma of coffee and *brioches* greeted my nostrils. The Opera was pointed out to me, the rue de la Paix. In the Place de la Concorde, the fountains were playing. I took a great gulp of air and light. We turned up the Champs Elysées. The chestnuts were in bloom. Pink and white tapers ascended the sky; revolving sprays like the tails of whirling birds of paradise watered the plushy turf; excited children rode demure little donkeys; there was even an ostrich harnessed to a tiny cart. *Nounous*, resplendent with gold pins and tartan streamers, pushed their small charges; here and there a comic Zouave, like a music-hall turn, swaggered past with a doting *midinette* on his arm; muffled music came from the pavilions; coachmen in shiny white top hats cursed, were mocked by impish *chasseurs* on bicycles, fussy little motor cars wound in and out of the traffic, whips cracked, newsvendors bawled.

A wordless exhilaration poured into my lungs. My heart missed a beat. It was love at first sight.

*   *   *   *   *

The next morning, I burst uncharacteristically into my aunt's bedroom without knocking.

"What is it, dear?"

"When I'm grown up, I'm going to live in Paris!"

The first outward manifestation of my new-born passion was an

[40]

illustrated diary; the second, a sustained effort to speak French without the blurred, slovenly, British accent.

I was taken sightseeing; I couldn't see enough. The Louvre was lyrically, if inaccurately, described in the diary, accompanied by a thumbnail sketch of the Venus of Milo; Napoleon's tomb was wept over, the Conciergerie, shuddered at. Aunt Jessie and Moiselle exchanged amused glances. Approving letters were written home. What had become of my *flegme brittannique*? Where would it all end? I was taken to see Buffalo Bill, rather staccato films for the young at Dufayel; I subscribed to *Le Jeudi de la Jeunesse*, became acquainted with Moiselle's niece, Germaine Caigné, a contemporary.

After a month in Paris, I was considered to have made sufficient progress with my French to attend French classes at the Faubourg St. Honoré. I can still see the toothless old charwoman, Agathe; still smell the freshly *encaustiqué* parquet. The head mistress was an intelligent Jewess, Mademoiselle Abraham. She wrote rather mediocre novels under a male pseudonym, which was then the fashion. The three allotted months passed all too quickly. Hardly had I returned to London than the Blight settled on me again. It could only be attenuated by bribes: if I was good at my lessons, I would be allowed to return to Paris the following year. No wonder my parents were exasperated. Whereas in Paris I had shown myself to be a high-spirited, gregarious child, always ready to play *aux quatre coins* or Colin Maillard, in London I kept myself to myself, shunning children's parties, snubbing my contemporaries, fighting with other little girls behind the sooty lilac trees of Portman Square. Then, of a sudden, everything changed. I made a friend.

One day I allowed myself to be dragged to a tea-party at Lady Kilmorey's. There I met a girl older than myself, but, apparently, every bit as unsociable. She was tall for her age, gawky, most unsuitably dressed in what appeared to be her mother's old clothes. I do not remember who made the first step. Anyhow, much to my family's gratification I asked if I might have her to tea. She came. We were both consummate snobs, and talked, chiefly, as far as I can remember, about our ancestors. I essayed a few superior allusions to Paris. She was not impressed; her tastes seemed to lie in another direction. She digressed on her magnificent home in the country, her dogs, her rabbits.

I thought her nice, but rather childish (I was then ten). We separated, however, with mutual esteem. The repressions of my short life immediately found an outlet in a voluminous correspondence. I bombarded the poor girl with letters which became more exacting as hers tended to become more and more of the 'yesterday-my-pet-rabbit-had-six-babies' type. Clearly, no letter writer. Our meetings, however, atoned for this epistolary pusillanimity. These were devoted mainly to the discussion of our favourite heroes—d'Artagnan, Bayard, Raleigh. We used to sit dangling our legs over the leather fender of my father's sitting-room (he was never in at this hour) until fetched by our respective governesses. Our friendship progressed all that winter. I was invited to stay at Knole.

It is not an exaggeration to say that places have played at least as important a part in my life as people. Indeed, it is almost as though the places had generated the people; equipped and apposite, they have sprung spontaneously from the background which created them. It was necessary to see Vita at Knole to realize how inevitable she was. Knole was committed to produce a Vita. Generations of Sackvilles, heavy-lidded, splenetic, looked possessively down on their offspring, a united chorus, finger to lip. These self-same features, painted by Van Dyck, Gainsborough, Lawrence, emerging from a ruff, a 'jabot', a 'choker', occurred in each generation. One thing was common to them all, a detachment, part morgue, part melancholy, which in the end drove them to seek in Nature the stable compensations they had failed to find in their fellow creatures.

Vita belonged to Knole, to the courtyards, gables, galleries; to the prancing sculptured leopards, to the traditions, rites, and splendours. It was a considerable burden for one so young. No wonder she wrote about rabbits!

For the first time, I became conscious, almost oppressively conscious, of the personality of her mother, of whom, hitherto, I had only been vouchsafed an occasional glimpse. She was as intermittent, yet omnipresent, as the Cheshire Cat. Her daughter, who admired and distrusted her, was, up to a point, the Cheshire Cat's plaything, but only up to a point. Knole, the Sackvilles, her charming, if unobtrusive father, watched over her.

There was much about her mother I was at a loss to account for. Her vivacity, effervescence, like new wine in an old bottle? She was a

woman of about fifty. In her too fleshy face, classical features sought
to escape from the encroaching fat. An admirable mouth, of a pure and
cruel design, held good. It was obvious that she had been beautiful.
Her voluminous, ambiguous body was upholstered, rather than
dressed, in what appeared to be an assortment of patterns, lace, brocades,
velvets, taffetas. Shopping lists were pinned to her bosom. She kept
up a flow of flattering, sprightly conversation, not unlike the patter
of a conjuror, intent on keeping your mind off the trick he is about to
perform. Like the conjuror, she fascinated you, more especially as
these monologues were uttered in a youthful, high-stepping voice, with
a strong French accent.

"Is she French?"

"No," her daughter informed me, "not exactly: my grandmother
was Spanish, a gipsy dancer, but mother was brought up in France."
All this, and a gipsy too!

My romantic heart overflowed. I immediately began to hunt for
the gipsy in Vita, some hint of the nomad; restlessness; a desire to
sleep beneath the stars; a crepitation of the fingers; drumming of the
heels.

But no. Vita, at that age, was stolidly, uncompromisingly, British.
In her deep stagnant gaze was no dawning wanderlust; far from being
the star of the dancing class we both attended, she had, rather, it must
be confessed, a *succès de fou rire* ('Now, Miss West, do your best!'),
hopelessly involved with a scarf of octopus-like propensities.

Perhaps it was a case of arrested development? Perhaps the gipsy
would lose nothing by blossoming late? To comfort myself, I would
tell myself stories of Pepita, relegated in her old age to a distant wing
of the great house where, reverting to type, she would squat on the
floor repairing pots and pans.

★   ★   ★   ★   ★

The following spring, I returned to Paris with Moiselle. This time
I was promoted to an apartment in the Quai Debilly (actually Avenue
de Tokio) which my mother had rented from a friend. It was full of
Empire furniture, engravings of *le Roi de Rome*; it pandered to my
Napoleonic cult. I saw myself as Josephine, endeavoured to slur my
r's *à la créole*. Lessons were a delight for the simple reason that they

were based on a love affair, my love affair with France. My entourage could not get over the change in the sullen, unresponsive child who, not content with attending classes in the Faubourg St. Honoré, was forever poring over a French grammar and a French dictionary. (One day, I threatened, I shall write a book in French!)

I revisited all the, by then, familiar landmarks; Napoleon's porphyry tomb lit by a perennial ray; Notre Dame, similar to some great galleon turned to stone, its flying buttresses spread with the rhythm and symmetry of perfectly timed oars; the daisied lawns of Bagatelle; the *quais* where we could buy goldfish and parakeets, rabbits, even ferrets, whose passion for secrecy was cruelly violated by being in a shop window. Then there was the Sunday treat of Versailles where the fountains looked as though they were spurted by subterranean whales; the Thursday treat of Rumpelmayer with its absurd mural paintings of the Riviera (still existent) and succulent chocolate éclairs. I loved the excitement of the rue de Rivoli, the shops full of enthusiastic rubbish and a kind of prancing tricolour truculence.

My mother paid me the supreme compliment of coming to stay at 'my' flat. In her opinion, a woman could not learn soon enough to serve food in its proper sequence. Accordingly, one day, she told me I was to order dinner for eight and gave me *carte blanche* as to the menu, with injunctions to the cook that it must be served exactly as I ordered it, on the principle that I could only learn by experience. To the embarrassment of her guests, mayonnaise sauce appeared not once, but three times; with the fish, the *rôti*, the sweet. It happened to be my favourite sauce at the moment.

I have vivid memories of the first time I accompanied my mother to the dressmaker, where she was received like a goddess, Monsieur Jean (Worth) supervising her fitting in person, the *vendeuses* quite shamelessly forsaking their other clients to vie with each other in flattering epithets. *Il y avait de quoi.* My mother was everything that could most appeal to them, lovely, vivacious, fêted, fashionable, with a kind word for each of the anonymous old crones who had been for years in the establishment.

Even I, *en plein age ingrat*, came in for a little vicarious petting. "*De Madame Keppel je suis la fille, je suis la fille!*" I chanted to the tune of Madame Angot as we were ushered out.

My mother took me to Fontainebleau. The last time she had

visited the château was, she related, with the Empress Eugénie, whom she knew as a very old lady. Mama was staying at an hotel opposite the Palace where she had gone to recuperate from a bout of influenza. One day her maid burst into her bedroom. "Madam! Madam! The wife of Napoleon the First is waiting to see you downstairs, she says she has only just discovered you were staying here!" The outcome of this unexpected call was that the Empress expressed the curious wish to show my mother over the château, accompanied by a guide and a bunch of tourists. Insensitiveness, or curiosity as to the official 'authorized' version of the history of the rooms she had known so well? Presently, they came to the *salon* where the first Napoleon had signed the Act of Abdication. "And this," said the guide brandishing a pen, "is the pen he used!'

"*Pardon, Monsieur,*" the Empress stepped forward, "you make a mistake." She approached the bureau, pressed an invisible spring. Out leapt a little drawer, in which was a pen. The Empress showed it to the gaping tourists. "This, I happen to know, is the pen His Imperial Majesty used!"

Such were the anecdotes with which she regaled our childhood. If the great lost the power to impress, they at least gained the faculty of endearing themselves.

A story in much demand was that of 'little Winston', whose Nannie had left on a well-earned holiday. The exuberant and exacting little boy of five was entrusted to the care of his mother, Lady Randolph Churchill (a friend of my mother's), who little realized what she was in for until night fell. . . .

It began with Hunt the Thimble, which led to Hunt the Slipper. Puss in the Corner was somewhat of an effort; Pirates were followed by Red Indians, which were followed by rebellion on the part of Lady Randolph, who, as the clock struck two, sank unnerved and exhausted on her bed.

"Winston," she gasped, "you are impossible!"

"Yes, indeed," endorsed the portentous child. "*A miserable business for both!*"

It was about then that I became acquainted with French country life. There is something opportune, uninhibited, about an average French country house. It is light, to begin with; the panelling is painted a light grey; the rooms are light and airy. The furniture, elegant, yet formal, is mostly made of blond woods, ash, wild cherry, *citronnier*.

Polish and prominence are given to certain accessories: the fire dogs gleam, the chandelier glitters, *girandoles* glisten redly. The unmuddled furniture, symmetry of pictures and ornaments, further enhance the impression of clarity, light, which permeates every branch of French creativeness, and which, when carried to extremes, becomes dryness, sterility, pedantry, frigidity.

I got to know a family of the name of Sourdun; it consisted of a handsome, taciturn, widowed father, and two daughters, aged twelve and thirteen respectively. They lived in what must have been a banal little white château in Seine-et-Oise, which appeared to my infatuated eyes as a haven of beauty and charm, merely because it was *different*.

The difference began as soon as you got up. You washed in a *cabinet de toilette* hung with *toile de Jouy*, representing the fables of La Fontaine and exhaling a smell that was both fusty and mysterious. On the frilly washing-stand were two cut-glass bottles containing *eau de Botot* and *fleur d'oranger*. (*Eau de Botot* mingled with the resinous fumes of *encaustique* is to this day the characteristic odour of French country houses). Then you went downstairs, where Gustave, the *valet de chambre*, would be performing a kind of gouty dance, his right foot encased in a piece of old carpet, on the drawing-room floor, which he polished until the lozenged parquet shone like a skating rink. Then we had breakfast; bubbly chocolate and soggy *brioches*.

I don't know if this is due to the enchantment of retrospect, but it seems to me that the summer was always orthodox and fine; there would be carpets of wood strawberries, and clumsy cockchafers zooming against our tennis racquets; the gardener, who wore an enormous straw hat, would rake the prim alleys until they smarted.

Déjeuner was at 12 in the panelled dining-room with tapestry 'let into' the panels. We children were given *eau rougie*—water with a drop of wine in it—and lumps of sugar dipped in the coffee of our elders at the end of the meal. After luncheon, there was a drawing class in the shrubbery, where our nostrils were agreeably titillated by the scent of syringa. One of us would be made to pose, and melodramatic profiles (they were easier) would be propped on vacillating easels.

[46]

Edmond Rostand was our god and we each knew at least one of his plays by heart. Antoinette, for example, would often be called upon to recite *la scène du balcon* out of *Cyrano*, waving an impassioned hand stained with ink and strawberry juice.

Later, whenever any of my contemporaries offended me either there, or elsewhere, I would indulge in a revenge which was as diabolical as it was pedantic. An *'oraison funèbre'*—obituary notice—in the manner of Bossuet, beginning, say, 'Après une longue et douloureuse maladie, *la si peu regrettée* Antoinette de Sourdun'—in a disguised hand would be slipped into her satchel.

At first, the formality of French country life struck me as being almost eighteenth century; the perpetual kissing of hands, curtsies to one's elders and betters (I quickly conformed to this custom), the prim grouping of the drawing-room chairs which were co-ordinated as for a figure in a quadrille, and which no one ever dared to disturb, the albums of bloomy photographs to be fingered reverently after meals, the elaborate ritual of saying good morning, saying good night, all this formed part of the 'difference' I found so intoxicating.

Sometimes I would go fishing in a small and treacly pond, where dragonflies skimmed, perch swam, and acacias trailed in the water. You tied a small piece of red flannel to a bent pin, and the frog would leap at it like a tiny athlete. (If my salmon-fishing uncles could have seen me, how ashamed they would have been!)

France, then, caught me young. Young enough to re-mould and compress a nature as fluid as a camembert cheese. By the time my only English friend arrived in Paris, the harm (or the good) was done. I saw her through French eyes, her height and gaucherie accentuated, *une asperge montée*. It annoyed me that she did not respond to Paris in the same way as I did. Her shrinkings and hesitations when compelled to cross the street filled me with a secret contempt. I felt old and worldly.

Literature, however, brought us together again. She had written a play in French as long as Swinburne's *Chastelard*, at least as unplayable. The costumes were Louis XIII and, needless to say, home-made; black satin bloomers trimmed with very prickly lace, much beribboned blouses, and corked moustaches (it was an all-masculine cast).

The audience consisted of our respective governesses, the concierge and his wife, the chef, and the butler. It speaks highly for their good manners that they sat it out. I am not sure if it was not performed on three successive days as it could not possibly be crammed into one afternoon. It took place in the apartment of Sir John Murray Scott in the rue Lafitte, an abode packed with the most wonderful furniture and bibelots worthy to compete with those he had bequeathed to the Wallace Collection.

My admiration for Vita's French knew no bounds. How was I ever to hope to rival her handling of syntax, her mastery of *l'imparfait du subjonctif*? Without the stimulus of Vita, it is doubtful whether I should have taken so much trouble with my lessons. Try as I might, she was always a class ahead of me in everything.

For three blissful consecutive years, I was allowed to return to Paris in the spring, where we would remain for three or four months, then, in my fourteenth year it was decided that my knowledge of French, now well above the average, must make way for another language: Italian.

I set out for Florence with my pioneer aunt and the inevitable Moiselle, without prejudice, but without enthusiasm. Aunt Jessie, alias Duckrus, was one of the mainstays of my existence, defying time and erosion. She was a pillar of strength, as, indeed, was my mother, but Duckrus was of a different period, a different texture. There were no flights of fancy, no chimæras about Duckrus. Architecturally, she belonged to the early nineteenth century. She first swam into my ken as the rather dim supporter of my exquisite grandmother: she and Mrs. Wells, Gabbata's maid, dressed in serviceable black, seemed the perfect foils to her delicate beauty.

I never knew my Uncle Ted, and was sometimes tempted to doubt whether he had ever existed? A born widow, Duckrus had all the authority, yet none of the responsibilities, of the married woman. What she said, went. She ruled her household of four with equity and moderation. Why was I drawn to Aunt Jessie?

To begin with, I liked her long, rather austere, ancestral face, the face I had so often met in a frame at Duntreath. She much resembled my grandfather, whose favourite daughter she had been; was accustomed to be held up as a paragon to that nonconformist, my mother.

At a very early age, I began to plan the downfall of Aunt Jessie. The result of my cogitations was that I one day announced that henceforth she would be known as Duckrus.

"Duckrus! What an odd name! Why Duckrus?"

"Because you are Duckrus to me. Don't you see? A mixture of a duck and a walrus, a duck, one day, a walrus, the next. Unless, of course, you prefer Borem-Manger."

"Borem what?"

"Borem-Manger. I thought of that name first, but I can't explain what it means."

"No, no," said my Aunt hastily, "we will stick to Duckrus."

And Duckrus she remained.

The name was but the thin end of the wedge. I must have realized that with 'Aunt Jessie' I would have got nowhere. If you give people a new name, it is a kind of annexation. A person called Duckrus has simply nothing in common with a person called Aunt Jessie. She grew more and more like Duckrus and less and less like Aunt Jessie. I loved her. Apart from her deplorable laxity with me, she represented every known virtue with a delightful, sampler-like, literalness. Her religion governed every minute of the day. She was what is known as High Church, though she had no patience with the Papists, but there was nothing mawkish about Aunt Jessie's religion, it had the inelasticity, the Old Testament virility of a John Knox. In other words, Aunt Jessie was tough.

She lived to be very old. In 1937 she had a mild stroke which confined her to her bed, which she was never to leave again. Her condition was stationary, there was no reason to suppose she would not live for years. One night, in Paris, however, I dreamt she was dying, although my parents had assured me she was no worse, and flung myself into the first available train for London. I shall not forget her face when I burst into her bedroom.

She could not talk much; soon I left her, promising to return the following day. As I turned to go, she waved confidently, vigorously, as one waves from the deck of a ship, to comfort those who remain behind. Before I returned, she was dead.

*   *   *   *   *

The pendant in my heart to Aunt Jessie is Nana, who had much in common with Duckrus, in fact she was a kind of rustic Duckrus. Reared in Northumberland, she had a charming North Country accent (Dooky, she would call us, in moments of expansion). Physically, she resembled Henry VIII, with glazed pink cheeks like cold salmon. She was addicted to ornithological hats, Bible-reading, and beer, a glass of which was sometimes kept behind my mother's photograph.

Her *bête noire* throughout her life was Moiselle, whom she once accused of having bitten her in the calf on her way upstairs.

I can still see Nana sitting up in bed in her starched night-gown, spelling out the outlandish names in the Old Testament under her breath, before going to sleep, which, in her case, was a jungle of snores. (Surely, no sound in the world is more earthbound?)

My sister gives an excellent description of Nana in a collection of short stories that was published in 1935. Here it is.

THE TAIL

To look at, my Nurse seemed to be as protected from ordinary attack as one of His Majesty's battleships. Her piqué shirt and skirt were so stiff with starch that they might have been made of armour-plating. In her watchful eye was all the confidence of a born leader of nursery-maids. Yet she had two vulnerable points of which I was sadistically aware. One was a 'toe' which acted as a weather-vane, presaging storm and disaster, and the other was a 'tail'. Most of the nurses I knew had 'toes', but none of them (as far as I could ascertain) had 'tails'. There was something individual and distinguished about it, something in it which retrieved her from the common herd of nurses and put her on a level with nurses of Royalty and Sir Ernest Cassel's grand-daughters. It was made of long coarse burnished hair and its main point was that it was detachable. It 'took off' to comb. On gala days, such as a birthday, or a day on which I had lost a tooth without making a fuss, I was allowed to touch it and even brush it, and on these occasions the ceremony was a solemn one. My nurse unwound it from the back of her head, whereon it had lain, coiled like a serpent, deter-minedly shook it out and shut its end in the dressing-table drawer. I was given a hair-brush and told to be careful. I can still remember my pride on the occasion of the first brushing. I went to my task with the devotion of a vestal virgin. I even made the suggestion of washing my hands first. Familiarity with the rite bred slight contempt for it and subsequently my nurse's pride was hurt when she found me driving her 'tail' to market. Fiendishly I used it against her as a weapon of blackmail. I wielded it over her with the ferocity of a Moujik manipulating the knout. Her life was made hell by it until my mother intervened. "Everyone wears false hair now. It is all the fashion," she comforted poor Nannie by saying, and with the rivet mended in her armour-plating, Nannie steamed ahead once more.

I bided my time.

One winter's afternoon I was banished to the night-nursery to do penance for half an hour. Nannie had discovered me slaking my thirst with her home-made recipe for chapped hands, and I was told to stay in the night-nursery 'till I was good'. Determined not to affect this metamorphosis too soon, I looked round the room in search of distraction and saw the tail hanging from the drawer. (In the winter, with fogs about, an extra combing was wont to take place before tea.) An idea, colossal in its daring, stabbed my brain. I tiptoed to the window, thrust it open, and looked down on the dreary square. Vague outlines of carriages and cabs passed underneath me, and from the right I saw approaching a large van drawn by two sturdy greys. Seizing the 'tail' from the drawer, I brandished it aloft and flung it from me. Down, down it went, curving and doubling and writhing as though in the extremity of fear. The driver of the dray saw it too late to avoid it. With a grinding of rusty brakes he pulled up his horses, but not before the offside grey and two offside wheels had crushed it into pulp.

Slowly he descended from his perch, peered shortsightedly at the bedraggled remains and sadly shook his head. Then he stooped and gathered them up and rang our front door bell. Ecstatically I leaned from the window and heard snatches of his conversation with the footman.

"Sorry, sir. Saw it just too late. Must've broken its back anyway, pore little dawg!"

*   *   *   *   *

It was inconceivable that Italy should take the place of France. (It never has.) We stayed at a pension in the Via Venezia which in those days was considered one of the 'healthier' quarters of Florence, inasmuch as it was a little-frequented street, far from the *Sturm und Drang* of the Via Cavour. It had a semi-detached suburban gentility; wistaria dripped over the wall in the best post-card tradition; the pension was shabby, decorous, spinsterish. Of course, it was kept by an Englishwoman.

The robust intrusive dome of the Baptistry was visible from the upper windows: I longed to linger in the ravine-like streets clubbed by bells, and thick with smells it was fun to try to decipher: old leather, older cheese, urine, coffee, frying oil.

Little by little, the grace, the beauty of the population began to impinge on my alert suspicious senses. The postman? But I had already seen him somewhere? Of course, in the Titian of the three musicians. He was the one who played the harpsichord. Gianina, the maid who waited on us, there was no mistaking the resemblance: she was none other than the Sixtine Madonna.

These people had a consummate distinction; they were primitive, exuberant, but never common. Would my loyalty to France be able to withstand so much beauty, so much charm? I was still in this freshly inoculated condition when Vita, accompanied by her French governess, arrived on the scene. The powers that be, not devoid of acumen, had divined that I should learn Italian twice as quickly with Vita to compete with. It became immediately apparent that Vita's reaction to Italy was exactly what mine had been to France. She was bowled over, subjugated. Inarticulate with love, she would wander from church to church, from picture to picture. She was staying in a villa infinitely more congenial than my pension. Villa Pestellini, to which one acceded by a bar of crochet-like umbrella pines, was a smallish ochre-coloured house with the usual Tuscan attributes of loggia and *limonaia*. The nights were lit by fireflies and serenaded by frogs.

I realized that Italy was as necessary to me as France, but for a different reason. Italy could be superimposed; France was the foundation stone without which nothing could have been accomplished.

*   *   *   *   *

It took me years to realize that I would never have anything but a small slick aptitude for drawing. I knew what to put in, but not what to leave out. Many people can draw a little, just enough to be in demand for a visitors' book, or a programme for amateur theatricals. Now and then, a really successful caricature, like an embarrassing byblow, would seem to hint that my talent lay in quite another direction. I mention this fact in connection with Florence, as this is where I began to long for some mode of self-expression, other than drawing.

Music was brought into my life by my father. Though he had never studied, he played delightfully by ear, Wagner, Verdi, Massenet, Saint-Saëns, Puccini, the latest musical comedy—everything was grist to his mill. In addition to this gift, he excelled in understanding children; nothing was too much trouble, matinées, Gunter's, bedtime stories, he left no stone unturned. No child in its senses ever resisted him; besides, it was thrilling to be taken out by this huge, handsome, elegant man! ("How tall is your father?" "Six foot one!" "Oh, that's nothing; mine's six foot four!")

Another year passed.

"If you learn enough Spanish in a month to ask for what you want, I will take you to Spain for a birthday treat," proffered my mother, boldly pandering to my collector's instinct which was never wholly dormant. This time, it was countries. France, Italy, —Switzerland didn't count—she knew I longed to add Spain to my collection.

After a month's drudgery at the Berlitz School, I was able to produce enough Spanish for my purpose. If France is cerebral, Italy sensuous, Spain is passionate—the country where the choice of desire is more involuntary than death and suffering. I got to know the tigerish, pitiless sun of Spain that has blood mingled with its stripes, the sun that rubs its hairy spine against hot marble, the sun that beats like a drum in one's brain, urging: Faster! Faster!

The Spanish dancer who travels immured in her dance, motionless but for those flickering hands; the dark, deep tides of the blood that clamour for violence and passion. . . . How ridiculous are the travel posters of Spain, Keiller's oranges and ogling gipsies with a pretty perspective of the Alhambra in the background. They attempt the impossible; not by any manner of means can Spain be made pretty: it is as ridiculous as dressing up a gaunt, hairy man in his sister's clothes. Spain can be superb, haggard, squalid, spectacular, macabre, amorous, bloodthirsty, but pretty, never.

The faces of two lovers pressed against the bars of a window, not touching, equal, as though the pulsation that began in one was continued in the other, gave me an insight into love that quickly made me blush and turn away. I had never seen anything so naked.

Spain has no use for compromise, dissimulation. Be yourself, it seems to exhort, let yourself go, be violent, cruel, ruthless, let go pretence! Into the jolly little international cocktail I was rapidly becoming, Spain shook a drop of angostura.

CHAPTER THREE

IN 1910, we moved from Portman Square to 16 Grosvenor Street; it was a great improvement. Osbert Sitwell has excellently described our new house in *Great Morning*:

"It was surely one of the most remarkable houses in London. Its high façade, dignified and unpretentious as only that of a Georgian mansion can be, very effectively hid its immense size. Within existed an unusual air of spaciousness and light, an atmosphere of luxury, for Mrs. Keppel possessed an instinct for splendour, and not only were the rooms beautiful with their grey walls, red lacquer cabinets, English eighteenth-century people in their red coats, huge porcelain pagodas, and thick, magnificent carpets, but the hostess conducted the running of her house as a work of art in itself.

"I liked greatly to listen to her talking; if it were possible to lure her away from the bridge-table, she would remove from her mouth for a moment the cigarette which she would be smoking with an air of determination, through a long holder, and turn upon the person to whom she was speaking her large, humorous, kindly, peculiarly discerning eyes. Her conversation was lit by humour, insight and the utmost good-nature; a rare and valuable attribute in one who had never had—or, at any rate, never felt—much patience with fools. Moreover, a vein of fantasy, a power of enhancement would often lift what she was saying, and served to emphasize the exactness of most of her opinions, and her frankness. Her talk had about it a boldness, an absence of all pettiness, that helped to make her a memorable figure in the fashionable world."

My mother's 'instinct for splendour' caused her in later life to buy a villa in Florence, with one of the most inspiring views in the world. It needed both her courage and imagination to convert a large, admittedly historical, but hideous, house, cluttered up with conservatories and verandahs, into the classic abode of beauty it subsequently became.

In the November of 1910, when the fog already sprawled witless, prostrate, across the city, I was gazing moodily out of the schoolroom window, thinking, O God, four months of this! when the door suddenly opened, and Mama appeared.

"I have good news for you, children. I am taking you to Ceylon for the winter. In my opinion no young lady's education is complete without a smattering of Tamil." She added with her customary twinkle: "You will have plenty of opportunities of picking it up. The boat leaves in four days, so you will just have time to do your packing."

We gasped. It was too good to be true. The fog could do its damnedest. What did we care? A procession of visionary elephants poured into the schoolroom with young, turbaned rajahs culled from Dulac on their backs. Cobras undulated, macaws screeched, sepoys salaamed. I looked after the retreating figure of Mama with superstitious reverence.

Once again, I set out on my travels, this time accompanied by my sister, Moiselle and Nana. My mother and some relatives were joining us in Naples. The boat was by no means a large one; the Bay of Biscay lived up to its reputation. Sandwiched between the kitchen and the 'Gents', I would have subscribed, had I known it, to Paul Morand's theory that nothing smells as stuffy as the sea; but at fifteen curiosity soon gets the better of seasickness. I couldn't wait for my first glimpse of the East which in this case turned out to be Algiers. I naturally insisted on visiting the native quarter, clinging to the arm of Nana. The streets were very narrow; a filthy old man carrying the carcase of a sheep on his back, brushed up against Nana, who turned on him furiously: "You dirty little black boy! I shall tell Mrs. Keppel about you!"

In the Red Sea, I had my first *corps à corps* with my enemy, the heat, a tangible, ubiquitous presence, exhibitionist, persistent as a beggar's whine. Pawed and mauled, I lay like a casualty on the stinging deck, too hot even to draw, longing for the solace of night with its phosphorescent waves and great blotchy stars. Far out into the Indian Ocean was wafted the smell of spices from Ceylon; long before we got into the harbour, we were mobbed by boats clotted with betel-chewing natives, which terrified me at first, as I thought they were spitting blood.

Our first night at the Galle Face Hotel was not an unadulterated pleasure. Curry was a condiment to be used sparingly, I had always imagined, not to be splashed indiscriminately over everything, including vegetables? Then there were the black beetles, ever so obliging they were; I even found one willing to act as a bookmarker.

By way of compensation, I reminded myself of the flying fish in the Indian Ocean; I looked forward to butterflies like birds, and birds like butterflies. Here at least, I was not to be disappointed. If the days were torrid, the mornings were heavenly, provided you got up early enough. We had pawpaw for breakfast, green of rind, pink of flesh. I became acquainted with precious stones, not grudgingly exhibited in jewellers' windows, but in little bags. Uncounted, you could pour them in a cool stream into the hollow of your hand: aquamarines, star sapphires, moonstones, peridots, catseyes.

We moved up to Candy. The Buddhist priests in their yellow robes, the sacred tortoises, white peacocks, appealed to me as a beautiful, if monotonous, frieze. I think I obscurely missed something with the possibility of change. I know now, what I inarticulately guessed then, namely, that I am essentially an Occidental. No yearnings for the East have ever plagued me, though I love travel. I like *hints* of the Orient, such as you find in Bucharest, Sicily, Southern Spain, an echo, a reminiscence; but the unmitigated East disturbs, without detaining me. Alas, I have never visited China, which was my mother's spiritual home, and which might well have proved to be mine also, for China had many affinities with France.

Our ultimate goal was Dambatenne, a bungalow some 6000 feet above sea level, in the midst of tea plantations, which had been lent to my mother by Sir Thomas Lipton. Monkeys gambolled on a small precarious lawn, parrots streaked from tree to tree, tiny humming birds skimmed huge greedy-looking flowers; I shared a room with a tame snake[1] and a wild governess. On a clear day, you could see the Indian Ocean with even a phantom ship or two on the horizon.

We had an old native butler, '*apoo*', I think, is the Tamil word, who would coyly waddle through the dining-room whilst we were having luncheon, with a pyramid of chamber-pots gracefully balanced on his head.

One day, my mother, as a great treat, took us all for a picnic. Despite the altitude, it was too hot for my taste. My sister and I sprawled, unrebuked, in glorious *dolce far niente*, whilst Mama and our two cousins, Ronnie and Eva Graham Murray, busied themselves with the preparations for the picnic. Presently we happened to glance down at our bare legs. You couldn't put a pin between the leeches! We met with no sympathy, the party had watched with glee the leeches accumulating.

On another occasion I begged to be taken on a big game-shooting expedition in the jungle some 3000 feet below. We slept in a rest house; all night long the most hideous unidentifiable shrieks and whistles literally made my hair stand on end. The following day I was privileged to have a shot (the only shot of my life) at a crocodile indistinguishable from a log of wood. There was a sudden plunge—I think I hit it in the tail.

The two impressions which remain were seeing fresh elephant spoor in a clearing in the jungle, and a shoal of butterflies which squashed themselves in a milky mess on the windscreen on the drive back to Dambatenne—oh, yes! and a great snake coiled like a necklace round a tree smothered in sybidiuns, for all the world like the snake in Douanier Rousseau's *Charmeur de Serpent*.

Taken as a whole, Ceylon was a completely irrelevant interlude in an otherwise coherent life, in which country-house visits alternated

[1] A domesticated one employed to catch rats.

with instructive European travel. On looking back, I realize that my education was entirely based on geographical bribery; my parents, being indifferent linguists themselves, were wisely obsessed with the ambition of having at least one polyglot daughter.

The greatest effort was yet to come. Our parents had planned to visit China; they had also planned that we should learn German, not as other English girls learn German, with an English-speaking governess and a contemporary compatriot. We were to be dumped down, like the Babes in the Wood, in an exclusively German forest, where we should be compelled either to sink or to swim, if I may mix my metaphors. After three months in Ceylon, we were accordingly put on a Europe-bound boat with many recommendations; my parents sailed in the opposite direction. Sonia and I were face to face at last without any other conversational outlet; I cannot recollect my opening gambit; for the first time in my life, I realized that I liked my sister.

*   *   *   *   *

When we arrived in Munich, it was snowing as it snows in those old-fashioned crystal globes when you turn them upside down; it was snowing so thick and fast you couldn't see out of the taxi window.

Moiselle and Nana, for once, were unanimous in condemning the parental policy of sending two defenceless children to fend for themselves in an alien, if not positively hostile, foreign country. Curiously enough, I did not share their gloom. Any change of atmosphere acted as a stimulant on me, my innate curiosity always getting the better of any other instinct.

On the threshold of the pension where we were to spend at least six months, stood a bulky pink flannel figure; its flaxen head was decorated with curl papers: "*Willkommen, Willkommen,*" it panted "*Willkommen* to our pension.*"

My sister was subject to asthma. The day after our arrival, the poor little thing was sitting propped up in bed with all the familiar paraphernalia: steam kettle, thermometer, inhalations. She was breathless, but game. I felt she was on my side. Snow agglutinated to the double windows, made it impossible to see out. Moiselle, in a towering rage, paced up and down.

"*Non, on n'a pas idée de cela,*" she spluttered, "*nous envoyer chez*

ces satanés Allemands en plein hiver sans connâitre âme qui vive, eet ees
a scandale!"

"I must thay, for onth, you're right, Madamthell," endorsed Nana,
who lisped. "Mitheth Keppel can't have known what wath in thtore
for uth. It ith not even ath if Mith Violet thpoke German!"

I whipped round. "All right, I will, I'll speak German before you
know where you are!"

Every day we went to German classes in a German school kept by
an Alsatian of the name of Savaète, who spoke French and German
equally badly. Every day on my way to school I would pass through
the Palace Gardens; the statues were muffled in snow; the Palace in
mystery.

The Wittelsbach legend began to impinge on my consciousness; in
some of the bookshops lurked fly-blown photographs of that ideal
couple, Ludwig of Bavaria and Elisabeth of Austria, he with his double
arch of hair and eyebrow, smouldering eyes, sulky mouth; she, vulnerable and aloof as a stained-glass window. Wagner's arrogant profile,
as virile as that of any old American hostess, generally escorted the
couple. Starnberg was only an hour's drive from Munich.

I did not mind the cold, I have always loved the snow; not the
snow you get in England, episodic, rationed, a pretext for pranks and
statistics; but the real snow of Central Europe, punctual, inescapable,
a mantle of oblivion impartially obliterating country after country.

The pension abounded in unfamiliar fauna. There was a fat lady,
Frau Leeb, who had an artificial leg. She and the leg were wheeled into
luncheon separately. The leg was laid on a china stove to be hotted up.
When it was *à point* she screwed it into its socket. The belle of the
pension, Fräulein Schultz, was a faded blonde who possessed two
tiaras, one made of wild boar's tusks for weekdays, and the other, made
of Beauvais tapestry, for Sundays.

Côté hommes, Pension Glocker boasted an Argentine youth, rather
surprisingly known as Herr Bunge (I have often wondered what his
real name was) and an extremely enterprising retired Oberst Lieutenant,
who immediately fell in love with Moiselle. Despite her antipathy for
his race, she played up, up to a point.

As the German language gradually became more accessible, my
spirits rose.

[60]

My sister, long since recovered from her asthma, made friends with a tough little American girl called Hildegarde Smythe-Martin. Incorruptibly alien, the two would post themselves on either side of the school-staircase where they would collaborate in tripping up the German children on their way down. A writhing hecatomb of German bodies was to be seen any morning at the bottom of the stairs, much to my embarrassment.

There were certain classes, notably chemistry, which I simply could not cope with. My nose tactfully took to bleeding when this was about due; but I couldn't absolutely rely on it after a time. My kind little sister stepped into the breach. She embroidered me a handkerchief with large red spots. A worried, strangely credulous mistress would burst into the class where she was working: "*Deine Schwester blutet*," was the invariable formula.

Needless to say, music came into its own. Nearly every evening I was taken either to the opera or to a concert. I became mad about Wagner, and soon prided myself on being able to pick out each motif of the 'Ring' on the pension piano.

At length spring burst on the Isar Valley. Every tree harboured a Waldvogel, the sky was cluttered with black scurrying Valkyries. I became acquainted with a young Wittelsbach prince with whom I fancied myself in love. He was a red-haired, foxy-faced youth, without any claim to interest, except as a distant connection of the House of Bavaria. It was not long before I saw myself as a mixture of Lola Montez and the 'Winter Queen'. We met at the Nymphenburg house of a lady called Pepita de Carmendillas, who specialized in pretenders and lost causes. It was bliss. The months slipped by. Suddenly, a cable arrived out of the blue from my mother, announcing her imminent arrival.

It cannot be said she took kindly to Pension Glocker. There was no disguising her distaste for its inmates, or her dismay at the metamorphosis wrought by Germany on her elder daughter. She had left a fairly presentable young girl, unobtrusively dressed in Woollands' coats and skirts; now a budding Gretchen met her gaze, fatuous, shapeless, wearing a silver watch-chain round her middle with a silver watch worn in guise of sporran. She took one look at me: "My poor child!" she exclaimed. "You can never leave Germany!"

I was much hurt.

"Why, Mama? Surely you wanted me to learn German and to like Germany?"

For the first time she was up against my fatal adaptability.

"Yes, darling, I know, I wanted you to learn German, but I never thought you would *turn into* a German. After all, I thought you had completely identified yourself with France; you can't be *both* German *and* French."

"Oh, yes, I can, one can like Sandkuchen and—and—*mille feuilles!*"

"That's exactly what you are, a *mille feuilles*; well, there's a *feuille* too many. It's time I took you both away, though I must say, Doey seems to have stood up to the Germans better than you have!"

"It's quite the other way round," I assured her with pride, "the Germans couldn't stand up to Doey," and I described the daily holocaust at the foot of the stairs.

She expressed a wish to meet our friends (if any). Sonia, of course, produced the muscular Hildegarde whilst I eyed mine with some misgiving. According to Anglo-Saxon standards, they did not seem all that attractive. However, I dubiously selected little Mitzi Schnurbart, the life and soul of the drawing class, who did such inimitable caricatures of her fellow draughtsmen, and Satinig Davidoglu, a broody Roumanian intellectual, who contrived to win all the prizes, but I had reckoned without her chronic bronchitis. When our friends were seated at dinner, I discovered to my humiliation that Mitzi's head only just topped the table. She was, in point of fact, a dwarf. How was it I hadn't noticed this before?

As to the saturnine Satinig, she scarcely uttered; her bronchitis seemed to have taken a turn for the worse. She appeared to be thickly padded in cotton-wool. As the maid was preparing to remove the soup, she turned her great mournful eyes to my mother. "I wonder if I might have another plateful, Madame?" She dived into her bosom, produced what had once been a compress. "You see, it is so important that I should have something *hot* on my chest."

Of course, America won, hands down, or rather, up. Apart from Hildegarde, Sonia had some other friends, English this time; the Molesworths. They were a large and devoted family, who appeared to spend most of their time sampling every known childish disease; whooping cough, mumps, chicken pox, and now last, and almost roguishly, German measles!

Childhood

The day they discovered this, they gave a party. They took us to the *Valkyries* where they had booked a small box in the same stratosphere as the pit. All we saw of the *Valkyries* was smoke, smoke from the dragon, smoke from Brunhilde's chaperonic fire. Just smoke. A week later Sonia and I both took to our beds with German measles.

In spite of the unfortunate impression created by my friends, in spite of the even more unfortunate impression created by my appearance, Mama consented to allow us to remain another six months, provided we moved to a decent apartment. This was found in the same street as the pension, Maximilianstrasse, a few doors higher up. It was a spacious sunny flat which I was allowed to furnish according to my taste, that is to say with furniture rented from the antique dealers for that period.

After my mother's departure, a new social phase set in. She had provided us with a set of friends whom she considered more suitable than Satinig and Co. Sir Vincent Corbett, our Minister in Munich, was, of course, familiar with what in those days was termed *die erste Gesellschaft*. Accordingly, Schönborns, Arcos, Friesens, invaded the flat, and we were invited back to their homes in town and country.

They were a jolly extrovert lot, given up to shooting and skiing, with a certain amount of music thrown in. Not very exciting, perhaps, but I induced them to act in a play I had written in German in which they performed with considerable gusto.

My life was blissful; painting most of the day, music most of the night. I had no wish ever to leave Munich. Papa came out; together we made various pilgrimages to Bayreuth, the castles. We would vie with each other in the identification of Wagnerian 'motivs'; hand in hand we sat through a wonderful performance of *Tristan*, conducted by the famous Felix Mottl, who subsequently collapsed in the arms of his wife, Zdenka Fassbender, one of the finest Isoldes I have ever heard. He succumbed to heart failure in the middle of the 'Liebestod.'

No girl of seventeen was ever dragged more unwillingly from her studies, no Backfisch ever turned her back on Munich more reluctantly.

*   *   *   *   *

Paris. The judgement of Paris. With infinite disdain, Paris looked me up and down. Nearly two years in Germany? No wonder, *cela se*

[63]

voit! Monsieur Gaston! Her hair! *Mais elle est grotesque, cette pauvre petite, vous allez me faucher ça!* No stays, no *soutien gorge?* But what was her governess thinking of? *Ne bougez pas, Mademoiselle. Il faut ce qu'il faut.* Her clothes! *Mais elle est vêtue comme l'as de pique . . .*

"Mademoiselle Mado!"

After a month in Paris, who would have recognized the Bavarian Backfisch? Patiently, tirelessly, my mother dealt with my appearance, item after item; complexion, hair, figure, clothes, adding here, subtracting there. A whole *quartier* concentrated on my uninviting person.

If only I hadn't got to return to England. If only—couldn't I come out in Paris instead? No, I couldn't. It was for London that I was being prepared, I was being prepared by Paris for London. Better get that straight. Please, couldn't I go to just one party in Paris? Only one? Just to see what it was like. Mama considered. "W-e-ll, I might perhaps take you to dinner at Boni de Castellane's. I don't suppose he would mind, he is such an old friend. It might even amuse him to see what you were like!"

Ce qui fût dit fût fait.

Boni de Castellane was, I suppose, at the zenith of his prestige. Regarded with the irreverence of seventeen he had fuzzy pink hair set rather far back on his forehead, a fair drooping moustache, heavy-lidded sleepy eyes, and the staccato walk of an automaton. But he was very kind.

His house, lit exclusively by candles, was lovely, full of exquisite bibelots and family pictures, including a portrait of his great ancestor, Talleyrand. Hypnotized by all this, I sat silently at dinner, conscientiously drinking the wine that was poured into glass after glass. Accustomed to the most spartan of evening meals based on biscuits and a glass of milk, I was determined to drink as to the manner born.

Presently, one of my neighbours remarked slyly: "You seem very young, Mademoiselle. Would this by any chance be your first grown-up dinner party?" This would never do.

"My first dinner party!" I snorted. "I would have you know, Monsieur, that I have just celebrated my twenty-fifth birthday!" As ill luck would have it there was a dead silence as I uttered these words. My mother heard, and threw me a look of unadulterated fury. I collapsed into a crestfallen silence, and took a great gulp from one of my glasses.

Was it my imagination, or were there two Boni de Castellanes, or had he a brother who was very like him, a twin, perhaps? I blinked again. Curious that I shouldn't have noticed there were two of them.

Now I came to think of it there were two of almost everything, two of Boni, two of Talleyrand—my neighbour again turned a mischievous eye on me. "As you have been *dans le monde* for so long, Mademoiselle, you doubtless remember our host's pink marble palace in the Bois?"

"N-no, strange to say, I have no reco—recollection."

I seemed to have some difficulty in articulating, could it be the wine? Horror! I put down the glass I was in the act of conveying to my mouth.

"If I were you, *chère Mademoiselle*, I think I would stick to one kind of wine," his voice was now definitely motherly, "mixtures are bad for the stomach. Personally, I drink nothing but Bordeaux."

But the harm was done. I experienced considerable difficulty in rising to my feet at the end of dinner. Both my neighbours by now converted into nannies, supporting me under each elbow, whispered a word into the ear of my host, who burst out laughing and led me to a tiny *salon* with a Directoire canapé. Presently, he brought me a large cup of black coffee and some smelling salts. I have never forgotten the shame to this day.

Part Two

YOUTH

CHAPTER FOUR

No such folly occurred on the night of my coming-out ball in Grosvenor Street. My unfortunate experience at the Castellane dinner prejudiced me against wine for years. We dined at little tables; the garden was spanned by a tent. Casano's band played discreetly during dinner. I was disposed to be cynical, critical, the blasée woman of the world. Yes, I had spent 'several years' in Munich, studying art. Painting. When I wasn't painting, I was playing the piano (I might have added, execrably), though I now looked upon music as my *violon d'Ingres.* "*Violon* how much?" The pink and white young man on my right eyed me suspiciously. "Paradoxical though it may seem, painting was originally a *pis-aller*—of all the arts, music appealed to me most." O Lord! A ruddy blue stocking! The young man's jaw dropped—he turned to his other neighbour.

Though I didn't care about débutante dinner parties, I discovered that I adored dancing. It was the dawn of the jazz. Astringent, syncopated 'chunes' (such as 'Who paid the Rent for Mrs. Rip Van

Winkle', 'On the Level You're a Little Devil', etc.) put new life into the decorous dance floors of London. Presently, the Charleston would disarticulate the world; meanwhile the fox-trot and the tango reigned supreme. Passionate plodders (counting audibly) propelled each other solemnly round the room.

The Russian ballet came into my life. So did frivolity, flippancy, futility.

I hadn't been 'out' a month before my mother informed me that we were spending the week-end at Knole.

Now, though I had not seen Vita for two years, we had kept up a desultory, somewhat misleading, correspondence. I think she was rather disgusted with my geographical flightiness, Bavarian rhapsodies. As far as I can remember, I had sent her a snapshot of myself as a fully matured German, complete with plaits and silver-watch sporran. That had silenced her—at any rate, for the time being. I was still very fond of her, however, and was looking forward to demolishing some of her insular prejudices.

If she expected a horizontal pseudo-Gretchen, I expected a 'representative Englishwoman', perpendicular, gauche, all knobs and knuckles. No one told me that Vita had turned into a beauty. The knobs and knuckles had disappeared. She was tall and graceful. The profound, hereditary Sackville eyes were as pools from which the morning mist had lifted. A peach might have envied her complexion. Round her revolved several enamoured young men, one of whom had presented her with a bear, inevitably christened Ivan. Bears had taken the place of rabbits.

She had all the prestige that two years' precedence *dans le monde* can confer. I felt resentful, at a disadvantage. Surely she might have kept me informed of her evolution? "Do you like my dress? *Tu me trouves jolie?*" I questioned eagerly, reverting to the French of our childhood, pining for praise. "*Tu as beaucoup de chic,*" was the cautious reply.

There was an attractive young man staying at Knole for the week-end, Michael X. I sat next him at dinner. He had the comet-like eyes of a Persian miniature, merry hair, charm, wit. I set out to see what I could do. The result was that we vanished into the park after dinner, only returning after everyone had gone to bed. I longed to tell Vita of my conquest; maybe she was still awake?

I groped my way down miles of passages, past the staterooms, through the long gallery, with its perennial smell of mothball. At last I reached her bedroom door. I didn't knock for fear she might be asleep. The moonlight poured through the uncurtained windows on to the carved historical-looking bed.

She was not asleep. "Hullo," she said in an unsurprised voice, "it's you, is it? I wondered what had become of you." I sank down on the step on which the bed rested.

"I've had such a lovely evening. He kissed me," I boasted. "You have no idea how attractive he is."

"Nobody is under any delusion as to how attractive you find *him*," my childhood friend commented dryly. "I think it's time you went to bed, your mother may be sitting up for you."

Before the week-end was out, my reputation as a flirt was firmly established. At last I felt grown up. Neither Michael nor I was in love with each other, but our mutual admiration was as intoxicating as a *pas de deux* on ice; we whirled, wheeled, dipped, in perfect unison, carved graceful hieroglyphics.

My old intimacy with Vita was, apparently, at an end. She treated the Michael episode with an amused condescension which I, for my part, found extremely galling. Six months later she married without letting me know. I had heard rumours of her engagement, but as long as she did not tell me herself, I attached small importance to them. I was stunned by what I took to be a piece of perfidy I did not deserve. As usual, Vita was a class ahead.

A year later, all was redeemed. I became godmother to Vita's eldest son, Benedict. Harold and Vita bought a Tudor cottage in Kent, very pretty in its way, but too selfconsciously picturesque for my taste. Life in a Tudor cottage is like living *under* the furniture instead of above it.

The blue stocking phase was over; I discovered I could amuse people in various ways; I have always been a good mimic, I could do caricatures, improvise imaginary conversations. In short, I could create an atmosphere. This was highly stimulating.

I was admitted to the scintillating Sitwell triumvirate; *enfants ter-ribles*, they sat on their private Olympus and pelted the Philistines, the Blimps, the Kinfoots, with the snowballs of their satire. Each, a genius in his way, seemed to belong to a different epoch. Edith was Gothic; Sacheverell, Renaissance; Osbert, Hanoverian. The ferocious author of *Before the Bombardment* was also the tender poet of the simple. It did not occur to people that he only loved the things that were worth loving. Osbert's *England Reclaimed*, his *Mary Anne, Mr. and Mrs. Hague, Phoebe Southern*, are as rustically beautiful as Chardin's *Ménagère*.

I made friends with Rebecca West who has a voice like a crystal spring and eyes like twin jungles; with Gerald Berners who was infested with talents, and a tease of genius; with Nancy Cunard who seemed the incarnation of youth and joy of living.

My wanderlust was temporarily lulled. In the summer my parents rented a place in Holland, near The Hague, belonging to a friend of theirs, Baroness de Brienen. Built over a canal, it was all that a Dutch house should be, benevolent, platonic, contemplative, philosophical. For three hundred years it had smiled at its lilied reflection. My father's family was of Dutch origin; Joost van Keppel and Bentinck had accompanied William III to England. Keppel, younger, more attractive, superseded Bentinck in the King's favour; he was given a miniature Versailles (Voorst), an earldom, the Garter. Bentinck was made Earl of Portland. Nowadays Keppels and Bentincks, the most orthodox of men, vie in competitive coyness when confronted with their distinguished, if slightly ambiguous, ancestors.

To return to Clingendaal: shoals of guests, including a suitor or two, came to spend August and September with us. We used to bathe in the morning at Scheveningen, sightsee in the afternoon, sometimes dress up for dinner. In the summer of 1914, all the brilliant, doomed young men the war was to annihilate, George Vernon, Volley Heath, Patrick Shaw Stewart, Raymond Asquith, Bim Tennant, flocked to Holland. Diana Manners, dazzling, disconcerting, came with her mother, the Duchess of Rutland. Diana appeared, as it were, to people, lighting up the room with her flawless, awe-inspiring beauty. So must the angel have looked who turned Adam and Eve out of the Garden of Eden. With a face like that, she should, I thought, carry a sword, or a trumpet.

Lady Oxford and the epigrammatical Elizabeth also visited us; in fact, they were there when the war broke out. We all crowded on the night boat to Newhaven. The following morning, we breakfasted at 10 Downing Street, which gave us the momentary thrill of being behind the scenes, though, of course, we saw nothing, not even the dumpy, grumpy figure of the Prime Minister.

Not immediately did I realize the horrible implication of war, how one contemporary after another would be picked off, sacrificed; how relationships planned to endure would be brutally severed; how the voices of a Rupert Brooke, a Julian Grenfell, would be stilled for ever. Men in their prime were taken; half-smoked lives, their talents scattered.

I met Julian in the spring before war was declared, at Taplow. He resembled a young gladiator with his curly, bullet-shaped head, projecting lip, cleft chin, magnificent physique. The loveliest girls in London were there for him to choose. His deep-set, implacable eye raked the room. I suddenly felt a hand on my shoulder. "Let's get out of here, come for a walk." Dumb with surprise and gratitude, I found myself being propelled at great speed through a still wintry wood.

"You see, I'm anti-social," he was saying, "I don't even possess a dinner jacket. I loathe parties. What the hell are you doing here?"

"But let me——"

"Yes, I know, you're a débutante and all that, but that's no answer to my question."

"As a matter of fact," I stammered, anxious to rehabilitate myself in his eyes, "I didn't want to come out, it was forced upon me."

"Oh well, there's some hope then!"

Before I knew where I was, I began to tell him the story of my life up to date. Of course, I fell in love with Julian. Who didn't? His manner of wooing, if anything so tempestuous could be called by so mild a name, was unconventional to say the least of it.

He would arrive at Grosvenor Street dressed in an old sweater and crumpled grey flannel trousers, with frequently a black eye, and, more than once, a split lip (having been boxing the night before); would sweep aside the terrorized footman, mount the stairs four at a time, and burst into my so-called 'studio' at the top of the house, which was in reality a kind of glorified house-maid's cupboard, decorated in the most ridiculous and pretentious Italianate style, chasubles on the wall, and an ikon over the radiator, the gift of a more honestly inclined admirer. (Let no one be under any misapprehension concerning Julian's intentions. He suggested everything, bless his heart, short of matrimony!)

A cloud of incense denoted my presence: as it wasn't of the best quality, people had to cough through a barrage of asphyxiating smoke before they could discern anything. Julian alternately fascinated and terrified me. On one occasion, I dragged him to a ball given by one of my relatives. Bursting out of hired 'tails', he lured me to the ladies' cloakroom, where he locked us in. An awkward moment arose when a member of the Royal family asked for her cloak. Had he been less precipitate he would doubtless have won my consent to—anything.

Alas! His courtship was too spectacular, the ladies' cloakroom incident did not pass unnoticed. My father was infuriated by his dress, his recurrent black eye, *sans gêne*. Julian was banned. The war was imminent; he was one of the first to go. The war saw to it that we never met again.

When I heard of his death, I refused to believe that anyone so vital, so gifted, so superb, should have to meet with the common fate. But I was soon to learn that the élite were Death's favourites.

My cousin, Willie Edmonstone, was the next I was to mourn. Popular, wholehearted, athletic, he was killed at the age of nineteen. George Vernon, Patrick Shaw Stewart, Volley Heath, Bim Tennant, one after the other, were struck down, their loves suspended, their soaring stayed. It required superhuman courage to open a newspaper. Mercifully, there were trivial incidents which created a diversion, such as when I was fired from the canteen where I was working, for making a cup of cocoa for a visiting general out of knife powder. My mother alleged that I was always to be found during the paltry air raids of 1917, lying full length under the dining-room table, tightly buttoned into a sealskin coat, sniffing a gardenia.

Sonia, the reverse of static on these occasions, would bicycle madly round and round the basement. I do not recollect her bicycling at any other time.

Round about the age of sixteen, my sister shed her chrysalis cocoon, and turned into a remarkably attractive young creature with hair like ripe corn, and a beautifully proportioned athletic figure. So far her studies had played but a small part in her life. We had both attended Miss Woolf's classes in South Audley Street at different periods of our lives. Fully realizing that the ability was there, should she choose to exert it, Miss Woolf remarked one day in a tone of idle speculation: "Isn't it interesting how two members of the same family can be so different? Your sister, of course, won *all* the prizes."

The result was electrifying. Galvanized, on her mettle, Sonia managed to atone in six months for the inattention of several years. Practically every talent was hers to develop; she was musical, possessed a lovely mezzo-soprano voice, danced like a dream, wrote with facility and verve, the only gift she did not possess—I think she would be the first to admit this—was the gift of drawing; and even that is not strictly true. She could produce very small, meticulous, painfully literal renderings of mostly utilitarian objects. Flights of fancy were not for her. When I decided to attend the Slade School, she begged to be allowed to accompany me. Considered too young and inexperienced for the Life Class, she was accordingly turned loose in the Still Life room; it contained some two hundred plaster casts.

When, in the course of the morning, Professor Tonks visited the Still Life room, he was confronted with a large sheet of cartridge paper, on which the largest possible percentage of casts figured in riotous juxtaposition—in fact there were the maximum of statues in the minimum of space. For the first time in history, the formidable Tonks was speechless; tears of helpless laughter coursed down his cheeks, inarticulate, choking, he left the nonplussed girl.

When he returned the following day, purity had taken the place of promiscuity. In the middle of a sheet of virgin paper, was one enormous eye, each eyelash assessed and distinct from its fellow, cornea, pupil, iris, as scrupulously delineated as on the optician's board.

"*L'œil était dans la tombe et regardait Caïn.*"

The professor fled, confounded.

*　　*　　*　　*　　*

It must have been during the autumn of 1917 that I was first invited to stay at Berkeley Castle, which in those days belonged to an octogenarian peer, Lord Fitzhardinge. A brown and nimble niece, half squirrel, half bird, kept house for him. Lord Fitzhardinge, despite his age, hunted four days a week with his own pack, and his elegant huntsmen dressed in saffron yellow. It was a fine sight seeing them streak across the water meadows to the Severn. I like to dwell on my first glimpse of Berkeley, that pink mammoth of a castle with its sullenly gleaming silver roofs (a twelfth-century Lord Berkeley had owned silver mines in Wales), tufts of valerian gratuitously springing from the crevices between the stones. The pink mammoth grazed in water meadows, a rugged and solitary old monster, the bull of the herd, to which we are as so many ticks; it is accustomed to the ticks feeding on it. One tick is exactly like another, century follows century, it continues to graze. I know this sounds nonsense, but I have never known this animal feeling about any place, save Carrouges in Normandy, which is also pink, shaggy, and horned.

Lord Fitzhardinge put me in mind of a crotchety ogre; he was practically stone deaf and wore a Persian cat draped like a boa about his shoulders; he conversed, via the cat, never addressing you directly; "Omar says he thinks it's time you got some roses into your cheeks, young lady. We must sit her on a horse and see what she can do!"

Pat Dansey, his niece, fitted in beautifully. She was small and quick and done in various shades of brown, her hair was the colour of potato chips, her eyes were like bees, her face had the texture and hue of a pheasant's egg. I have made her sound edible, but she was too brittle and furry to make really good eating. She had a stutter that sounded most incongruous in her small neat person, for it gave one the impression she was slightly intoxicated. Her life was given up to Berkeley, hunting, and her ancient uncle. How well I could understand her cult for Berkeley, of all the places I knew the most richly suggestive; part historical, part legendary, wholly Shakespearian. I never heard the screams of the unfortunate Edward II, neither did I meet with any of the ghostly habitués. A motherly chronic smell of strawberry jam permeated the whole place in these days, than which nothing could be more reassuring; perhaps it was a kind of ghostly disinfectant?

Meanwhile, the war went its weary way. One could scarcely open a newspaper without coming across some familiar name in the casualty lists. My mother ran a hospital in Boulogne with Lady Sarah Wilson. I envied her going so often to France, even under such dreadful circumstances, but as I clearly had no vocation for nursing, I was not allowed to accompany her.

I got engaged more than once, with varying motives; compassion, curiosity, boredom, physical attraction. I got engaged, but somehow shied at matrimony. "*Jamais*," Rostand said, "*la barque ne vaut la passerelle.*"

Then, the last year of the war, I met Denys Trefusis, who, like Julian Grenfell, was an Elizabethan. He had a pale arrogant face, whose logical conclusion would seem to be a pointed beard; I mentally added a ruff and one pearl earring. It was impossible to look better bred, more audacious. Slim and elegant, he could not help dramatizing his appearance; like Lord Ribblesdale, he made the most ordinary clothes appear picturesque. Intrepid, rebellious, he had led an adventurous, exciting life, having run away to Russia when he was little more than a schoolboy, refusing to accept money from home, living on the proceeds of half a dozen improvizations. More Russian than English, he returned to England at the outbreak of war, where he joined the 'Blues'.

Who was I to withstand such nomadic prestige, such intransigence, so many challenges to my imagination? In fact, the only time I ever succumbed to *le charme slave* was with Denys. I was by no means the only girl to set her cap at him. Never did I work so hard. At long last, he began to respond, taking care to explain that, like Julian, he was anti-matrimony. It was most unfortunate. I might have married a budding genius, a cultured and domesticated future duke; why did I always want to marry people who had a prejudice against what is called 'settling down'?

On his return to the front, I wrote innumerable, and, judging by the result, successful letters. On his next leave he reluctantly proposed. We were married on June 16th, 1919. Melba sang the 'Ave Maria' at our wedding.

Marriage can be divided into two categories; those that begin well and end badly, those that begin badly and end well. Mine came (roughly) under the latter heading. It was not until a full year had elapsed that we were able to establish a *modus vivendi*. I hasten to add that the fault was entirely mine. I was spoilt, egocentric, insensitive, odious.

At the end of a year Denys was given a job in Paris. As usual, the spell began to work. We had a tiny flat in the rue Fourcroy. It is situated in the lugubrious 'Ternes' quarter, but the mere fact of living in Paris was enough to atone for any local shortcomings. Denys spoke rapid idiomatic French with a Russian accent. He had masses of Russian friends, notably Grand Duke Dimitri, but recently escaped from the Bolsheviks. At a dinner party at Boni de Castellane's the butler, about to pour out the champagne, had bent over him with a magnum of Mumm, "*Brut Impérial*," he boomed in the best French tradition. Poor Dimitri hadn't yet recovered.

I liked many of Denys's friends, but cared not for their nocturnal peregrinations. I have always been what the French call *couche tôt*. Not so my husband, the darling of the Caveau Caucasien and other night-clubs. "Can't you yawn a trifle less ostentatiously?" he would bark at me, when at about 2 a.m. everyone was getting into their stride, and I was pining for my bed and hot-water bottle. (Besides, I was jealous.)

Apart from nightclubs, we were often amused by the same things. A year later, fed up with the drabness of the rue Fourcroy, we moved to the rue Laurent Pichat which, although it boasted proximity to the Bois, was an apartment in a shabby tumbledown house with an asthmatic lift which had a tendency to linger between floors. However, we were by no means unhappy there, and occasionally gave makeshift dinner parties.

Rue Laurent Pichat is chiefly associated in my mind with a farcical row we had there. Denys, as befitting a *noctambule*, would frequently ring up late in the day to say that he was not returning for dinner. I had no objection to his dining out, but did not particularly relish a solitary meal; it was not always easy to find someone to dine with me at such very short notice. One day, after a week of this, I arranged to dine with a friend and to go to a ball afterwards. (I had not lost my taste for dancing, merely my taste for nightclubs.)

It so happened that Denys had nothing on that evening; he tele-phoned from his office to say he would be in to dinner. Whereupon I rang up my friend, asking him to fetch me after dinner, and proceeded to put on my smartest frock, at the sight of which Denys's face darkened. "What are you all dolled up for, may I ask?"

"I am being fetched after dinner to go to a ball."

"The devil you are! On the only night I arrange to have dinner at home! Typical."

"But you have dined out every day this week," I protested.

"No doubt I have. I dislike going to bed at 10. The night I decide to go to bed at 10, you decide to go on the tiles!"

"How could I guess you would suddenly elect to come in to dinner?"

"Well, you're not going out, anyhow. You can just ring up your friend and tell him he need not come and fetch you."

"I shall do nothing of the kind!"

"I think you will." So saying he picked up a bunch of grapes off the dinner table and flung it at my dress. It made a beautiful splash on the bodice. Our tempers were of an equal violence. Inarticulate with rage, I made for the door. "Where are you going?" he stormed.

[78]

Without replying, I tore out of the flat, snatching up a coat as I passed through the hall. It was snowing. I ran up the street, across the desolate Avenue Foch. Our distinguished and charming lawyer, Maître Hélène Miropolska, lived not very far away, in the Avenue Bugeaud.

"*Miséricorde!*" she exclaimed as she opened the door. "You look like something out of an old-fashioned film. What do you want?"

"Divorce," I panted, "I want to be divorced. Look what that brute, my husband, has done to me!" I pointed melodramatically to my chest.

"If it's blood," remarked Maître Miropolska philosophically, "you don't seem much affected by the loss of it."

"It's not blood, it's grape juice."

"*Dieu de dieu!* What a waste, and grapes so expensive nowadays! Come in and calm yourself, my child. I will give you a cup of coffee to warm you up before sending you home."

"I am not going home, ever, ever!"

"Well, you can't sleep here, except on the divan in Gaston's study." (Gaston was her husband.)

"I don't care where I sleep, but I am not going home; *je demande le divorce.*"

She cast an oblique look at my distraught countenance.

"*Allons, allons,* we will discuss this tomorrow, *à tête reposée.* I am far too busy to listen to you tonight. You had better sleep on the divan after all. I will go and prepare it, and Gaston."

Tired out with frustrated rage, it was not long before I fell asleep on the divan in Maître Strauss's study. My sleep was so sound that I was not disturbed by a peremptory ring at the front door some hours later. The next morning, I was called by my involuntary hostess. "Get up, and go and titivate in the bathroom. I have arranged for you to have your breakfast in the dining-room, as you dislike solitary meals."

Ten minutes later, she flung open the dining-room door. There, grinning from ear to ear, sat Denys. Needless to say, I burst out laughing. The laughter became a *fou rire,* when he confessed that he had called on the previous night to ask for a divorce.

I'm afraid we both rather enjoyed these Noel Cowardian episodes, which would sometimes end in a *fugue à deux.* He was a remarkable linguist. Russian is child's play compared to Magyar. After a few weeks in Budapest he would casually ask for things in the language of the country. He was also extremely, and, a trifle pedantically, musical. Here I could not keep pace with him.

"Your taste," he would say, "is impeccable in literature, painting, decoration. In music, no."

"But I love all music, including bad music," I would protest.

"*Especially* bad music," he would rectify. "When I say 'bad', I mean music which appeals solely to your emotions. Now Bach——"

"*La mathématique voilée?*" I would quote. "Well, no doubt, I am a musical lowbrow."

★　　★　　★　　★　　★

In 1923 we found the home we had always longed for; a diminutive house in Auteuil, facing full South, looking on to a garden full of gnarled old trees, uneasy to find themselves in Paris. A magnificent chestnut towered over them as a conductor lords it over his musicians. In winter, with its denuded branches (I had nearly written 'antlers'), it put one in mind of a vigilant stag; in March, the young sticky leaves drooped like the ears of a bloodhound; later, it turned into a periwig. We hastened to furnish the house, regardless of nationality or period. There were Chinese rugs with geometrical patterns, Venetian mirrors full of reminscences and plots, glass pictures, one of which was given me by my mother. It represented a Chinese lady smiling at a small grey parrot perched on her arm. She attempts nothing to detain it. Its cage is in her eyes.

After a year or two of relative content I realized I was married to Lohengrin, or Odysseus? His latent nostalgia for Russia asserted itself more strongly. Roused and anxious, I would accompany him on his nightclub expeditions. I awoke to the fact that the wasp-waisted Caucasian dancers had probably more in common with him than I had. Not for nothing did they sing: "*Ulié tai na Krilieh viétra.*"[1]

Go he must. It so happened that a friend of his, Fred Cripps, was being sent to Russia on a mission. Denys, with his knowledge of the language, would be invaluable. He did not hesitate. For several months I was practically without news of him, owing to no fault of his: the posts were irregular and his letters censored.

In a half-hearted way, I tried to pick up the threads of the life I had lived as a *jeune fille*. I was unhappy, more especially as I had now given

[1] Approximately, 'Let us flee on the wings of the wind.'

official recognition to my sentiments by jotting them down. I still possess a diary I kept at that period. It is entirely given over to that eternally adolescent couple: *Weltschmerz* and *Schadenfreude*. Here are a few reflections selected at random:

'An artist makes use of his sorrow; he makes it sit to him. Unfortunately, it takes its revenge during the "rest".'

'The sea in which we drown may be of a ravishing shade of blue.'

'Everyone flies from the solitary: one must pretend to be several.'

'Which is preferable? The hardness of virtue or the softness of corruption?'

'Courage: the virtue of the ruthless.'

'Our separation has left a draught in my heart.'

'Why go on living? I have loved much, suffered much, travelled not a little. I would die rich in love, rich in suffering, rich in countries. I would say: "Take, O God, the remainder of my life, I care not for small change." Etc., etc. *Très jeune Werther.*'

I had no intimate friends. Those of my childhood were married and busy rearing families. Marriage, in France, is practically inescapable. All categories and circumstances are catered for. There is an unofficial tariff founded on the laws of compensation, which works out something like this:

A plainish, richish girl	= A country bumpkin (*hobereau*) slightly titled.
A plain, rich girl	= A ruined or rakish title, or a coming politician (*chef de cabinet*).
A pretty, penniless girl	= A rich roué or a crazy young man, i.e. Love.
An extremely well-born girl	= A millionaire—*industriel.*
A ravishing, rich girl	= A duke or a prince, she can even marry for love.
A rich widow of a certain age, with a good cook	= A handsome penniless young man, or a prosperous contemporary.
An elderly adventuress with 'economies'	= An old lover.
An old maid	= An invalid or a widower with six children.
A penniless, *déclassée* girl	= The convent, or the streets.

But away with cynicism. Founded on common interests and mutual advantage, supplemented by a sense of decorum implanted in both parties since the age of puberty, French marriages often work out better than ours in the long run.

As marriage is considered indissoluble, husband and wife labour much harder to make it a paying concern. Faithfulness is not expected; loyalty to one's family, is. However much they may quarrel in private, in public (and especially in front of their children), a French couple try to give the impression of a *ménage uni*.

There are, of course, exceptions; suspicious, inbred, frightened little men who seem to be the result of a hundred hate matches, and who look upon grand alliances as a substitute for sensuality.

No, I had no intimate friends. I was intimate with Paris, which replaced them. Presently, a small germ of ambition sowed itself in my dissatisfied mind. Paris? Paris, failing people, could give me all I craved. Surely success is an excellent substitute for happiness? My technique of living, if any, had been acquired in France. No elusive and dazzling bird flashed across the high bland sky, for the torment of her populations. Smug is an odious word—how to reconcile smugness with charm, charm with accessibility?

Her pleasures were immediate and proffered. '*Le viergé, le vivace et le bel aujourd'hui.*' No nonsense about being elsewhere and waiting until tomorrow. '*Cueillez dès aujourd'hui les roses de la vie.*'

All Latin countries are more or less positive. It takes a Nordic to be interrogatory. The English reproach the French for not liking, or experiencing, the need to travel. Why travel when all countries are reproduced within the limits of your own? Brittany, racially and geographically, is but an annexe of Cornwall. The Spanish element meanders through the Basque country; from Grenoble to Turin, Italian and French mingle, despite the frontier; in the North, France melts into Belgium; in the East, into Germany. A Frenchman who knows his own country thoroughly has an approximate idea of what other countries can offer him, and what can they offer comparable to the *agrément* of French culture, conversation, cuisine, clothes, love-making? The grandeur of Rome never atoned to Du Bellay for his *douceur Angevine*.

I got to know a few writers, names to conjure with, Paul Morand, Anna de Noailles, Giraudoux, Colette. The first time I met Colette she asked me to repeat my name. "Violette Trefusis," I replied sheepishly.

"*Moi,*" came the bucolic Burgundian voice, "*je vous appellerai 'Géranium'.*"

Giraudoux shared Colette's love and understanding of animals, especially birds. He was rather like one himself: a crane, shy, elegant, exotic. Though his wit and *espièglerie* were typically Gallic, there was a nordic element in his imagination. "*Ondine,*" with its Germanic insistence on knights and naiads, gives us abundant proof of this.

By the time Denys returned from Russia I was more firmly 'installed' in life. I attended lectures at the Sorbonne, first nights. The rue du Ranelagh teemed with *littérateurs*, many of whom found favour in Denys's eyes. There was more give and take, less friction. I did not interfere with his Russians, he encouraged me to write.

Occasionally, we broke away from the routine of Paris, we visited Vienna, Budapest, Berlin. We went to Poland, to stay with the Potocki. Lançut was a legend of international scope.

I had been reared on stories of how you drove in a coach and four, straight into the hall, how you dined in a different room each day of the month, how the Potocki were waited on by hereditary giants, and hereditary dwarfs, whose families had served *their* family for generations.

We accordingly set out with great expectations. I forget the name of the Polish frontier, but not the station *samovar*, or the *zakouskis* spread out on the buffet. Russia seemed very near.

When we got out at the station where we were to be met, horror! There was no conveyance of any kind, let alone a coach and four. We hadn't a word of Polish between us. Denys began expostulating in Russian. People gave one look at the incensed Muscovite and slunk away. "*Anglishanin,*" he shouted, "*ya Anglishanin!*"

Anglishanin, my foot; we weren't born yesterday!

"*Lançut,*" he stormed, "*kudà Lançut?*" At last the reiterated *Lançut* produced some sort of reaction in the station master. Could it be that the Potocki were expecting Russian guests? Highly improbable, but just possible. Better not take risks with the Potocki. Temporizing, with the beautifully international word 'telephone', the station master disappeared. We sat hunched on our luggage, with an impressive and unimpeded view of Poland stretching for hundreds of miles. Were there Polish steppes as well, I wondered with sinking heart. My French maid was heard to mutter something about *les vautours, les loups.*

"*Ne dites donc pas d'idioties,*" I snapped. "*Il n'y a pas de loups en cette saison.*"

"I bet you put the wrong date in your telegram," Denys suddenly rounded on me, blue eyes blazing. "It's the sort of thing you *would* do."

Alas, it was only too plausible. I nodded dumbly, humbly.

"Well, there's not much to be done," he giggled, as suddenly placated. "We may be here for several days. What about singing something to pass the time away?"

> "Watching the trains come in,
> Hearing the porters shout,
> Then when we've watched all the trains come in,
> We watch all the trains go out,"

I quavered.

"Only there aren't any trains *in* or *out*," deplored Denys, looking down on us. "Anyway, I *will* say you have acquired local colour. I have never seen a more convincing pair of Polish refugees!"

I don't know how many hours we sat there—long enough for Denys to pick up Polish, no doubt. At last a tiny speck appeared on the horizon. "A ship! a ship! I mean a car! a car!" I exulted.

A few minutes later a huge American limousine drew up at the station. The station master, bent double with servility, bowed us into the car. Obviously the Russians *had* spoken the truth for once. They *were* expected to stay at Lançut.

Though awed by its size, we were not, I am sorry to say, impressed by the beauty of the place. It was a typical Austrian *Schloss* with bulbous pepper pots and rococo flourishes. What was staggering were its contents. The cream of Versailles, selected by a discriminating ancestress, Princess Lubomirska, was spread over salons and suites (each guest was allotted a suite, ours consisted of four rooms). Watteaus, Lancrets, Fragonards, furniture signed by Jacob, signed by Oeben, Riesener; monogrammed carpets, bindings stamped with the arms of the Kings of France: then, in the middle of all this refinement, would suddenly occur the portrait of a Polish ancestor with shaven head and jewelled scimitar.

Two huge attendants with astrakan 'toques' mounted guard over our door. So intimidating were they that we seldom ventured to cross its threshold. Another delicate attention on the part of our hosts was a brass band (culled from the ranks of the personnel) which, not content with following us about everywhere, would burst into 'God Save the King' at the most inopportune moments—especially in the morning.

Here foregathered the *élite* of four or five middle-European countries: Roumanians, who stood out for their perfect mastery of the French language, their Oriental standard of flattery and their taste for power (this especially applied to the women), which was only equalled by their thirst for intrigue; Hungarians, handsome bores; Viennese, graceful, anglophile, frivolous; Poles, chivalrous, heroic, with here and there a woman of outstanding beauty and vivacity, central Europeans all, with a background of great rivers and jagged fir trees, resonant with languages richly incomprehensible and mutually aggressive, furred, frogged, feudal, the envious onlookers of the East!

Countess Betka came of princely Viennese stock; her mother had been a famous beauty, and her father one of the crack shots of Europe. She was persona grata at the surviving courts of Europe; was wafted, without inquiry, without comment, from embassy to embassy. Most ambassadors were either distant cousins, or hopeful candidates to the shooting parties at Lançut. Great men abounded in her ancestry. Shorn of prestige, bereft of legend, Metternich was merely *der alte Clemens*, the not-too-faithful husband of Tante Mélanie; Talleyrand, also a connection of the ubiquitous Potocki, was spoken of as a testy, though diverting cripple, chiefly to be remembered for his excellent cuisine and his amusing, though equivocal correspondence with his niece, the Duchesse de Dino.

Every morning, a programme would be submitted to the guests. It was a programme of the recreations of the day: golf, tennis, polo, shooting (pheasant, roe deer, hares), you only had to choose.

"I should hate," Denys confided to me, "to be looked upon as a spoil-sport, but I somehow cannot forget the squalor of the Jewish village at our gates, the ringleted gaunt men with the foxes' tails hanging from their hats, the women who go to earth with a hand over their eyes (for all the world like in *Ivan the Terrible*) when they hear us coming. Maybe they are scared of cars?"

[85]

CHAPTER FIVE

THE visa to Denys's friendship, or, at any rate, interest, was music. I very soon realized that I was merely tolerated in his musical circle, a profane, though doubtless well-meaning, hanger-on. His Egeria was Princess Edmond de Polignac; together they would attend concerts, rehearsals, the score under their arm; together they would curtail elaborately prepared dinners, so afraid were they of missing any part of the programme.

Madame de Polignac was a remarkable woman. Imperturbable, inscrutable, she hung over life like a cliff; her rocky profile seemed to call for spray and seagulls; small blue eyes—the eyes of an old salt—came and went; her face was more like a landscape than a face, cloudy of hair, blue of eye, rugged of contour. Although she had lived all her life in France, she spoke French with a strong British accent, which, however, merely rendered her observations more piquant, playing the part of ketchup to her dry, caustic utterances. Like all fundamentally shy people, she was infinitely intimidating. People quailed before her.

The story was told of an unfortunate young woman with social ambitions who had inquired ingratiatingly, *"Vous êtes pour quelque temps à Paris, Princesse?"*

"Pour trente ans, je pense," came the annihilating reply.

She was in the habit of giving supper parties in her studio, usually to celebrate the début of some young musical discovery. On one occasion I found a small piece of glass in the dish I was eating which I parked as discreetly as possible on one side of my plate; but nothing escaped the eye of my hostess who had, apparently, found a similar piece in her helping. "Cinderella, or the little glass supper," she muttered between her teeth.

There is also the well-known story of the fancy-dress ball. A guest who was not exactly celebrated for his virility, emboldened by many cocktails, called to the Princess across a crowded drawing-room :

"Bonsoir, Tante Winnie!"

"Tante vous-même!" was heard by everyone present.

This immensely rich woman led a curiously unluxurious life. She was potentially an ascetic, openly proclaiming that all she needed was a comfortable chair and a piano. During the 1914 war, anxious to make a donation to the poor of her *arrondissement*, she set out for the local *mairie*, with a cheque for a million francs in her shabby little bag. The secretary gave her one look which absorbed the valiant hat, woollen gloves, devoted old shoes. *"Si vous venez pour la distribution de vêtements, c'est au premier!"*

Winaretta de Polignac was not only musically gifted; painting was her *violon d'Ingres*. Always a pioneer, she had bought a Manet at the age of sixteen for 2000 francs. No artistic manifestation left her cold. The muses, *'neuf filles unanimes à qui la musique plaisait et qui portaient en leur sein un coeur tranquille,'* never found more diligent a worshipper.

Madame de Polignac's *salon* was rightly known as *'le carrefour des arts'*. Here I first became acquainted with Valéry, mumbling almost unintelligible epigrams beneath his chewed moustache; Madame de Noailles was also an habituée. Tiny, brilliant, restless, she lived in a tropical turmoil of flowers and furbelows. Never relaxed, never silent, she twittered, twitted, perorated. She was always to be found at any hour of the day in precisely the same room, in precisely the same chaise-longue, in precisely the same state of combative inanition,

[87]

vowing she would be dead before the year was out—to a philosophical audience who knew perfectly well that on the stroke of eight she would leap to her feet, galvanize her servants, don veils and feathers, and be fetched by two doting slaves who would conduct her to some restaurant which she would dazzle and bewitch until two in the morning, when she would suddenly recollect she was a dying woman and would practically be carried to her grave by the conquered diners. The French are creatures of habit; the unexpected makes no lasting appeal. They liked to feel that Anna was always to be found in her bedroom from 12 a.m. to 8 p.m. It was comforting to know that she died all day and dined all night.

I find it difficult to do justice to the verbal eloquence of Anna de Noailles. It began as a kind of incantation, like the preliminary drumming of the heels of a Spanish dancer, little by little, it gathered impetus, the rallying words poured in from all sides, the inescapable, elected, irresistible words, rained like blows on her audience, never pausing in their inspired frenzy. Her listeners were as riveted as Oedipus by the tirade of the Sphinx.

She had a genius for *cocasserie*. A witty though fatuous young man, Stanislas de la Rochefoucauld, greatly daring, stood up to her once in my *salon*. "*Ce garçon m'excède*," she exploded. "*Il a un œil qui applaudit l'autre avec un bruit de castagnettes!*" On the telephone it was not always easy to grasp her meaning. "*Mais je suis, Roland*," she would wail, "*Roland tout entier suspendu à son oliphant!*"

*   *   *   *   *

Madame de Polignac would take a mischievous delight in confronting what she called the 'thoroughbred' with the 'percheron'; in other words, Anna de Noailles with Colette. Colette on these occasions would behave like a somewhat grumpy gardener who has been dragged away from his work. The thing that bored her most was talking shop; or, at any rate, discussing her own books, philosophy or death, a favourite topic with Anna. "*La mort*," Colette would grumble, "*ne m'intéresse pas, pas même la mienne!*"

But get her on the subjects of flowers, trees, animals, or food, and there was no limit to her knowledge. She had all the peasant's cult of *le labour*, his fatherly solicitude for the vine; she was a connoisseur of

[88]

wine of the first category. That is to say, she could tell a *grand crû* from its aroma, and, approximately, the year of its *mise en bouteille*, by tasting it. She was not a native of Burgundy for nothing.

I need hardly say she had a horror of cocktails, and other *boissons frelatées*, though in winter she favoured hot aromatized red wine with a dash of cinnamon and a soupçon of nutmeg. In all this she was as fastidious as she was frugal. A genius for comfort characterized her dwelling-place. The chair was exactly the right height for the writing-table, the reading-lamp at the correct angle for reading, the pencils would be always sharpened, her blue writing-paper with its blunt emphatic handwriting is already part of her legend. She was essentially domesticated, *une femme d'intérieur*, who loved receiving in her own home. She dreaded parties. To use a word that must astonish those who do not know Colette, she was 'cosy'. She loved mixing the sauce vinaigrette that accompanied her home-grown salad; her kitchen was more familiar to her than her drawing-room. She adored comfort and disdained luxury. She had many phobias; any kind of snob, social, literary, political. Especially she disliked women whose conversation was as skimpy as their diet.

Ever since I have known her, she has been devoted to the same man, her husband, Maurice Goudeket. He was some fifteen years younger than she and worshipped the ground she trod on. Colette has im-mortalized him in what I look upon as her greatest masterpiece, *La Naissance du Jour*, in which she describes the love of an aged and lucid woman for an obstinate and infatuated youth. It takes a brave woman to count each wrinkle, to compare her swollen and rheumaticky hand with one smooth and supple. At the risk of disappointing those who take an entirely misguided view of Colette, which is imputable to her early and reluctant association with that elderly satyr, Willy, I would whisper the suspicion that the three people she has cared for most are her second and third husbands, Henry de Jouvenel, at one time French Ambassador in Rome; Maurice Goudeket; and her mother (Sido). Earthy and pagan, sensible and sensuous, she evokes the Georgics of Virgil rather than the Chansons de Bilitis. Her almost mythical love for her mother substituted itself early in life for other dogmas. I am convinced that even now she is incapable of taking a decision without asking herself whether 'Sido' would approve.

The last time I saw her was over two years ago, *en pleine apothéose*, though crippled, poor soul, with arthritis. The film *Gigi* was the success of the season; *Chéri* was playing to crowded houses, the much-coveted ribbon of Commandeur de la Légion d'Honneur garnished the lapel of her coat. Despite her seventy-seven years—and her infirmities—the same foxy face looked up at me through a fuzz of hair that might have been undergrowth.

I expressed surprise at seeing no animals hovering about her chair. "What," I enquired, "has become of *le chat si caressant* described in your last book?"

"*Erreur*," rumbled the rich Burgundian voice, "*un chat n'est jamais caressant, il se caresse à vous.*"

Her apartment in the core of Paris overlooks the Palais Royal. Her couch is built into the embrasure of the window so that she is, as it were, in the stage box of a theatre. Often, a ball, thrown by children, leaps up at her; she instinctively holds out her hands to catch it. In summer, the swifts almost graze her face; she speaks to them in their own language, never attempting to teach them hers; in this, I think, resides her power over all wild things. She has written of snakes, owls, monkeys, peacocks, with an uncanny intuition. On the theme of love, she is a virtuoso, playing on our heart strings with the fearful familiarity of a Kreisler. She is one of the rare people who have given me the impression of being an *aliment complet*, both tender and brutal, experienced and incorruptible. I have no hesitation in setting her down as a genius, a genius in the art of loving, and in the art of living, and of describing those arts.

I got to know Poulenc, the most typically French of the famous 'Six' which included Erik Satie, Darius Milhaud, Arthur Honegger, Georges Auric, Germaine Taillefer. Sheer *joie de vivre*, malice, wit, fantasy, spouted from his every work; impish as a young apprentice, contortionist as Valentin le Désossé, lyrical as a troubadour, Poulenc, full of verve and devilry, whether it was in *Les Biches*, *Aubade*, or *Le double concert pour piano et orchestre*, had us all bewitched. He was, apart from his music, an incomparable raconteur; through his stories, rich in surprises and compensations, ran a comforting fairy-godmother element which was the outcome of a rare vocation for happiness. He was so eclectically, collectively sensual, so diffuse, so diverse, that it would have been impossible to sever all his pleasure-absorbing tentacles at one blow. You suppressed the theatre, there remained the cinema.

You suppressed his cuisine, there remained his vineyard. You suppressed Paris, he was just as much diverted by his village in Indre-et-Loire.

Georges Auric, taciturn, mordant, would occasionally drop a telling ingredient into the sizzling pot of Poulenc's conversation. The Serts, too, were always welcome in Tante Winnie's *salon*. His titanic paintings adorned the walls of the most *avant garde* hostesses in those distant days. Physically, Sert resembled a portly Franz Hals, with his splashed-on moustache, his jovial baldness; a fat cat purring by a well-fed fire, fed by his wife, Missia, whose terribly intelligent eyes sparkled with wit and ferocity. A mixture of Puck and Sans Gêne, she would overturn with a shrug doctrines hatched in the morning of Time, canonize with a word artists no one had ever taken seriously. Queen of burlesque, she whisked the spectacles from the nose of the sage. Under her tuition, people behaved as in a ballet; the universally respected statesman would suddenly discover himself to be animated by a Petrouchka-like passion, the dowager forsaking her train for pink tights.

I was attached to the esoteric couple though I couldn't help feeling they would have liked me better had I had an eye in the middle of my forehead, or the merest soupçon of a hump. Though their life was a perpetual *mardi-gras*, as they grew older they acquired the vindictive, faintly sinister air of stage properties no longer in use.

More often than not, in the wake of Tante Winnie waddled the adipose, top-heavy, figure of Mme Legrand, née Fournès, universally known as 'Cloton', 'hydrophile', somebody added, as her hair had the consistency of cotton wool, her cheeks, that of marshmallows, well floured. Gallant as an old *cantinière*, greedy as a Chinese eunuch, she reminded one of those stately though oscillating figures you see in carnivals, precariously supported by human feet. In her youth she had been beloved by many, Maupassant amongst others. As generous as she was impoverished, now and again she would give dinner parties to which the greatest *gastronomes* in Europe were proud to be invited. Weeks were spent composing the menu, hours choosing each ingredient. She was to be seen inoculating strawberries with a syringe filled with Armagnac. As the day of the dinner drew nearer, Cloton's anxiety mounted. Would the trouts' *cheeks* be sufficiently full or not? Would the tarragon for the sauce béarnaise be fresh or merely bottled?

Could she really count on her wine merchant to produce the 1894 *framboise* he had promised?

Then there were the chucks.

How could she possibly replace Armand de Gramont? True, there were other dukes, but none as handsome, none as eloquent, none as courtly! Then the never-failing anguish about Anna who would, of course, be dying all the day of the dinner-party, possibly to revive on the stroke of eight, but one could never be quite sure. How eighteenth century were these dinner parties! All they lacked was a flirtatious *abbé* and an *encyclopédiste*!

After the collapse of France in 1940, I often wondered what had become of poor old Cloton, who took care of her, who saw she had enough to eat? It was only on my return to France, in 1945, that I learned that she had gone to live with her equally ancient maid in a little village by the Loire. There, people were very kind to them. Now and again a poacher would bring them a rabbit; they would *trinquer* with the postman on his daily round.

Her memory became obligingly blurred; the recurrent horrors perpetuated by the Germans only reached her in a blunted and woolly condition, wrapped, as it were, in *coton hydrophile*. The thing from which she suffered most was the cold. This was invincible. Night after night, wrapped in rugs and old newspapers, she and her old maid shivered in front of a practically non-existent fire. One night, Cloton had a bronchial chill—the supply of fuel was exhausted—Hortense dismembered a chair. There was no paper left of any description. "My letters! Those piles of old letters!" her mistress suddenly wheezed. "*Nous sommes sauvées!* Go and fetch them, Hortense!"

Together they set fire to sheet after sheet, letters from royalties, Cabinet Ministers, academicians, even Maupassant, were not spared, though the hand that held the letters trembled. There was only one small packet left. Hortense was about to add it to the rest. "*Non,*" croaked Cloton, reaching out her hand, "*pas sca!* I know he was no one in particular, but he was such a sweet boy, absurdly young. Well, of course, I couldn't consent . . . he got himself killed in 1915."

Thanks to Denys's restlessness, we visited Greece. The Islands confirmed my suspicion that Beauty was the triumph of elimination, a lesson in self-denial, a strict diet for the mind. Temples reduced to two or three columns, continued to suggest entirety. (There is surely an astringent quality about Greece that is lacking in the fleshier countries?) A tree, no longer one in a multitude, became the shade and protector of mankind. In spite of its frugality, or perhaps because of it, Greece seemed more alive than other countries. The land might be bare, but it was the bareness of the athlete stripped for the Stadium.

There was a curious tautness about everything. In that tingling atmosphere a word spoken assumed the sharp significance of an arrow —even the ruins seemed winged, lightly resting on the earth which bore them. "*Rome s'enfonce, Athènes s'envole,*" Cocteau once rightly said.

Surely nowhere was death so ignored, in such low repute? Philosophers and sculptors snubbed it perpetually. Steles with a shocking, but consoling, levity, adorned themselves with exquisite bas-reliefs representing a lady at her toilet, two friends having a comfortable gossip. How beautifully Greece explained my grandmother! On landing at Corfu, the first thing that met my gaze was a statue of her father. No wonder Gabbata had seemed like a being from another world! The difference between Northern and Southern mythology, I discovered, was that in the North men behaved like gods, and in the South, gods behaved like men. Greece made other countries look as though they should go in for a slimming cure. I remembered how gross and clumsy quite good-looking people had appeared in the presence of my grandmother.

"How is it," I inquired of Denys, "that places make me happy, and people make me miserable? My irresponsible and elusive nature staggers under the too heavy trappings of love; it is as grotesque as a child dressed up as a grown-up. We are flattered by your interest, we will momentarily produce all the gestures required of us, but we stumble over our train." He gave my arm an impatient little shake.

"Come off it. Cease strutting about in front of the looking glass. Cease, my little scuttle fish. We are not taken in. You are like someone who owns a really good picture of which she will only exhibit a shoddy reproduction; why aren't we shown the original?"

"Because I'm the caretaker."

In 1927 we visited America; a large party of us. Denys vaguely toyed with the idea of finding a job there, but he did not toy for long. Though people were kindness itself, we quickly realized we were not for export. We were too lazy, too undemonstrative, too choosy, too introspective, too critical, above all, we were too thickly incrusted with European barnacles, in a word, too old. We felt like a couple of misplaced adults in a rollicking nursery. We felt that we must get out before the monosyllable FLOP blazed in neon lights across our chests. We got out. We went to Cuba.

We had not been there for 24 hours before we felt we were back in Europe, South-Western Europe, Malaga, Lisbon, Cadiz. Some people see only the American side of Cuba; bars, jazz country clubs, sky-scrapers, but I can assure you that in 1927 the spirit of the ancient *conquistadores* was not dead. The island had all the opulence of a Gobelins tapestry, crowded with fruit, conches, dolphins, palm trees. Those chubby cherubs, the trade winds, emerging from a baroque cloud, puffed prosperity. This flowery sloth, this God's holiday, had none of the makeshift atmosphere of a colony. It is an end in itself, neither rung, nor substitute. Its inhabitants are preposterous, charming, and— durable. The overfed houses were decorated with niches, pilasters, balconies, busts and pineapples. Our European habitations would look like sour old maids in comparison. Everything is voluptuous, beginning with the food, black *Moro* crabs with hooked claws like parrots' beaks, saffron-coloured rice used as a background for scarlet pimentos, green papoi with black seeds, small scented pink bananas as stubby as a sculptor's fingers.

We had an audience with the President whose name was, of course, Machado. We were introduced into a torrid ballroom where, despite the fact that it was only three o'clock in the afternoon, all the chandeliers were lit. After five minutes wait, the door was flung open. Enter the President accompanied by his wife, a duenna by Goya, coquettish, mauvely powdered, and his daughter, who had rich rolling vegetable eyes, like plums. They did not speak a word of anything but Spanish, except the Señorita, who made conversation in guttural French.

Meanwhile Mamita, who visibly comprehended nothing, hummed 'pian piano', an old Cuban refrain, beating time with her fan on the arm of her chair, her great velvety cowlike eyes ruminating, doubtless, a sentimental past; the delicious aroma of fresh tobacco was wafted through an open window. In the middle of all this I suddenly remembered the walls of our old schoolroom were decorated with prints representing the naval capture of Havannah by one of our ancestors, in 1772. Would the President have received me had he known? To stifle my feeling of guilt, I hastily summoned a few words of half forgotten Spanish to my aid.

Immediately, Niagara was let loose, my Spanish was mobbed, overthrown, trampled on. It never recovered, but the tangible result was that the following morning a white Rolls Royce, driven by a huge black chauffeur with a bridesmaid's bouquet of cattleyas pinned to his left shoulder, drew up in front of the hotel where we were staying and, hat in hand, announced that he had been sent by the President to fetch la Señora Trefusès.

I think my most Firbankian memory of Cuba is of an early walk by the sea. We had made a habit of going out before breakfast, it was so delicious. Suddenly we saw coming towards us a young Negress. She wore a white satin ball dress generously décolletée, in her right hand she carried a long piece of sugar cane, which she used as a walking-stick. As she passed us, she honoured us with a smile, benevolent, yet a trifle haughty, as much as to say she had no objection to our trespassing provided we realized *she* was the boss.

*   *   *   *   *

All my life, I had longed for a home in the country, hence these intermittent lusts for other people's houses. I think (perhaps wrongly) that had I always lived in the country, instead of in towns, I should have been a nicer person.

The year before Marcel Proust died I had the privilege of meeting him at a luncheon party given by Walter Berry. He was a disappointment, only emerging from his shawls to complain about his health, which was manifestly deplorable. A pair of Indo-Persian eyes, so heavily-lashed, so gaudy, as to make their owner appear overdressed, were imprisoned in a face the colour of tallow. At the end of the meal he became more objective. Turning to me, he inquired if I knew *les environs de Paris*? Without giving me time to reply, he amplified:

"I'll wager you have never heard of St. Loup de Naud, though perhaps you are familiar with the person of that name in my book. Yes? Well, you should visit the place which inspired it. It is about eighty kilometres from Paris, on the road to Provins. A lovely surprise. It is an aquiline little hamlet perched on a hillock *en pleine plaine*. The steep village street leads to one of the finest Romanesque churches in France. Poor church, it is sadly neglected; some allege it is disfigured, I would say it is embellished by great smears of green mould which make it look as if it had been reclaimed from the sea, *la cathédrale engloutie.* Go to see it—*vous m'en direz des nouvelles!*"

I forgot all about St. Loup until many years later. I happened to be re-reading Proust. St. Loup! The name smote me like a reproach. It was as though the author had given me an appointment I had failed to keep. I decided to waste no time in making amends and set out accordingly on one fine January morning, in the direction of Provins. It was freezing. The cold always makes me feel cruel and gay. The road was so French that it seemed almost a pastiche of France; flanked by towering poplars, it was like driving up some Gothic nave. (Did I but know it, it was the kind of French landscape that lodged itself most firmly in people's minds and that which, in exile, would produce the cruellest nostalgia.) Ploughed fields, limitless as the waves of the sea, stretched away from the road; the *plaine de Brie* is as monotonous as the Steppes, but more fruitful. At length, hunger made me draw up at a village called Coubert, which appeared to be doing an extremely self-conscious imitation of an Utrillo, with its duck's egg green shutters, denuded plane trees, black shawled housewives carrying a *quiche* of bread a yard long under their arm. "Where," I enquired of one of these persons, "can I have luncheon?" Her face was dry and wrinkled as the earth in drought, her coffee-coloured eyes were full of pride and prophecies.

"I know of a place," she said darkly, "but it is not for the likes of you. (One felt that she was feeding the feud of a lifetime.) No, you must go straight on, till you come to 'Auberge de l'Ecureuil'. It is not much to look at, but one eats well." She nodded with the air of a connoisseur. I did as she suggested. The obese patron of the Ecureuil loomed on the threshold and, noticing my hesitation, beckoned me in. The only clean thing about his vast person was his cigarette, but somehow I trusted the ménagère.

If the exterior resembled an Utrillo, the interior was pure Cézanne with two workmen in corduroy trousers, drinking out of bubbly blue glasses, a pack of greasy cards splayed across the table and an eel-blue knife stuck in an apple with one mauve cheek. My attempt to order lunch was quickly nipped in the bud.

"*Laissez-moi faire*," begged the patron. I was rewarded for my docility. An exemplary *omelette chasseur* was succeeded by a succulent steak *au poivre*. Half a bottle of Château Ausone 1918 accompanied this feast. "*C'est le petit Jésus en culotte de velours*," he tenderly murmured, as he poured it out. His slovenly attire, unshaven chin, I was ready to acknowledge, seemed all part of the business. With a shudder I recalled the antiseptic nursing home face of English provincial hotels, the listlessness, the lack of initiative. Above my head hung a huge stuffed pike, with the sort of hooked protruding jaw I always associate with the more enterprising female globe-trotter. The proprietor leaning over me noticed my concentration.

"You're admiring my pike, *hein*! Fine fellow, isn't he? The largest one caught in these parts, over a hundred years old, they say."

A century of mud beneath the water lilies, undulating and stationary, he would lie in wait for the little fish. What a rich slice of summer, the juicy summer of the ponds. I saluted this aquatic suckling of a hundred summers. He had the cunning of the crocodile in his eye, the Buddhistic composure of the tortoise and the elephant.

The pale sun made zebra patterns on the wall, the grandfather clock ticktocked, a bluebottle buzzed. But it was time to keep my appointment; my appointment with Proust. In Provins I was directed to St. Loup de Naud. Was there by chance any house to be bought in the neighbourhood? My informant scratched his head dubiously. "There is, I believe, an ancient tower, but it is very dilapidated."

We absorbed almost twenty more kilometres of undiluted plain, and there, sure enough, on a turn of the road, we came face to face with Proust's 'surprise', a village perched on a hillock, like an illustration from some fifteenth-century missal, words frothed about it, and, crowning the whole, rose the spatulate admonitory finger of a Romanesque church tower. Behind it, almost choked with trees, sprang another tower, the one that was to be mine.

France does not, as a rule, go in for being either mysterious or romantic. Mystery provokes a taunt, romance, a smile, superstition, a shrug. St. Loup was both romantic and mysterious. It could even lay claim to a certain magic all its own. It was not obvious, for magic, to be successful, can never be obvious. It was passive, immutable, like sensuality—a climate, not an episode. It lay coiled within the massive walls like a snake, which only rears its head when trodden on, but it was there, none the less.

I'm afraid the character of St. Loup cannot be described as 'nice'. It is sensuous, greedy as a Venetian courtesan, with the same insatiable taste for velvets the colour of rotten peaches. It is ruthless, vindictive, capricious. If it takes a dislike to you, you are done. A pipe bursts in your room before you have been there five minutes. You fall, twisting your ankle badly, down the corkscrew stairs, the fire in the bedroom smokes to such an extent that you are reminded of the last act of the Valkyries. If, on the other hand, you have the good fortune to please St. Loup, it is equally unscrupulous. No *scène de seduction* is too crude, no posture too audacious. It beckons, importunes, detains.

It has been called by many names. La Tour Prends Garde, Le Chequers français, La Mélisandière. Yet the soul of St. Loup is rugged and unfathomable. It is not duped by its recreations.

In moments of solitude, in the winter months, for example, when it is surrounded by skeleton woods, and sullen snows from the East swell the skies, it is apt to remember that it has been a contemporary of *le posvre petit escholier qui eut nom François Villon*. Many a barn, many a cellar, in l'Ile de France must have sheltered his shivering, persecuted figure, *plus mesgre que chimère*. I would like to think he found sanctuary in my village church, where, like the penitent thief he so much resembled, he, perchance, devised the lovely prayer which even now cheats the Devil of his prey.

I was not the only one to have *le coup de foudre* for St. Loup. Denys was also subjugated: it was exactly the kind of house he could understand and appreciate; it was in keeping with his Shakespearian character. He came there often and willingly, but he was fundamentally restless. Russia never left him in peace for long.

In 1928 he went there for the last time, at the risk of his life. He knew he was suspect (wrongly, of course, but no matter). He was even compelled to submit to a kind of farcical trial, during which he pretended not to understand the questions levelled at him. He was finally made to choose between a fine and imprisonment, needless to say, he chose the fine. They must have been naïve to allow him to return, under escort, to his hotel, where he crammed all his clothes into one small suitcase, cutting off anything that protruded with a pair of scissors. (I could not think why some of his shirts had only one sleeve!)

[98]

He somehow managed to dodge the waiting police, and reached the Polish frontier, travelling under the seat. By the time he joined me in Italy his nerves were in a pretty frayed condition.

Never robust, his sorely taxed constitution began to show signs of wear and tear, but moderation was foreign to his nature. His declining health never succeeded in obtaining any concession; with him to live dangerously was not merely a picturesque axiom, he really shunned security. In 1929, his undaunted young life came to an end. The previous autumn, he had to undergo an operation for appendicitis; the operation in itself was a success, but he had subsequently started to cough. All through the winter he coughed, a small undramatic cough, as quietly persistent as Scottish drizzle. Let it not be supposed that the cough was allowed in any way to interfere with the routine of his life. He continued to go to bed as late as ever, sometimes even neglecting to take an overcoat on the wildest winter night; precautions were not for him, I could not but admire his lordliness. Then, what was bound to happen, happened. The cough got suddenly worse, he was X-rayed. Galloping consumption was the diagnosis. He was taken to the American Hospital in Neuilly, where for months he languished, with the sudden spurts of optimism characteristic of his disease. One of the people whose visits he seemed to enjoy most was Madame de Polignac. I can only suppose they talked about music, as I was not encouraged to be present.

All my life I have had a superstitious dread of summer, season of catastrophes, promoter of wars, instigator of accidents. The summer of 1929 was a particularly merciless one. All day long, Denys lay gasping for breath in his white and torrid room. If only I could have taken him to Switzerland—but he was too ill to be moved. Up to the end he craved for music, music and a horse. They were the things he had cared for most. Russia began his destruction, the summer completed it. Russia, like Revolution, is a comrade who cannot forgive.

I have known many remarkable men, I have never known a braver, a more prodigal. He had all the ballad-like qualities I most admire, I, all the defects it was most difficult for him to condone. Nevertheless, there was a great link between us, we both loved poetry, France, travel, being insatiably interested in foreign countries. We were both Europeans in the fullest sense of the term. The same things made us laugh, we quarrelled a lot, loved not a little. We were more to be envied than pitied.

CHAPTER SIX

SHORTLY before Denys's death, I had published a mediocre little
book, a patchwork affair, aphorisms, maxims, annotations, loosely
woven into the shape of a novel. It served its purpose, it was a loop-
hole, an outlet, above all, a piece of blotting paper which absorbed
my obsessions.

Sortie de Secours led to *Écho* and *Écho* led to—many things. *Écho*
was a novel about the Scotland of my childhood; it was romantic,
nostalgic, with a sublimated incest motif running through it like an
alien thread. Much to my surprise, it was a success and nearly won me
the 'Prix Femina'.

Apropos of this, it is customary to make a series of calls before the
award of the prize, exactly as it is necessary to 'canvass' academicians
before 'standing' for the Académie Française. Madame Alphonse

Daudet, widow of the great Daudet, was one of the most influential members of the jury; a visit to her house was indispensable. "Whatever you do," my friends recommended, "do not let her think you're well off." I accordingly borrowed an old suit from my maid, taking the métro, not a taxi, to her distant *quartier*. A few days later I sent the old lady a few mangy marigolds. "*Quand je pense*," she bewailed, "*que cette petite veuve si méritante a dû se priver de manger pour m'envoyer ces fleurs!*"

Alea jacta est. Henceforth my road was clear: I had been put into the world to write novels.

Echo brought a lot of new friends in its wake. I realized I was a self-made woman, and also, in spite of appearances, a lonely one. I received a proposal. Max Jacob, poet, painter, libertine, dandy, wit, who was doomed to die the death of a martyr at the hands of the Germans, called on me one afternoon, dressed, he imagined, for the part of a suitor. A small dapper Punchinello, he wore a top hat, white spats, gloves the colour of fresh butter. He hung his hat on his stick which he held like a banner between his legs. He was irresistible. I longed to take advantage of his proposal which was couched in terms that sounded as though he had learned them out of a book on etiquette. We examined the pros and cons. St. Loup, far from being an asset, proved a stumbling block.

"*Je déteste la campagne*," said Max, "*tout y est trop vrai!* The nearest I ever get is the Bois, and that is bad enough, because it *reminds* me of the country."

"What about travel?"

"That is different, the place doesn't belong to me, there are no responsibilities. *C'est comme si je mangeais au restaurant.*"

A great advantage, he pointed out, was his being about twenty years older than me. "I have waited forty years before proposing to anyone. I am not likely to propose to anyone else."

Had he begun to suspect that all his roads, his devious dissembling roads, led to God, that the same stone which the builders refused was to become the headstone in the corner? For years, Christ lived, so to speak, incognito, in the 'wings' of his thoughts; an anonymous, delicate presence which somehow managed to interpose itself between Max and his pleasures, a diversion, an irrelevance, which seemed to cast a doubt as to the value of what he was about to undertake; would it really be so enjoyable, worth the plotting, the effort?

Max's conversion comes, apparently, under the 'exogenetic' category, founded, that is to say, on an apparition. Exogenetic, miraculous and sudden, as nothing leads us to suppose he went through a period of 'incubation subliminale'.

On Christmas Day, 1886, in Notre Dame, Claudel was also transformed by a conversion as abrupt as it was unpremeditated, but his enlightenment was interior, rather than exterior, not, as in the case of Max, who saw Christ with the eye of the body and not with the eye of the soul.

He was baptized at Notre Dame de Sion, a church founded by a fellow Jew, P. Marie Alphonse Ratisbonne, for their conversion. He was given the name of Cyprien, in preference to the name of Fiacre, patron saint of gardeners, suggested by his godfather for the occasion, Pablo Picasso, who incidentally presented him with a copy of the *Imitation*.

In 1931, he went definitely to live at St. Benoît-sur-Loire, where his long-repressed vocation for saintliness lost nothing by flowering late. The Germans arrested the happy prisoner of God in 1944. He died in the concentration camp at Drancy, where he had been singled out for privations and ill-treatment.

There appears to have been no conflict between the artist and his religion. The satirist and the believer, the cynic and the 'devot' lived side by side, like people in semi-detached villas who feign to ignore each other's existence.

★　　★　　★　　★　　★

I will not pretend that after a year or two had elapsed I was not seriously tempted by the thought of remarriage (the truth is seldom in the best of taste.) As usual, the candidate was fantastically unsuitable, he was already married and unlikely to get a divorce, let alone an annulment. I endured torments of jealousy; love turned me successively into a spy, a beggar, a virago, a bore.

The kind of devotion I could supply was as old-fashioned as bustles, or the operas of Gounod; we live in a period of small sensualities; mansions are only tolerable when split up into flats. 'I'll be a mansion to you', has no longer the appeal it had fifty years ago.

"Your love," he reproached me, "is too vast, too draughty, you are driving me to seek a stuffy little episode, vile and cosy."

As others take sun baths, the loved one bathed in fatality. He saw in me someone to whom one brings one's worries to mend, like broken toys. I was not so much his love, as his lap.

"You see, *chérie*, I only tell you lies in order to spare your feelings. The truth is always wounding, sometimes fatal. One must avoid the truth, one must 'cut' it without seeming to do so!"

He had a latent snobbishness, the snobbishness of unhappiness. Happiness was bourgeois, dowdy. As usual, I was only reassured when travelling.

Months before the projected trip I would rattle the names of unknown cities which I looked upon as my accomplices. Once I had got him away from Paris all would be well. He became the charming, if wayward, child he was in reality. During the first 'fitting' my mind would be full of pins, a readjustment might be necessary. He was comparable to those *malades imaginaires*, insufferable in their own home, who, when a stranger appears on the scene, behave just like other people. If only I could have stopped caring for him when he returned to Paris, I would have spared myself much misery.

Sleep, always a delightful surprise, forsook me utterly. Now and again, after several sleepless nights, I would stand myself a sedative as one stands oneself a good dinner. Full of impatience, I would close my eyes; I was glued to my bed as to a stall in a theatre when the play is too long. I would hear twelve o'clock strike, then, hazily, one. My thoughts were no longer in the least painful. It was as though a smaller, nimbler me, shook off the hampering folds of too ample a garment.

Quick! On all fours! The word *déclassé* suddenly confronts me like a game-keeper. Perhaps this is its only true meaning? Who cares? I have slipped under my worries as under a barbed-wire fence. Diminished and free, I lie listening to sounds not intended for human ears. Presently the sun will show itself like a sovereign on his balcony; long before then, I shall have fallen asleep like a respectable person.

* * * * *

All my life I have wrestled, not with the Devil, but with the Angel. To the Devil I have gone quietly, with many a wistful backward glance. The Angel is much more arresting. The Devil was, merely a bad habit (nearly everything is a bad habit, including life).

And like all bad habits, practically incurable. Solicitous, international, he rushed to meet you half way.

"The usual table, Madame? I have kept you one by the window. ... And a bottle of the usual?"

Immediately I was surrounded by a welcoming appreciative crowd. There is nothing daredevil about *my* devil. All he has is technique and a 'wonderful memory for faces'. I never knew him when he was young and handsome.

The reason which originally lured me there and made me an habituée of that smoky crowded room, was the 'coompany'. You met all sorts of interesting people, they were gay (if the Devil was not), witty, attractive, gifted, they put you at your ease at once, made you feel one of themselves; it was like the most exclusive kind of night-club. You felt it was a privilege to belong to it; besides, it cost nothing.

Then, in the small hours of the morning, intoxicated by the fumes of their conversation and the compliment of their fellowship, you would reel out into the icy street. There, in his full regalia, stood the Angel, towering over the squalor, astringent and thrilling as the sound of the sea. No, I was never tempted by the Devil. He is old and fat.

The place is cosy, though. ...

*   *   *   *   *

Paris, during the ten years which preceded the Second World War, was enough to go to anyone's head. It has been so much written about, sung about, messed about, that I feel disinclined to add my quota of praise.

Nevertheless, I will describe a party given by me on the Eiffel Tower as symptomatic of the period. The Eiffel Tower is not to be had for the asking. The Eiffel Tower keeps itself *to* itself. It is prudish and mulish. It had to be wooed, cajoled, humoured, made much of.

Minister rang up Minister. Contemporaries of the Inauguration were consulted as to its powers of resistance, climate, hobbies, recreations. The Tour Eiffel, which for so many years had been taken for granted, suddenly found itself *la vedette du jour*. It was interviewed, tested, talked over, walked over.

People said: "You're mad to want to give a dinner party on the

Tour Eiffel, *and* a fancy dress ball into the bargain; you will be pelted with rotten eggs, if not worse, by the Communists of Belleville."

"It's not a fancy dress ball," I objected, "my guests will only come in the dress of the period, the period of the Inauguration. It is out of politeness to the Eiffel Tower, so that it should not feel old-fashioned once we are all up there." People shrugged, people tapped their foreheads significantly, but they came.

My more unconventional friends were beside themselves with delight. We were not pelted with rotten eggs by the Communists of Belleville. On the contrary the crowd which had collected at the foot of the Tower, clapped itself silly. People arrived in tandems, in 'spanking' dog-carts, on bicycles, in bloomers. They had muffs, feather boas, buttoned boots, fans, carnets de bal, hats with sea-gulls, swallows, humming birds, aigrettes. Jewels were mostly astronomical —crescent moons, comets, constellations.

Gentlemen who looked as though they were protected from the world by their moustaches, bent over ladies who drew patterns on the floor with the points of their parasols. There were dashing cavalry officers with throttlingly high collars, *très Gyp*; a contemporary Colette, with a tiny waist and a boater, flirted with a 1900 Boni de Castellane. I made an unrehearsed entry with Serge Lifar; we polkaed round the palms of the first floor where my guests were assembled.

In the middle of all this, an ancient friend of my mother's, who must have been in her prime when the Tour Eiffel made its début, was announced. Chignon, tortoise-shell lorgnette, feather boa, *galbe*, all were perfect. Lifar rushed up to her in his effusive way: "Ah, Madame, do tell us who made you that wonderful wig *et la merveilleuse poitrine postiche?*"

There was a deathly silence. Madame de L—— put up her lorgnette and glared at Serge as though he were a hair in the soup. "I was not aware, Monsieur, that this was to be a fancy dress ball."

In spite of this, and other incidents, the party was an unqualified success. The personnel of the Tower got so carried away that it attempted to substitute (in a smear of purple neon) the name of Violette for that of Citroen, whose advertising background it normally was.

The June night was perfect. Paris, pricked by a myriad diamond antennae, throbbed at our feet. The silver scimitar of the Seine carved its way to the gentle slopes of St. Cloud. Multi-coloured balloons floated up from between the iron shafts of the great Tower, which was mine for the night. All summer in a night. My childish wish had come true: I was one with Paris.

*   *   *   *   *

Charm: that which replaces everything, and which nothing can replace.

I was rather pleased with this definition. Definitions formed part of my French education. Why was I so keen on defining charm? Because my mother possessed an unfairly large stock of it: charm oozed from her every sentence, every gesture. At the age of five, her elders decided it was time to make a stand against this irresistible, but deplorably naughty child. She must have sensed what was coming to her.

With downcast eyes and wilting curls, she confessed: "I have a wicked heart"—a sigh of gratification went up from her family—"and *so has Jessie!*" she outrageously completed. My mother's iconoclastic statement caused a stir of reprobation. Jessie was the family paragon, by whom all the others were judged. Fully conscious of the enormity she had uttered, the *enfant terrible* was off, with a toss of her golden curls, off to torment her doting brother, off to play with the gillies' bairns, off to ride her Shetland pony 'upside down' as she had seen it done at the circus. Stories of my mother's charm are legion. The most telling, perhaps, is the Story of the Burglar.

One day she had gone to a ball with my father; being tired, she returned home early, and alone. When she entered her bedroom it was not unoccupied. A burglar was gloating over the contents of her violated safe.

'Hands up or I shoot' is, I believe, the correct formula on these occasions. My mother, resplendent in her ball dress, sat calmly down, opened her cigarette-case, offered a cigarette to the dumbfounded man. "Suppose you tell me why you do this for a living?" she suggested conversationally.

"Well, I'm b——!"

"I wish you would. I'm really interested."

"Why aren't you scared?" he burst out. "Why don't you 'oller?"

"No doubt I'm not the hollering kind." She actually smiled.

"Well, of all the——!"

"We will take that for granted. Now do tell me, instead of standing gaping there. Are you quite sure you don't smoke?"

He mumbled something which sounded like: "Well, I don't mind if I do," sank into a chair. With many a pause and sucking of the teeth, the man's squalid, banal story was unfolded. When he had finished, he whined: "Now I s'pose you'll send for the perlice?" His heart was no longer in it; somehow the story had sounded terribly flat.

My mother's unfathomable blue eye dwelt thoughtfully on him. "I shall do nothing of the kind. You can go, if you wish. I have no intention of sending for the police."

The man was undone. He sat open-mouthed, staring at the lady who sparkled like a Christmas tree. Then he got up, silently picked up the things on the floor, replaced them in the safe.

"There!" There was a note of triumph in his voice. "There! I don't want nothink, nothink from you, that is to say."

He glanced at her slyly, shyly.

"But I'd like to take somethink, all the same."

"What?"

"A pickshur, a pickshur of you—that photo, for instance, somethink ter remember you by."

*   *   *   *   *

It would have been difficult to find two people more dissimilar than Virginia Woolf and my mother. Yet, strange as it may seem, they were deeply interested in one another, and longed to meet.

Raymond Mortimer got wind of this, and with typical mercurial mischief offered to sponsor an encounter. He was to bring Mama to tea with Virginia in Tavistock Square. Meanwhile, Virginia had steeped herself in Edwardian memoirs, while my mother struggled manfully with *Mrs. Dalloway* and *To the Lighthouse*. Off we set. Raymond and I had agreed that it would be more tactful, after the first *échange de politesses*, to eclipse ourselves; there was a drawing-room, at the extremity of which we sat, well out of earshot.

After about half an hour's spasmodic conversation, we were longing to see if the experiment had been a success—we unobtrusively moved nearer—they certainly seemed very animated. "Personally,

I've always been in favour of six cylinders though I know some people think four are less trouble."

"My dear Mrs. Keppel, you wouldn't hesitate if you saw the *new Lanchester with the fluid fly-wheel!*"

Neither knew a thing about motors; both thought they were on safe ground, discussing a topic on which they could both bluff to their heart's content.

Some people have charm, others have Romance, or what the French call *poèsie*. It is to be found in the most unlikely places: you can be penniless; an orphan; a failure; you can possess Titian hair, a Byronic profile; tapering fingers; a limp; a cough, a facility for fainting, and yet be without a vestige of romance, and, stranger still, you can be rich, well born, well covered, and yet be romantic.

I have known very few romantic people in my life. Denys Trefusis was romantic. He *looked* romantic, came of romantic stock. The name Trefusis is supposed to be of Phoenician origin. (The head of the family, Lord Clinton, is the 21st holder of the title.) But that in itself would not have sufficed. Russia was grafted on Cornwall, the balalaika took over from the mouth organ. He went from Nijni Novgorod to Tidworth. If he had the blue, sea-roving eye of the Cornishman, he had also the wasp-waist of the Cossack. Romance is contrast.

Take Vita Sackville-West, a great poet, an heiress, the bearer of a great name. All the ingredients of Romance, you would have thought, were there, but it was not enough. There must be a dissonance, a flaw somewhere, Romance resides in the flaw, Romance is devious; double-faced; it is thanks to Pepita, the slums of Malaga, the reeking cauldron of *puchero*, Pepita's rascally thieving brothers, that Vita is romantic.

Surely a young woman who is rich, young, lovely, and a duchess to boot, could lay little claim to romance? Yet the friend in question contrived to look like a displaced person, an orphanage leaflet. One expected to find her lying across one's doorstep. One saw her in inverted commas. 'Too proud to beg', 'Stolen by gypsies', 'Homeless, hopeless'.

Take another case, an Englishman, and a great friend of mine. He enjoyed good health, good food, good music, bad language, low company. He was gregarious, yet anti-social; intelligent, yet illiterate; a boor, a bohemian, and a bourgeois. Undisciplined, he would not

have hesitated to walk down Piccadilly dressed in a fig leaf if he felt
like it. On the other hand, he was so conventional that he would not
fail to write a letter of condolence to a mere acquaintance.

He lived in a small room on the top floor of a banal hotel, only his
room was cluttered up with statues! The only piece of furniture was
a pitch-pine cupboard. One was reminded of an early Chirico. Physically, he resembled a moose, a large, lone, rogue moose. His hands
were so aristocratic and beautiful that they seemed borrowed. His
mind was encumbered with picturesque impossible schemes for
making money, in contrast to which the White Knight's little gadgets
seemed quite American. In a word, he was romantic.

Yet I have known unfulfilled writers, undernourished musicians,
dethroned kings, forsaken ballet dancers, with not an ounce of romance
between them. In what measure does wishful thinking influence my
judgement?

Colette's talent as a water-diviner is well known. She would
readily take a *baguette de coudrier* with her, on a country walk; presently,
she would stand stock-still, while the twig writhed in her hands like a
living thing. Maybe I am a romance-diviner? On the other hand, it is
just possible that the romance exists only in my own mind. In our
emotional wardrobe there is a stock of dresses of which we alone
possess the key. Customers come, customers go. We dress them as we
feel inclined. You? Cut out for Castlereagh. Try it on. Yes, I know
it looks too large, but it can be taken in. (So can you.) Madame
Récamier? Why not? You are just the type, etc., etc.

There is a story by Barbey d'Aurévilley, which perhaps illustrates
the point I am trying to make. It was New Year's Eve in the Quartier
Latin. Three young students had pooled their resources, in order to
have the semblance of a *réveillon*. Pierre had bought a bottle of wine,
Bertrand, a *pâté de campagne*, André, a cheese. The party was in full
swing when groans were heard proceeding from the floor above.
"*Tiens!*" exclaimed Bertrand. "What can that be?"

"Oh that! That's nothing, it must be that old Jewish money-lender
who, on counting his ill-gotten gains, finds out that he is five francs
short!" André shrugged.

"Rather far-fetched, isn't it? I would say it is merely a gentleman
who has dined not wisely, but too well."

"I don't agree," Pierre, who had said nothing so far, interrupted.

"I believe it is an Eastern potentate, *un roi en exil*, who was obliged to flee his country which had been invaded by barbarians. He was able to save his skin, but not his lovely daughter, whose loss he is even now lamenting."

Scarcely were the words out of his mouth when the door opened slowly. A majestic, turbanned figure, akin to one of the Magi, appeared. Great gems blazed on his fingers.

"*Messieurs!*" he said, addressing himself in a deprecating tone to Bertrand and André, "*vous n'aurez jamais de talent!*"

★   ★   ★   ★   ★

In 1927 my parents had bought the Villa dell'Ombrellino in Florence. What amused my mother was turning a house that was practically a lost cause, into a thing of beauty. In this case, the house, though of historical interest, was purely a pretext for the view. This was both unique and dual; like Janus, it had two faces, one turned towards the city, the other towards the country. From the terrace, it was like being on the deck of some great ship about to set sail. A cortège of graceful statues accompanied it; busts of Galileo and Ugo Foscolo, former tenants, shared the loggia. The buildings which have inspired more clichés than any other in the world, the Duomo, Baptistery, Palazzo Pitti, Ponte Vecchio, lay sprawled at our feet; it was stupendous, overwhelming. "*C'est comme,*" Jouvet once remarked, "*si vous aviez une baignoire sur l'Acropole.*"

Nothing can be more tyrannical than a view. It is always straining its ear to catch what you say about it. *A la longue*, I preferred the less spectacular one, overlooking the countryside, pastoral, Virgilian, cliché-provoking though it could not fail to be, 'just like a Florentine primitive'. So it was, gentle, acquiescent, with its festooned and girlish vines. (So different from their stunted French counterparts which might be the clenched fists of a buried population.)

The villa itself was furnished with magnificent French and English furniture (the cream of Grosvenor Street), Chinese pedigree porcelain, serenely remote, ruddy eighteenth-century ancestors, tapestries, chinoiseries in the Venetian manner.

It had quality, beauty, spaciousness, but no intimacy.

My mother had excellent taste; she felt not the need of privacy.

She liked large handsome rooms, leading out of each other, *salons en enfilade*, geometrical Chippendale chairs, uncompromising Régence settees, perspectives, statues. For a woman, her taste was grandly objective. She had a horror of knick-knacks. When she first settled in Italy she had only one Italian sentence: *"Bisogna begonia"*. . . . Well, '*bisogna begonia*' worked marvels. On every side, flowers, shrubs, trees sprang into life, vistas were born in the night; where yesterday had been a croaking puddle, to-day a fountain tossed back its veil of water, like a bride. No wonder we christened her 'La Nôtre'!

A touching pantomimic intimacy existed between my mother and her gardener. Full of imagination and initiative he understood her slightest gesture. When her deep voice echoed through the loggia, 'Dindo' would come running like a flattered boy.

As for my father, who had scarcely glanced at a picture in his life, he now haunted the picture galleries; his friends teased him, "In six months you will be disputing Berenson's attributions!"

L'Ombrellino is temporarily mine. No one could own two houses more dissimilar than l'Ombrellino and St. Loup. I would compare the former to a full-strength orchestra on a gala night, every chandelier ablaze, decorations, I mean constellations, worn, nightingales *de rigueur*. Fireflies, with the zeal of programme sellers speed from spectator to spectator. The frog claque croak. We pant, we swoon, we expire— night after night.

How can the infinitely more sober, less obvious charms of St. Loup compete? Chamber music compared to an orchestra? A meagre quartet scarcely constitutes a gala night. Must we then replace fireflies by glow-worms, constellations by a paltry star or two?

Was that a nightingale? Just one, a soloist, not a chorus?

How exquisite. What quality. At last, we can relax. Do you see what I mean? Italy for an occasion, a celebration, apotheosis; France for everyday. *Le triomphe du quotidien.* As well compare a Chardin to a Tiepolo, a beret to a tiara.

With flowers it is the same thing. A flower, in France, is an encounter; in Italy, it is a mob. The seasons jostle one another, overlap, commingle; spring is not a long convalescence, a difficult progress, it is a passionate struggle to prevent itself being overtaken by summer.

Italy is not beautiful on purpose. Her beauty is effortless, gratuitous, largesses for all.

Is it my Northern atavism which subconsciously demands that we should work in order to achieve beauty? The slow savouring of the Seasons like the savouring of dishes, successive, different, seems to me more desirable than having them all spread out almost simultaneously with no regard for timing or precedence. Seventy per cent of my compatriots prefer Italy to France, of which they know nothing, or next to nothing. Paris, a shopping centre, with an element of 'naughtiness' thrown in; the Riviera, grinning, invariable as a waiter in perpetual evening dress; perhaps Breezy Biarritz as an epilogue to influenza—and that is all.

With Italy, on the other hand, they are prepared to go to endless trouble. Baedeker is ever by their side, they compete with each other in discovering long-discovered beauty spots; not a campanile escapes them, not a fresco goes unsaluted. The philosophical inhabitants, blasés about invaders, treat them with indiscriminate patience and courtesy. (The Spaniards and the Italians, let it not be forgotten, have the best manners in Europe.)

Why, apart from her beauty, and the quality of her manners, does Italy appeal so much to the British? *Because Italy meets them half way.* Because Italy is like a lovely comic opera, all smiles, (on the surface) no problems. Nobody makes fun of their pidgin Italian, nobody criticizes their idiosyncrasies, it being universally accepted knowledge that the British are mad, and must be humoured at all costs. In France, we also pass for mad, but nothing in France escapes criticism.

It is thought a pity we are mad. Besides, should the insane be humoured? Ah! That is the question, etc., etc.

Moreover the Italians are beautiful, the French are not. The English prefer Beauty to Elegance, Colour to Form, Song to Speech. The Oak and the Cypress: a love match. The Oak and the Poplar: a *mésalliance*.

*   *   *   *   *

I am in the extremely fortunate position of having one foot in Italy, the other in France. Both are indispensable.

My heart goes out to the Italian people. In Italy, a peasant is nearly always a gentleman; a gentleman is sometimes a peasant. In either case, nothing derogatory is intended. It would be idle to pretend that the Italian is as cultured as the Frenchman; he is also less introspective, less analytical, in a word, far happier; but if the Italian may envy the Frenchman his superior education, God knows we can all envy the Italian his beauty, distinction, unconscious feline grace. They make modern clothes look as ridiculous as the frills on performing panthers; besides, beauty in Italy is by no means confined to one class, as I suspect it always was, say, in Russia. It is evenly distributed throughout the population.

My parents were very happy in their Florentine home. Perhaps, just as a great talent is spilt in the transmitting, the younger generation inheriting merely facility where there had been genius, my grandmother's love of Greece revived in an attenuated form in my mother's love of Italy. Not that I wish to make an invidious comparison between Italy and Greece, but maybe the blinding Attic blaze was too strong for her slightly modified vision; Italy was kinder.

In my case the love of the South, the sun, appeared in even milder form. I chose France, which combines the rigours of the North with the sensuousness of the South. My children, had I had any, would no doubt have been content with England.

CHAPTER SEVEN

EVER since Denys's death I had been haunted by Russia. I was never allowed to accompany him on his more or less hazardous fugues. More than any woman, Russia had been my rival. What was the secret, what the attraction, besides which all others paled into insignificance? I considered myself inoculated against *le charme slave*: many were the Russians, outwardly charming, who had exasperated me by their fecklessness and sloth.

In the summer of 1936 I set out on a cruise of the Scandinavian countries, culminating in a week in Russia, Leningrad, Moscow. The Nordic capitals sped past, bland and blameless. Stockholm alone seemed to have character, pith. Did the Swedes resemble pre-Revolutionary Russians? Is their lovely capital paved with bad intentions? It was impossible to tell in 48 hours. Who's afraid of the Guépéou, the Guépéou, the Guépéou? I chanted to the tune of the 'Big Bad Wolf', as we sailed into Cronstadt.

I had suspected Russia of many things but, I am bound to say, that *smugness* was not one of them. Where I had expected tragedy, the tragedy of contrast, I found the smugness, nay, the boredom of *lack* of contrast, the nightmare of monotony, of conformity, everyone dressed alike, thinking alike, expressing the same opinion.

The Moscow Metro was, of course, the only metro in the world; it was interesting to learn that the X-ray was also a Russian invention, likewise the wireless, all the more surprising as Marconi(vitch) had married a distant cousin of my father's!

I was, however, agreeably surprised by the apple-cheeked state-owned children, who were only too happy (like the brats in *High Wind in Jamaica*) to have escaped from the ministrations of their parents. There is no sillier fallacy than that the in-tourist was not allowed to see anything. Short of being blind and deaf, the in-tourist could see quite a lot, merely by walking the streets of Moscow and Leningrad, which no one prevented him from doing. Much, surely, can be deduced from the aspect of the streets? If you landed at Naples, you would immediately be accosted by a guide who would not necessarily start by showing you the slums. The first thing you discovered was that there was nothing you could conceivably want to buy in the shops (this was in '36; they have certainly improved since), that is to say, if machinery is not your main interest in life.

Food was plentiful and nasty, salt fish, gherkins, black bread, were the principal ingredients, washed down by tepid beer or vodka. We in-tourists would all be herded together in a restaurant which catered for the foreigner; a pseudo-tzigane band deafeningly played all the old favourites: 'Otchi tchorni', 'Sadko', 'The Volga Boatmen', etc., so that you could scarcely hear yourself speak. This pandering to pre-revolutionary airs was surely rather infra-dig?

"Haven't you any new tunes?" I inquired of our quite nice little tow-haired guide.

She threw me a quick suspicious glance. "Why? Don't you like these?"

"They are so old-fashioned," I complained; "such bourgeois old tunes!" Again she flashed a look at me, but no, caviare would not melt in my mouth; besides, there wasn't any; another grievance; all the best caviare was for exportation, all we got was the greasy black treacle, known as pressed caviare; it was not even called caviare, it was called *ikra*.

Now and again, I could understand a few words of what was being said around us. Greatly daring, I decided to risk one of my scanty Russian phrases. Immediately the guide pounced: "But this cannot be your first visit to Russia?"

"It is, though."

"I do not believe you, you have a very good accent."

"Ah, yes," I hastened to assure her in French, "but it is all accent and no vocabulary, my vocabulary is limited to about twenty sentences." Her face positively sizzled with suspicion. I had a brain-wave. "And I think you will find most of them in this book," I added, producing a small Russian conversation manual which I carried about with me. Her face cleared. I was able to show her the phrase I had used.

One day I was walking down the Nevsky Prospekt, when I saw a cloud of smoke coming to meet me which I could not account for. All at once my eyes began to water and I was seized with a violent fit of coughing. Passers-by, I noticed, were similarly affected. They quickly took refuge in a cavernous doorway, while the cloud swept by.

"*Chto eto?*" I inquired of one of my fellow shelterers.

"It is a new gas," he replied with indifference.

"No warning?"

"It is not necessary. It is not lethal."

The palaces and museums were beautifully kept: an army of Anglo-Saxon housemaids could not have done better; in fact, an officious lady with a broom shooed me away more than once when I exhaustedly sank on to one of the stools presumably intended to seat the tired proletariat. But in Russia one may take no such liberties. Never have I seen more diligent sightseers, many, from the Eastern provinces, wearing brightly-coloured skull caps like the Polovtsian dancers in Prince Igor. The most beautiful objects I saw in Leningrad were the Scythian jewels in a small museum whose name I have forgotten. Composed in three shades of gold, on the same principle as Fabergé's cigarette-cases, they represent animals, birds, stylized, hieratic; a panther, a stag, a peacock. Fluent and flexible, these metallic frescoes form necklaces and bracelets; they speak very highly of the degree of taste, not to say civilization, which produced them.

No greater contrast can be imagined than that which confronts the perplexed traveller when he steps from the robust eighteenth-century palace of Catherine the Great to the greenery yallery Grosvenor Gallery atmosphere of the nineteenth-century annexe lately occupied by the Imperial Family at Tsarskoé Sélo.

The eighteenth century in Russia: the ogre in powder and patches, gigantic in stature, encrusted with diamonds and filth. A hairy Gargantua, strong enough to fell an ox, yet striving to be 'dainty', to crook his little finger, to force his cosmic convulsions into a shrug, his ungainly tongue into quip and epigram. . . .

The barbaric practical jokes of Peter the Great still haunt the more delicately nurtured visitor; Peter with his scissors, guffawing with cruel laughter as he clipped the beards of his boyards, Anne's shriller titters as she escorted the hapless Prince Galitzin and his *kalmuk* bride to their icy nuptial couch, are perhaps merely the forerunners of Stalin's ogreish satisfaction when he compelled his foreign guests to drink themselves silly during the Moscow peace banquets? *Plus ça change——*

But to return to the tourist of 1936. His inner eye still feasting on Baltic ambers, on the porphyry, malachite, lapis-lazuli, scattered about Catherine's palace with contemptuous profusion, fulfilling the function of stone and brick with the servility of enslaved Oriental princesses, the bemused visitor, whose imagination is still pleasantly busied with Catherine's favourites, flighty Saltykov, faithful Poniatowski, stupendous one-eyed Potemkin, suddenly finds himself in—Kensington, a Kensington of fifty years ago.

The Tsaritsa's Art Nouveau boudoir is painted a swooning green. From every doorpost, dado, cornice, the straight line has been triumphantly banished; the vegetable kingdom with its undulations and fluencies has been the sole inspiration of this tentacular room in which everything ripples, writhes, clings, chiefly clings.

Brass represents the male element around which all this greenery winds itself. Laocoon—like brass lamps stoically put up with the embraces of convolvulus, vine and ivy. Everything that is not made of art-muslin, serge, or unbleached linen, is made of brass. Brass are the bellows, poker, tongs, coal-scuttle, chandelier, coffee-table. The possibilities of noise in this room are truly terrifying.

It is nevertheless a skimpy, genteel, frightened room, on the subject of which Dr. Freud would no doubt have found much to say. Flotillas of photographs, mostly of the Alice Hughes period, all boas and fringes, adorned with high-stepping signatures, clog shelves and tables. The only reminder that you are in Russia is supplied by chaplets of Fabergé Easter-eggs, bell-pushes, little animals made of quartz, jade, cornelian; the Grand Dukes were wont to lavish such presents on their intimates. If the Tsaritsa's boudoir took one by surprise, what must I say of the conjugal bedroom? Two twin beds, more suitable to a young ladies' dormitory than to an adult couple, stood side by side. The usual family 'snaps' littered the furniture; ikons, in which the features of the Imperial family had simply been substituted for those of the saints, adorned the walls; but, facing the twin beds, so that it should be the first thing that struck the Imperial eyes on waking, was a life-size photograph of Rasputin with his head bashed in.

In their tiny island of detached domesticity, the Imperial family led an exemplary, if narrow life. A complacency worthy of the three little pigs defying the Big Bad Wolf, possessed them. They were not interested in Russia. The letters they exchanged might have been posted in Kensington and delivered in Hampstead.

Viewed through the Empress's Edwardian lorgnette, Rasputin becomes a kind of heroic and misunderstood suffragette; the Metropolitan, a meddlesome vicar. The great winds of the Steppes never so much as ruffled 'Sunny's' sleek waves; as for 'Nicky', he had much in common with our Charles I, who was also essentially a 'family man'. "It is not the best part of Charles the First's tragedy," wrote John Drinkwater, "that he never could be persuaded he was not, at all times, a kindly father to his people; not indeed that it was easy to find anyone with the courage to attempt seriously to persuade him. It is true that except in the formal way, he knew nothing about his people, but he believed seriously that he wished them well."

Nicholas II suffered from similar delusions. Outside the prim precincts of Tsarskoé Sélo, Russia groaned and travailed, cried for bread and was given sweets, clamoured for a leader and was blown kisses.

What would a Catherine II, whose constructions have so splendidly survived every cataclysm, have thought of this Swiss Family Romanoff, she in whose breast beat the intrepid heart of our Elizabeth, and who always lent a maternal ear to the sufferings of her people?

I am attracted by historical analogies; surely the resemblance between the two great queens is flagrant? Both were cultured, hard-working, practical, humorous, vital. Both Elizabeth and Catherine were suspected of doing 'nothing to prevent' the disappearance of the two people who were obstacles to their happiness.

One was Amy Robsart, wife of Leicester, who died of a mysterious 'accident'; the other was Peter III, husband to Catherine, whose murder was by no means inconvenient to Gregory Orlov, though carried out by his brother. Leicester and Orlov each aspired to marry his Royal mistress. Both sovereigns refused for the same reason, because as Elizabeth phrased it 'unmarried, she was king and queen'.

Recently, I had the good fortune to come across a book which supplied the answer to many unformulated questions. Sir Bernard Pares has written an excellent introduction to the myriad of hitherto unpublished letters the Empress wrote to the Emperor from 1914 to 1916.

The cloying girlishness of the unfortunate woman's outpourings, their illiteracy, crass sentimentality, can only be compared to the early letters of Marie Antoinette to her mother, Maria Theresa, but even those were partly redeemed by a certain eighteenth-century veneer, a touch of mischief, the petulant pride of a young Hapsburg Arch-duchess who rather charmingly boasts that she knows how to keep the King's mistress in her place.

The poor Tsaritsa had none of Marie Antoinette's gift for snubs. Her notorious inarticulateness which vented itself in a spate of mindless observations, did not lend itself to this. In one of her letters we come across this revelatory phrase: "Our Friend wants me to go about more, but where?" We visualize Rasputin as a kind of beery old procuress, not devoid of social acumen.

On another occasion she has the indignations (and the style) of a kitchenmaid.

"Botkin told me, as Gardinsky (Ania's friend) was returning from the South, where he had been to see his mother, in the train, he heard two gentlemen speaking nasty (*sic*) about me, and he at once smacked them in the face and said they could complain if they liked but he had done his duty and could not allow them to speak so. Of course, they shut up."

And this other extract in the same vein:

"We travelled well, it was so *cosy* having N. P. with us, and reminded one of the Headquarters so much. Lovey dear, please don't let them present Madame S—— to you. You remember I told you I had the conviction Grabbe wants to do it. And fancy that nasty man had the idiocy of telling Nini his friend he hoped I would not be going to Headquarters, so as to get you acquainted with her, so that she might become your mistress!"

One does not know which is most deserving of pity, her blindness with regard to her 'Friend', her sustained triviality of mind, her physical courage (she was very often in pain), her doting solicitude or her stubborn Anglo-Saxon conviction that they will somehow contrive to 'muddle through'.

In the end, Russia breaks through, splashing the persecuted couple with the glorious colours of martyrdom and romance. As their life had been the most unimaginative, their death was to be the most spectacular. History has no more poignant figure than Nicholas II shielding his beloved wife with his own body, surrounded by dead and dying children.

'*Tout rentrait dans le désordre*', a warning to anyone who should be naïve enough to attempt to lead a bourgeois life in a country swayed by Excess, swinging indiscriminately from sadism to masochism, from extreme self-indulgence to supreme renouncement.

Is Lenin embalmed, or is it a wax figure? We shall never know. Out of his chin sprouts a foxy little beard akin to that of the Emperor Charles V. Hushed crowds still queue up to view his tomb. Leningrad, more homogeneous than Moscow, has a grave deep beauty no amount of shabbiness or neglect can impair. Perhaps a humorous Providence ordained that the concerted shadows of Peter the Great and Catherine should have the last word?

*   *   *   *   *

My all too rapid visit to Russia had a consequence that no one could have foreseen. On the principle that the shorter the stay, the longer the book, on my return to France I published two or three entirely superficial articles on my first (and last) impressions of Russia in *Le Temps*. The following spring took me to Italy where to my amazement I was informed that if I desired an audience with Mussolini, it would not be refused me. Curiosity is perhaps my most strongly marked characteristic, it has even been known to get the better of my cowardice. Of course, I replied that an interview with the Duce was the apex of my ambition. I accordingly filled in the customary form for Alfieri. Meanwhile things were going from bad to worse. There was talk of the Italian journalists being recalled from England before the Coronation; our Ambassador had not been received by Mussolini for quite a long time; there seemed little chance of my request being granted. However, one fine morning, the butler, with goggling eyes, brought me an envelope on which was conspicuously printed 'Ministero della Propaganda'. I opened it with trembling hands. S.E. il Capo del Governo would be pleased to receive me the following Wednesday at 5 p.m.

My next step was to go to Rome. It was arranged that I should stay with the Vitettis who owned a magnificent apartment in the Palazzo Orsini.

Overwhelmed with the perils of my 'mission' I arrived one lovely May evening, full of the bronze clamour of bells, the plashing of innumerable fountains. The great cyclopean palaces frowned down on piazzas gay with flowers; a synthetic smell composed of frying fish, coffee, cheese, clung to the narrower streets, the criss-cross of *cortile* and *vicolo*, septic and sinuous. The Rembrandtesque ghetto had, of course, been cleared away to make room for the charmless modern thoroughfares of which Mussolini was so proud. The Roman policemen in their solar topees had gentle old-fashioned faces like the heroes of the South African War. A feeling of constraint weighed on the great city which is governed by a thumb, once Caesar's, now Mussolini's. Up or down? Down, down! Rome sinks ever deeper into the greedy earth. Meanwhile the master had omitted to muzzle the statues; uncensored, the rhetoric which flowed from their sculptured lips. . . .

Vitetti had been recently moved from the Italian Embassy in London to the Foreign Office in Rome. A brilliant future was predicted for this subtle, diminutive, olive-skinned diplomat; he belonged to a type which had been superseded by the tall, frequently blond, athletic Italian of to-day.

[121]

In the sonorous salons of the Palazzo Orsini, all Rome assembled, conspired, gambled, defamed, flirted, disputed, was reconciled. Here, Christians were thrown wholesale to the lionesses, who beautifully mangled them before devouring them. Lioness, or better still, the French term *lionne* strikes me as a not inappropriate term in dealing with these superb, destructive, feline, patrician ladies.

The next morning, I awoke with a feeling of panic which made me seriously contemplate slipping out of the house with one small 'grip' and taking the train for—anywhere; that or a sudden recurrence of the malaria I had had as a child, or would this be taken for a perfidious allusion to the perfected draining system of the Pontine Marshes?

People began to stream into my room, each with a piece of advice as to how to comport myself, terrifying reminiscences as to what had happened to *them*, or to their uncle, or their cousin, on a similar occasion.

"The audience chamber is as slippery as an iceberg. I nearly sprained my ankle before reaching the desk."

"He has eyes that bore into one's brain. *Lo zio* said they made him feel all dizzy the first time he was received."

"He will doubtless prefer to speak Italian, though his French is impeccable. Of course, you speak Italian quite fluently, *tesoro*, but it is so important not to say the wrong thing, for instance——"

God alone knows how I contrived to get up, to totter downstairs, where the Princess of T—— was waiting to give me a final coaching.

"How long," I nervously questioned, "do you think the audience will last?"

The Princess had the narrowed voluptuous gaze of the shortsighted, to which is given so many exciting interpretations, and which nearly always means, "Now, where have I left my spectacles?"

"It depends," she ruminated, "on whether he is interested—or not. A quarter of an hour, I should say—half an hour at the outside."

This depressing information was allowed to sink in. Then: "Be careful not to make any gaffe; for instance, whatever you do, do not mention anyone in connection with the Fontanges episode."

It was not very long since Mademoiselle Magda Fontanges, after a presumed 'adventure' with the Duce, had been hustled across the French frontier; suspecting my friend, the ex-French Ambassador, Chambrun, of having been party to this, she had subsequently shot him in the stomach as he was preparing to take the train into Brussels. I shuddered at the possible effect of the gaffe insinuated: "No, indeed, that would be fatal," I agreed. G. unbent a little.

"No, I am sure you would not do anything so silly. Coraggio! You must try to interest him. After all, you are not stupid. You can talk about France, you know most of the members of the French Government, I'm told. (What curious tastes, you have, dear child. Still, it will supply you with a topic of conversation.) I will call at six to hear how it went off; no doubt you will be kept waiting. And now——" She rose majestically.

Luncheon was agony. The Italian journalists had been recalled that day from London. With any luck, the dreaded *udienza* would be cancelled. Three-thirty, four. It was not. At four-thirty the car came to drive me to the Palazzo Venezia. With syncopated heart and whirling brain, I gave my pass to the enormous official at the door. I was taken upstairs through miles of echoing corridors, shown into a small room pessimistically draped in bottle-green velvet. It boasted two highly uncomfortable chairs, and the sort of Renaissance table on which death warrants are usually signed on the stage.

I sat down, longing for a stroke, a heart attack, anything that would suppress both me and the interview.

> 'It matters not, Lord, where or how,
> Only let him have it now!'

But no. My heart, though running in a sort of insensate Marathon race, refused to stop. The stroke, with equal coyness, held off. Meanwhile, the little Italian I ever knew deserted me. I couldn't have strung two sentences together, and I doubted if I should understand a single word of what was said to me. I had already been there half an hour. That half-hour was so chock-full of apprehension, that it passed like a minute.

. . . Mussolini. The Regenerator of Italy. One of the most powerful men in Europe. For years I had liked him for his virility, dynamism, a certain peasant honesty. . . . Of all the dictators, he had seemed to me the most human. . . . Hitler had been his undoing. . . . Oh God, why had we interfered in Abyssinia, interfered without interfering, brandishing threats, recoiling before acts? Either we should have closed the Suez Canal or kept out of the whole wretched business. . . .

I stopped dead in the middle. Was this what I was going to say to the Duce? I had better marshal my thoughts into safer channels, otherwise the slightest jolt might spill the disastrous ones aforementioned— I had better—at this juncture, the door opened, a huge *huissier*, no doubt chosen for his bulk, filled the doorway: "*Volete seguirmi Signora.*" I dragged myself up on chattering legs. We passed from tapestry-hung room to tapestry-hung room, miles of 'needless perspectives', as Rebecca West calls them. I followed him with lagging footsteps. Ushers stood at every door. At last to my dismay, the giant stepped aside to let me pass. I found myself on the threshold of an immense and naked room which seemed twice as long as the Galerie des Glaces at Versailles. The *oeils de boeuf* that pierced the walls did not exactly make for intimacy. The carpetless marble floor was so slippery, it might have been made of glass. For several seconds I was obliged to concentrate on my equilibrium. When I looked up I found myself within a few yards of a bureau behind which rose the dreaded silhouette.

A dreadful thing happened. My foremost foot skidded! I fell, scattering the contents of my bag, lipstick, cigarettes, bills, compact, love letters.

What could Mussolini, who prided himself on his 'way' with women, do but help me pick them up? We met on all fours, face to face, under the writing table. His photographs had not lied. His eyes, black, round and *exorbités*, reminded me of the peppermint bull's-eyes we used to buy as children on the Glasgow platform. His bullet-like, completely bald cranium suggested a cannon-ball. His dignity, alas! was irrevocably impaired, a fact he could not fail to realize.

"You are English, aren't you? Why do you write in French?" he asked somewhat breathlessly, after the last cigarette had been retrieved. The ice was broken with a vengeance.

All trace of timidity had left me. "Because I have lived for twenty years in France. I love France and the French."

"And you are soon returning there?"

"*Si, Eccellenza.* I only came to Rome to see you."

He ignored the last part of my sentence, though he looked slightly mollified.

"In six months," he remarked sententiously, "France will go the way of Russia."

"I must beg to disagree, *Eccellenza*."

"On what grounds?" he flared.

"The French are stable in their instability. France is a wayward, fickle country, hard to handle—a blood mare. She must be given her head. She gallops along on her mad course, and generally stops of her own accord."

His face suddenly assumed a vindictive, passionate expression.

"How can you say that? France has completely changed, she is no longer the same country, her fine qualities are atrophied through lack of use. She is *morbida, decadente*."

This man spoke of France as a lover speaks of his faithless mistress. Only *jilted* love could speak as he spoke.

I ventured to say in French: "*Ne vous y fiez pas, Eccellenza*, France is the country of eleventh-hour recoveries, the tide may turn at any moment."

"And you think that such men as Monsieur Léon Blum, Monsieur Daladier, are the right specialists to call in for a death-bed consultation?" (I could not help transposing: "And is this man going to make her happy?")

"Frankly, I don't, but there are others in the offing; Reynaud——"

"You are acquainted with Reynaud?" he barked. My brain sent out a danger signal. I recollected that he had refused to receive Reynaud in audience a few months previously.

"Yes," I continued gingerly, "he is a man of great resource, inventiveness, dexterity, a duellist in fact."

"I see," he said in French, which he spoke fluently with a strong Italian accent. "The typical *débrouillard*, witty little Frenchman. France has no need of *esprit*, what she needs is *esprit de corps*. *Esprit* will be France's undoing."

"Then I have badly expressed myself."

He swept me and my argument aside. "France needs a master, not a jester, on the assumption that France is a Woman, which the French themselves are the first to admit. You remember Michelet's definition: England is an Empire, Germany is a Nation, France is a Person. A second Napoleon (he visibly saw himself in the part) a Napoleon—Pygmalion is required for this Galathea. Do you see either M. Blum or M. Reynaud in this function?"

His face relaxed. He looked almost humorous. Meanwhile, I was accumulating a little dossier of data. He had loved France, which had disappointed him; Germany was no doubt a *pis-aller*; he reads Michelet, probably all the French classics. He is accessible to reason, Napoleon is his God. "What," he suddenly swooped, "is in your opinion (it would be idle to pretend I was not flattered) the chief vice of the French working-class—and their chief virtue?"

I felt like Oedipus confronted with the Sphinx. "The same," I got out at last. "Economy, or, as some would have it, avarice. It is their chief vice and their chief virtue. May I relate to you, *Eccellenza*, a little anecdote? In my country place I have an old gardener, he is about sixty, his wife is perhaps ten years younger. I was at a loss to know what to give them for the *Jour de l'an*. So, lacking imagination, I gave them a few hundred francs, thinking they would probably spend them at the local *trattoria*. A few days later, I returned, and said to the gardener: 'Well, I hope you had a good time with my present.' He looked shocked, and remarked sententiously: 'We put the money aside for the *dot* of our daughter.' 'But,' I objected, 'I didn't know you *had* a daughter.' '*Non, mais on ne sait jamais!*'"

I was rewarded for my daring. Mussolini, to my surprise and gratification, threw back his head, and laughed long and loud, displaying strong white teeth, peasant's teeth.

When he spoke again it was in a different voice, an unofficial *méridional* voice, with a rustic intonation. "It sounds like something out of Maupassant."

"Hoarding and communism are an ill-assorted couple," I insinuated, "France is far too bourgeoise, too self-indulgent to emulate Russia."

"What was your general impression?" he demanded with a return to his examination-paper phraseology. I told him, warming to my subject. He spoke of Russia with a cold contempt, quite unlike the avidity he had displayed in connection with France. It was quickly brought home to me, after two or three abortive attempts, that England was a forbidden topic: to insist would have been to commit one of those monumental gaffes against which I had been warned.

Our conversation ricochetted from politics to travel, from travel to his latest architectural innovations in Rome. Here, he put me in a quandary; I was expected to say that they eclipsed the beauties of the past. A quotation released me:

"I cannot remember who said: '*l'Antiquité, c'est la jeunesse du monde*'," I proposed as a substitute for my own opinion.

"*Ottimo*," he applauded, "I must make a note of that." His ardour, the ardour of the art student, was communicative. Where was the ominous Dictator of half an hour ago?

"Do you know," he presently observed, "you are the only person of your nationality I have ever met who speaks Italian with a Florentine accent. Have you lived much in Italy?"

"My parents own a villa in Florence. I go there as often as I can, but my home, as you know, is in France, my greatest friends are French; you know one of them, Charles de Chambrun." *Ça y est!* I'd said it. The gaffe was out at last, full grown, irrevocable; all the lightnings of Jupiter would now descend on my defenceless head. Sick and mute, I waited, not daring to look up. Then:

"Caro Chambrun! You are a friend of Chambrun's? I always held him in great esteem. *Per Bacco*, you will be able to give me all the details of this attempt on his life." Truly, God was with me, the execution would *not* take place.

Feeling lightheaded and slightly drunk, I poured forth every 'detail' I could muster. "If he is still alive," I prattled, "it is thanks to his embonpoint." Was I mad, or did I discern a twinkle in the dictatorial eye?

"You will doubtless have heard that I was a friend of the lady in question? If this is true, it's time I got a little fatter!" And chuckling, he patted the place where, presumably, the bullet had traversed Chambrun's anatomy.

The miracle had happened; the Duce had made a joke! Emboldened by the joke, I addressed him abruptly, "May I ask you for something?"

"A photograph, no doubt?"

"No, something belonging to you, something you have used."

"*Volentieri*, what, a calendar, a pencil?"

"A pencil."

"Choose then," he indicated a tray containing every conceivable type of writing device. I shook my head.

[127]

"No, not just *any* pencil, your favourite pencil; one that is probably chewed and stumpy."

"*Ho capito!*" He smiled, dived in his pocket. "Take this one then. It fulfils all your qualifications; it is both chewed and stumpy."

It was. It lived in a little box with Mussolini's name on it. The Germans stole it in 1940.

"One other request. Will you show me the balcony from which you harangue the people?"

"*Venite pure.*" He rose; he was a little taller than I, more brawny than fat, with massive shoulders and too short legs. He was meanly, cheaply, dressed in a suit that looked ready-made. He stepped out on the balcony. Rome, reared on martyr's bones and pestilence, its paws sunk in sepulchres, lay couchant, carnivorous, like a superb lion, at our feet. The invading hordes had passed through Rome like so many grasshoppers, all they got was a flick of that tawny tail.

His arm swept the great, raucous city. "*Che bellezza. . . .*" Then: "It is not easy to create beauty, where there is so much already. . . . *Che bellezza,*" he repeated, and this time his tone was wistful, envious. He had mastered many things, his country, colonies, conferences, languages, strategies. Beauty was more elusive. Beauty had outstripped him. Not for nothing was he a Latin. Beauty had made him doubt. To show his responsiveness to her claims, he had written two indifferent plays; he knew in his heart they were indifferent. Was he not missing something, he, one of the Titans of the world? Art is a dangerous repression. Nero was a frustrated artist; likewise Hitler. A massacre can be a substitute; crime: a mere derivative. I am a second Napoleon, the world is mine, millions cringe at my name, but in the watches of the night, I wish I could forget that drawing by Leonardo, the one with the averted profile——

With a short sigh, my companion turned away from the balcony, stepped back into the audience-chamber.

"I hope you are satisfied?"

I murmured something entirely genuine about this 'unforgettable hour', followed him back to his bureau. It was quite a walk from one end of the room to the other.

Entered a flunkey carrying a tray which he deposited on the writing-table. On it was a covered cup, presumably containing soup, a bunch of grapes, a goat's cheese. That was all. (The abstinence of dictators is a theme which has never been properly exploited.)

"I will not ask you to share my dinner," Mussolini grinned, "it is hardly, as you see, a feast of Lucullus."

This clearly meant that the audience was at an end. I rose to go. He grasped both my hands in both of his.

"*Addio, Signora*, I have enjoyed our conversation. If you should again apply for an audience, it will not be refused you"—he paused significantly—"whatever happens." Again he walked the whole length of that vast room. As I turned to go, he said: "Send me your books; I would like to read them."

That night, I sat next to Ciano at a dinner party at the Princess de San Faustino's. "I know that you have been received by the Duce," he said, as soon as we sat down. "Did he keep you long?"

"*Non mica tanto*, no, not very long."

"The usual quarter of an hour, I suppose?"

"A little more than that."

"Half an hour?" He was furious at not being in the know. "What! More than half an hour—an hour?" His black protruding eyes vainly plagiarized his father-in-law's. I decided to put an end to his misery.

"An hour and twenty minutes," I enlightened him. In his astonishment, all diplomacy deserted him.

"An hour and twenty minutes! Incredible! What on earth did you have to talk about?" The other guests, who had been listening to our conversation, tittered.

Ciano had none of the culture, the *envergure* of his father-in-law. He was petulant, prejudiced, inordinately vain. Your heel of Achilles, my boy, is, as with most Italians, your vanity. You are as touchy as an old governess, whom I once nicknamed '*Soif d'Egards*'. Appeal to your vanity and one could make you do anything. This brought me to more general thinking. Surely our whole technique in dealing with the Italians was misguided? There is an old French saying that one cannot catch flies with vinegar. Italy is a young, ambitious, highly sensitive nation, the thing she dreads most is ridicule, the thing she covets most, admiration.

Talleyrand would have known how to deal with Italy. I re-remembered the advice given by a very clever woman to a young, inexperienced man who was courting a lady as elusive as she was fastidious. "Admire the one thing which has always caused her misgivings. Praise her for qualities you know she does *not* possess. She will possess them."

To return to Ciano: the origin of his aversion to France was two-fold: he was not given the *Grand Croix de la Légion d'Honneur* on his visit to Paris in 1935; the Frenchwoman he fancied on this occasion had not responded to his advances. Whereupon he stamped his foot and declared that France was 'beyond the pale'.

After dinner, there was a *ricevimento*. A little crowd gathered at the feet of Edda Ciano, daughter and Egeria to the Duce. Angular, square-jawed, sallow, this lady was singularly lacking in feminine graces.

As my talk with Mussolini had been of a more or less confidential nature, it was impossible to satisfy the questions that were rained on me from all sides. The result was that I was disqualified as an idiot or put down as a monster of duplicity, according to the nature of my interlocutor. I was glad when the party broke up in the small hours of the morning and I was driven home through the prowling and ominous nocturnal Rome, nightly dominated by Colosseum and Catacomb.

Later, as I lay in my high gilt bed, I reviewed the singular day, the crammed hour with its tiny though complete career, beginning in mistrust, developing into exchange of ideas, ending in sympathy. Such contacts, tragic in their enforced brevity, must have been struck up in tumbrils, more than once.

*　　*　　*　　*　　*

The winter of 1936 took me back to Budapest. I enjoyed the solitary drive across Europe, the stupid regimented fir trees stuck in snow, the frozen lakes, like white jade. Now and again, we would disturb some great bird in its intimacy. It would flop clumsily away from a negligible carcase. The morose hirsute frontiers of Central Europe—fir trees so crowded that they might be green hair cut *en brosse*—creep as near as they dare.

White and green. Green and white. Green everywhere on the clothes of the people, clinging to their hats, their buttonholes. The colour of the chase, the *battues* of dead and gone Highnesses. All these more or less ugly countries (no painter of note has ever bothered to paint them) are adorned by Music. Here the harmonious inclination of ten string instruments constitutes a fresco more decorative than any mural painting. The luxury of sound compensates for the austerity of sight.

I see through the Devil. He is as prompt as a bell-boy the day of your departure; as hyperbolic as a *vendeuse*; persuasive as a man who is trying to sell you a second-hand car; versatile as Ruth Draper; adaptable as a Neapolitan tout; ubiquitous as a gossip writer; encouraging as a psycho-analyst; intuitive as a successful clairvoyante. Sometimes he gets his own way, but I am not taken in. In the recesses of the human mind stalks an animal. It can become tame, domesticated, can even be made to sit up and beg. On the other hand, it can devour the mind.

In Budapest, I fell in love again, or perhaps it would be more accurate to say that love was 'wished' on me by the décor, the cold (always, in my experience, an aphrodisiac), the environment. It appealed to the comic opera strain in my make-up that I have never entirely succeeded in quashing: when I was not being Wittelsbach, I was being Offenbach.

Love, or its understudy, is a tribute exacted by Budapest of the unwary foreigner. Look at me—and love. It was all too easy; every conceivable 'aid' to love was available, proffered. Shakos, tzardas, spurs, gypsy bands, twirled moustaches.

The Hungarians, how good looking! They would be photographed standing behind rows of game, pheasants, hares, partridges, stags, wild boar. Game. That's what they were: game for anything. Then the excitement of the Danube, those bloated waters which had witnessed the death of Attila, the Scourge of God! At night you could hear the clink of ice block meeting ice block like the moves of some gigantic game of chess.

A lot of nonsense has been written about the Danube. It has little of the facile romanticism of the Rhine, or the bacchanalian impetus of the Rhône. It is morose, overwhelming, misanthropic, sulkily tamed, it renders the grudging service the Niebelungen gave the gods. No flippant Western river this, gay with bunting, and ladies trailing their white fingers through the green waters.

Even as Attila, the Danube is a scourge, a monstrous power to be reckoned with, conferred over, brandished, used as a threat and an ultimatum, made to serve this purpose and that: a policy, a sword of Damocles. As though realizing this, it sometimes rears in its course, like some runaway Tartar horse trying to throw its rider. But not for long; it is soon compelled to return to its great commercial vocation of linking country with country, tributary with tributary.

Budapest was more virile than Vienna. It had less charm, more fire; less taste, more zest; Vienna was Maria Theresa, Budapest Second Empire, with an Ottoman past. Bucharest, on the other hand, was a fortune-teller married to a fortune-hunter, trashy, flashy, as the gilt tubes of scent you buy in an Oriental bazaar.

Sometimes, of an evening I would go and call on my friend, Elisabeth C——. She was the wife of an eminent Italian diplomat, one of the most dynamic women I ever met. She had been a great actress in her day, the Duse of Hungary, it was said.

I had seen her in many parts, as prima donna, as Elisabeth of Hungary, Madame Sans-Gêne, a pillar of the Church, a pillar of the State; a wit; a wag; a rake; a prude; but I had never seen her on the stage. She had the persuasiveness of a cardinal, the portentousness of an Erda; a mental Fregoli, her experiments were purely intellectual; she will go down to posterity as one who deserved well both of her own and her adopted country. Elisabeth owned a little house in Buda, not far from my own.

Harried by the hurrying snow, I would battle up the steep street, past a kind of stone parapet from which you looked down on the great river. It filled me with a curious elation, like all untamable things, or persons. (Something Turkish still clung to Buda, the small houses drew together with an air of complicity, they nodded over old, old seraglio secrets.)

In Budapest, the pitiless cold would sharpen my wits to needle points, the coachmen would be wearing their frogged leather coats, now and then I would encounter a man with an oblique Mongolian face, hair sleek as a crow's plumage.

No wonder I fell in love with Horthy Estvan, the Regent's son. He had eyebrows like swallows' wings, and the figure of a Caucasian dancer. No wonder I took a rococo house in Buda, which might have belonged to the Rosenkavalier, with its china stoves and convex balconies.

Night after night, the tziganes would bend over us, 'milking' their violins; night after night, we would dance in beautifully organized *boîtes* with revolving floors, cubicles for two. Up and down outside, the detectives would pace, up and down, for Horthy's escapade with an Englishwoman was not approved of. It was lovely while it lasted.

Poor Pishta! His plane was shot down over Russia in 1942. I never saw him again.

The Hungarian comic opera was doomed, middle Europe was about to turn into a tragedy.

*   *   *   *   *

In 1938, our King and Queen made the conquest of Paris. Instead of the tall commanding blonde the French had somehow expected they were given *une petite brune qui parle le français avec l'accent de chez nous.* They took her to their hearts.

I was present at the Quai d'Orsay entertainment (Chevalier had just sung 'Ma Pomme') when thousands broke through the police cordon and swarmed, raucously clamouring: "*Au balcon,*" under the windows of the Ministry. From inside, it sounded distinctly ominous. The Minister of the Interior paled, whispered something in the ear of the *chef du protocole.* If my memory does not play me false, the King and Queen consulted no one; they exchanged a look of mischievous complicity, took hands, and raced through the room like a couple of children. When they were seen, hand in hand, and unaccompanied, on the balcony, the people of Paris went mad.

Later, I overheard the Minister of the Interior say: "Henceforth public protection is entirely superfluous. They could go anywhere, nobody would lift a finger against them."

*   *   *   *   *

Few months were to elapse before we had a preview of invasion, an undress rehearsal of the *exode* that was to be performed in earnest in 1940.

People put their mistresses in, their mattresses on, their cars, and rushed off to tend long-neglected properties in the South, or South-West of France. The sky was clotted with French and British Cabinet Ministers, hurrying to, and from, Berchtesgaden.

The telegraph wires hummed with appeasement.

In Munich, Daladier was serenaded by a band of facetious German students:

> *"Talatier, Talatier, komm' heraus,*
> *Sonst gehen wir nicht nach Haus?"*

The relief of the French when the appeasement appeared to have succeeded was only second to the relief of the British. People returned gratefully to Paris with their mattresses and their mistresses.

I, who have never been anything but a pessimist by nature, was by no means reassured. Besides, I knew the Germans. Our ignorance of German psychology was at least equal to their ignorance of British psychology. It is fatal to give in to a bully, or a bluffer. The Germans are both. I knew we were 'in' for it. *Ce n'était que partie remise.*

The moment has perhaps come for a stocktaking. I was at the apex of my life. Literary fumblings were at an end. I had poise, experience, friends, possessions. Romance was, at long last, disciplined, *coups de tête*, rationed. Then, as ever, I believed in three things: God, France, my mother.

If my character was complex, my faith, if not strictly orthodox, was simple. Like Wilde, I had, for a time, been misled by what Koestler calls 'pantheistic heresy'; like him, I thought that compassion was the essence of Christianity, but it had now acquired a harder, less vulnerable surface. Who was it said: *"Il y a des esprits qui vont à l'erreur par toutes les vérités, il en est de plus heureux qui vont aux grandes vérités par toutes les erreurs"*? My faith had been, if anything, reinforced by an accident, in which I had nearly lost my life by drowning in the Seine. I was completely dual, the physical me shrieking with terror as it rose to the surface only to sink again, the mental me detached and, yes, curious, as though bending over an unfamiliar map. I was fished out just in time and had to be given artificial respiration. My first thought on reviving was: I so nearly knew. What a pity, *tout est à recommencer.*

At the risk of appearing flippant, my beliefs can be resumed in three definitions of a Voltairean brevity:

> A cemetery : a cloakroom.
> Death   : a turnstile.
> The body : a container.

I see no reason to give it more importance. I try to see past it, it is like peering past an obstructive hat at a play.

Please, will you remove your body?

I hope I shall not blubber and squeal when the time comes to part with mine, and that I shall have the dignity to disentangle myself gracefully from the shabby old thing. After all, it is not as if it were young and pleasing. It has not been improved by an accident which has left me with a slight limp for life.

My trouble is fear of pain. I am a terrible coward; all the more so, as I seem to be what is called 'accident-prone'. Years ago, I broke my leg, dancing a *pas seul* to some new records I wanted to try out. It is a gay way of breaking one's leg. I think that in my case there must be some correlation between dancing and fracture (from rapture to fracture?), as when I broke my hip at the ballet, trying to get away before the rush. I didn't notice there was a steep step to the box I was in. The French comic newspapers made fun of my accident. '*On dit que les nouveaux ballets ne cassent rien, c'est faux, ils ont cassé un fémur.*'

I don't blame them. This was also the occasion for a fine display of sensibility on the part of a French audience. As I was carried out in the arms of a Titanic friend, a press photographer rushed forward to photograph the stereotyped first night 'faint'.

A growl went up from the onlookers.

"*Vous ne voyez donc pas qu'elle souffre?*"

A protest which the pressman prepared to disregard, whereupon the crowd surged forward, and, without a word of warning, wrenched the camera from his hands, trampled it to pieces. I wonder if this would have happened in America?

I have no words to tell of the sympathy and kindness lavished on me during my long period of immobility. Somebody said that my bedroom might have been the scene of the (public) *accouchement* of one of the French queens.

I have never been a gossip; still less, I trust, a mischief-maker, but I discovered during that time that the sick and disabled are the world's confidants. Is it because it is assumed that the motionless have lost their memory, or because the horizontal position creates a kind of ethical *faiblesse oblige*? For the first time in my life I knew everything that went on in Paris. It was intoxicating.

One of my nurses was an Englishwoman who had nursed both French and English during the war. The French, she said, were incredibly tough. They must be, judging from the degree of pain you are supposed to endure without an anaesthetic.

My surgeon was a handsome, witty, altogether charming, brute. Small wonder that his patients fell in love with him. He designed a minor torture for me that was worthy of the Middle Ages—or the Gestapo. A redhot skewer, similar to that which you use to roast a chicken on, was driven through my knee without a local anaesthetic. I was trussed by my knee to the ceiling. Every time I moved a millimetre, it tore my knee open. Sleep was impossible. I became subject to hallucinations in the small hours of the morning: I was a fox caught in a trap by my leg; I was chained to the Mont Blanc, impersonated by a white and mountainous knee. However, I forgave him everything when after a week's torture, accompanied by a bevy of love-sick nurses, he blew in to remove the skewer, crying:

"*Andromède, me voici!*"

My convalescence was littered with richly burlesque episodes. My window at the Ritz Hotel 'gave' on to the Place Vendôme; it commanded an excellent view of Van Cleefs, the jewellers. One morning the shop was burgled, in a smash and grab raid, a fact of which I was blissfully unconscious, being asleep at the time. The same evening my visiting friends said temptingly: "*Tu étais aux premières loges*, you will be able to tell us exactly what occurred."

To the first, I replied that I had seen nothing. To the second, that I had heard a few stifled screams. To the third, that of course I had seen everything from the word go, the smashing of the plate-glass window with a hatchet, the hold-up by masked men, the headlong dive into the *traction-avant*, the pursuit of the *traction-avant* by Police Secours.

"What a life you lead, in spite of your immobility," sighed my envious visitors, "never a dull moment!"

This incident took place just before Christmas. I thought it would be fun to have a tiny *réveillon* in my bedroom; to dear Poulenc I scribbled on a blank sheet: '*Venez sabler le champagne le* 31 *décembre chez la recéleuse d'en face.*'

Now, *recéleuse* in French means receiver of stolen goods. My maid, I subsequently discovered, had put the wrong address on the envelope. Anyway, he never turned up, much to my disappointment.

A week or so later, whilst he was dressing for dinner, came a knock on the door. Two very large policemen, such as you only see on the stage nowadays, with moustaches like ram's horns, stood on the threshold. "You are requested to present yourself tomorrow morning at the Commissariat du VII arrondissement." Poulenc blanched.

"Can you tell me the reason?" he faltered. "A *contravention*, no doubt?"

"*Affaire criminelle*," barked the moustaches in unison; turning on their heels, they clattered downstairs.

Poor Poulenc was mute that night at the dinner party, he neither ate, drank, nor spoke.

The next morning, sleepless, haggard, and unshaven, looking very much like the criminal he was not, he presented himself at the Commissariat du VII arrondissement. He was immediately taken to the Bureau du Chef, a small man with eyes like a gimlet. "Perhaps," said the Chef, with a supercilious smile, preparing to enjoy himself, "perhaps you can tell us where you spent the evening of the 31st of December?"

"With some old friends; we dined in Montparnasse."

"What a pity, when a much more alluring invitation was in the post!"

"...???"——

"Yes, we are aware it did not reach its destination. As it bore the wrong address, it went to the lost letter office; otherwise you would not be here; but between the old *copains* and the glamorous receiver of stolen goods, we assume you would not have hesitated, *hein?*" My letter was then thrust under his nose. Poulenc, frightened as he was, could not refrain from bursting out laughing.

"That," he beamed, much relieved, "is from a respectable old friend of mine, a writer; she is temporarily living at the Ritz."

"A most ingenious alibi, we are dealing with *her* later."

Francis gaped.

"But I simply don't understand what you're driving at?"

"Really? You must be less intelligent than we suppose, *cependant*, '*la recéleuse d'en face*' can only mean one thing. Your accomplice, it appears, had taken a room overlooking the Place Vendôme, where she obtained an unimpeded view of the smash and grab raid at Van Cleefs. What more simple, than to summon, under some trivial, social pretext, a man of the world such as yourself, with a hitherto untainted social reputation? It goes without saying she intended to hand you the goods."

It took Poulenc two hours to convince them of his, and my, innocence. Things looked very bad for me, when an investigation at the Ritz disclosed that I had left the previous day for the country.

They were not a little disappointed, when, thanks to the manager, they discovered I was the elderly and respectable English writer Poulenc had alleged.

Speaking of accidents, I had a third, a more melodramatic one: motoring back to Paris, one winter night from St. Loup, I heard a sharp detonation. Thinking it was children amusing themselves with squibs, I lent forward trying to see out. A bullet whizzed through the side of the car burying itself in the upholstery. If I hadn't ducked it would have got me. There were more reports, I saw two men running, one on either side of the car. The chauffeur, fortunately, had the presence of mind to accelerate. I was not frightened, as I had not had time to realize what was happening. Now I am less impressed when I read of the wonderful sang-froid of dictators, who carry on as though nothing had occurred, just after an attempt has been made on their lives.

There was a comic sequel to this episode. I was dining at the British Embassy that night. Having stopped at a café to give a drink to my hysterical maid and overwrought chauffeur, I was not a little late for dinner. "My car," I explained apologetically, "is riddled with bullets."

"Can't you think of a more plausible excuse?" came the sceptical reply. It had to be seen to be believed. Truth is often more improbable than fiction.

Because the most fantastic occurrences select me as their stage (or as their stooge) I have, I know, the reputation of being an accomplished liar. This, again, is not true. When, for instance, I arrived half an hour late at a pre-war Paris luncheon party, my excuse, if spectacular, was genuine enough. "Well, if you must know, it is because I have just killed a lioness." Chorus of: "*Vraiment, elle exagère, cette Violette!*"

This was the explanation. I had been for a walk in the Jardin des Plantes with François d'Harcourt. In those days there were a certain number of tame deer who were in the habit of being fed by the visitors. One of these charming little creatures followed us around everywhere. From time to time, absentmindedly, I would give it a piece of bun out of a paper bag. At length we found ourselves, all three, in front of the lions, who were sunning themselves on a kind of artificial rockery, separated from the public by a ditch. On being suddenly confronted by what had been, no doubt, a favourite dish in the past, a huge lioness began to tremble with covetousness. "Look out," warned François, clutching my arm. A second later, she came hurtling through the air, only to land with a splash within a yard of the concrete bank: the safety margin had been gauged to a nicety. I was under the impression that all the members of the cat family could swim. I was mistaken. After a brief and futile struggle, she sank like a stone. François was dismayed. "*Il y en a bien pour dix mille francs,*" he calculated. "*Disparaissons!*"

"We can't. We must tell the keeper what has happened." Very reluctantly he accompanied me, and much to my surprise, the keeper burst out laughing.

"*O celle-là,*" he jerked a derisive thumb in the direction of the roe deer, "*c'est une allumeuse! Depuis le temps qu'elle s'amuse à faire le mannequin devant les fauves, elle en est à son cinquième lion!*"

★　　　★　　　★　　　★　　　★

During the period immediately preceding the war, I saw a lot of Paul Reynaud.

I had originally been introduced to him by my friend, Gaston Palewski, whose chief he was. Since I have known him, Palewski has put his incorruptible loyalty, integrity and imagination at the service of three men: Lyautey, Reynaud, General de Gaulle. It takes either death or war to part Palewski and the person to whom he has dedicated himself: had it not been for the war, he would still, no doubt, be Reynaud's private secretary.

It would, perhaps, be an exaggeration to quote loyalty as a typical French quality; it must therefore be put down to Gaston's Polish antecedents; an Oxford education is no doubt responsible for his sense of humour which sometimes takes the form of a Puckishness incompatible with a French sense of decorum fundamentally as operative as in the days of Louis XIV.

To cap it all, Palewski is a Romantic, an unmercenary mercenary, a kind of beneficent genie, with nanny-like propensities. (I'm sure that he sees to it that the General does not get his feet wet.) Women find it hard to resist him.

It was extremely diverting to see Gaston's flexible international imagination, his rainbow-like experiences, being decanted and made palatable for Paul Reynaud's staccato little beak. Not that I wish to decry Reynaud's capacities. He had a charming tenor voice; a quizzical eye, a caustic wit. He had been an outstanding Minister of Finance. He resented being short, and practically walked on tiptoe. His clothes were always ostentatiously neat; an immaculate white handkerchief invariably protruded from his breast-pocket; his wavy black hair was parted down the middle, and nearly rejoined Mongolian eye-brows. He suggested all kinds of similes to be rejected impatiently one after another, a Chinese Mercury, a Japanese wrestler, a bellicose *bibelot*.

The first time I met him was, curiously enough, in Vichy. Who would have guessed the tragi-comical destiny of that hygienic spa, the paradox of France's octogenarian defeatist seeking stimulus from the Source Hépar; the anti-climax in the Casino, so suitable a setting for the government in which *rien ne va plus*, whose motto should have been: *Ce n'est que le premier spa qui coûte?*

I was not to meet him again until he was *Garde des Sceaux*. Palewski had arranged a luncheon party at Lapérouse, the world-famous restaurant on the Quai des Grands Augustins. Paris was in its most disenchanted Verlaine mood. The barges sailing up the Seine hooted with nostalgic reiteration; the trees outside seemed to be made of charcoal. My mother was present at the luncheon, and chaffed him in a way to which he had certainly not been accustomed; they parted in amused and mutual esteem.

After that, I was constantly to meet Paul Reynaud. Like most Frenchmen, he found social life diverting, but took it for what it was worth. We talked about England, where his duties carried him more and more frequently. He was Anglophile without snobbishness, appreciative without awe, a sentiment I may add, which was foreign to his nature. He took immense pains to learn English, which he spoke with great precision and such a curious accent that it seemed to gambol in unsuitable fancy dress, like a respectable matron disguised as a *mousmé*.

"Why do you, an Englishwoman, care so deeply for France?" he asked me one day abruptly. Should I pay him some foolish compliment or give him the plain unvarnished truth?

"*Parce que, cher ami, la France est le seul pays qui me procure toutes les sensations de la fortune et de la faillite;* because when we have definitely made up our minds that France is corrupt, decadent, she suddenly does something which causes us completely to revise our judgment, and vice-versa."

What were his real convictions? He was, in point of fact, an *homme du Centre*, with little or no political backing. Excess was both alien and suspect to his frugal, fastidious mind. When he became Minister of Finance and proved himself a brilliant success at the job, he rallied friend and foe. He was really in his element; even the recalcitrant extreme Right had to admit his abilities; if only Mandel had been Prime Minister and Reynaud had remained at the Ministry of Finance, the fate of France might have been different.

I was at St. Loup when war was declared. There was not much excitement; rather, a sombre resignation, an air of fatality, anti-climax. Countries which have been invaded as often as France turn to war with a fatalistic shrug. "*Autant en finir,*" they mumbled, "it had to happen." Throughout the phoney period, there was never a whiff of the *on les aura* spirit which won Verdun.

Month after month, men sat in the Maginot Line, bored stiff watching the Germans a few yards away, seemingly equally bored. The casualties did not appear to exceed the number of road accidents on a fine Sunday afternoon. Interest flagged, courage, from lack of use, became atrophied.

My home was on the direct line of invasion, *la route de l'est*, which leads straight to Nancy, Alsace, the Kehl bridge. How soon would the road be encumbered with shuffling, homeless figures, fleeing in the opposite direction, how soon?

Then, of a sudden, all changed. The monster which had been feigning apathy, sprang to life. I was in Paris when the news of the Sedan break-through reached us. There was a deathly silence. The silence of calamity. I think even then we realized there was no hope.

As early as the 17th of May, Gamelin gave out that he could contain the German armies no longer, and that, Pilate-like, he washed his hands of the situation. *Sauve qui peut!* A few days later I was given half an hour to clear out by the French Red Cross where I was working. They knew I was anxious about my parents, still in Italy; that I wanted to devise some means of getting them home.

I had the incredible good fortune to encounter my friend, Gilone de Chimay, who was about to try to 'make' her little house near Bergerac with her younger son, Elie. I provided the car, she the petrol. There was no question of returning to St. Loup. My career as the Scarlet Pimpernel had begun.

Never shall I forget the exodus from Paris, the cars, lorries, buses, bicycles, trailers, wheel-barrows, perambulators, the sweating bewildered population carrying bundles of every shape and size, the wild-eyed refugees from Belgium and the North, the exhausted men who fell asleep in any position, the old women who sat as though turned to stone in the swaying, stinking *camions*. Then the terrified scrutiny of the skies for dive-bombers which would suddenly swoop down on the convoy, leaving a shambles in their wake. Now and again, we were reduced to hiding in ditches until the dive-bombers overhead had dispersed. The first night we spent on the floor of an hotel in Evreux, the second in a small château near a large powder factory near Angers. Throughout we had the radiant weather which, in my experience, invariably attends catastrophes. '*Mai qui fut sans nuages et Juin poignardé.*'

Our relief on reaching Gilone's little property can be imagined. There I found a telegram from my parents (I had wired to them before leaving Paris) saying that they had left Italy and arrived in Cannes. I promptly replied suggesting that they should meet me in Bordeaux, only a hundred kilometres from where I was staying; there it should be easy to find a boat to England, but they were not convinced of the imminence of the danger and contrived to waste a week in Cannes, where I refused to join them, alleging it was foolish to waste the last gallons of petrol available on a journey I knew to be futile. Every day the news got worse. It was anguish to listen to the raucous bars of the Marseillaise on the wireless: '*Aux armes, citoyens!*' had become the despairing cry of a nation at bay with the enemy at its throat.

Ever since Reynaud's urgent call for 'planes' to England, we had hardly dared give voice to our apprehension. "*Je sens qu'on nous cache des choses!*" Gilone used to say after each evasive communiqué, but the possibility of a French surrender was undreamt-of, the worst that could happen was the taking of Paris, and even *this* fear seemed too monstrous to formulate.

Then my parents wired me to join them at Dax, a small watering-place fifty kilometres from Bayonne, which was, at any rate, two hundred kilometres in the right direction. Special permission was required to get to Dax, but I knew that the Red Cross badge on my car would get me anywhere. An ancient chauffeur, heavily bribed, was forthcoming. As I went further South, the natural insouciance of the population reasserted itself; Dax is only some sixty kilometres from the Spanish frontier; the narrow streets were faintly redolent of the cinnamon-flavoured chocolate which is so popular a beverage in Spain. A small forsaken arena almost jostled the much-frequented hot spring; wistful postcards of matadors garnished the shop windows.

I felt the repressed effervescence I always feel in Spain, but it is a Spanish effervescence, local, intestinal, fratricidal bubbles that have nothing to do with the vast European conflicts of France.

For the next few days, the march of events seemed to be arrested. Here, the bombing of Paris had made much more impression than the Sedan 'bulge'.

Many of the local plump ladies with cabochon eyes, nails, shoes, had friends or relations in Paris, and such a scandalous occurrence brought the war home to one. The atmosphere was oppressive *à l'heure du communiqué* in the hotel bar in which the bloated *clientèle embusquée* assembled. They did not care what happened as long as they were safe. "*Ici on est tranquille,*" they would complacently state, and all the time the Germans were creeping nearer and nearer.

On the 14th of June, a day sooner than Hitler had predicted, they made their triumphal entry into Paris. This gave the curetakers a nasty jar. Many of them had an apartment or pied-à-terre in the capital. What would happen to their furniture, cellar, *bibelots*, Pekinese? The post office was taken by storm, and hundreds of anxious, interrogatory, admonishing, persuasive, peremptory telegrams were sent.

Three days later, Pétain announced that he had asked for an armistice. "*Du moment que c'est le Maréchal, on a confiance,*" somebody sobbed. "He will only accept an honourable peace."

I could not believe my ears. France! It wasn't credible. Of all countries the least compliant, the most refractory, the only country which takes nothing for granted! Incalculable France, all meanness one moment, all generosity the next; soaring helicopter-like, without transition, from the ignoble to the sublime—and back. And this *enfant terrible* among nations, this spoilt child of Europe, with its impudence, cussedness, spunk, is to be surrendered without a murmur to the spirit breaker, the giant bully, the ostracized gate-crasher of Europe, all because the 'hero of Verdun' hasn't the courage to face the music! God! What folly, what criminal folly. What had possessed Reynaud to send for Pétain? Why hadn't he tried a *levée en masse*: it was not too late?

Blind with tears of mingled despair and fury, I stumbled from the room.

The British, it was said, were to be herded into concentration camps. It was clearly time we left. At Bayonne, we were told there was a British Consul who would give us advice. At Bayonne, we were told the last boat for England had left that day; there might still be another, but the date of its sailing was uncertain. There was only one solution; to attempt to gain the Spanish frontier, thence Portugal, where we would have no difficulty in finding a boat to England.

As opposed to this, it soon transpired that acquiring a visa for Spain was like getting blood out of a stone; the visa for Portugal was unobtainable under two or three weeks. Mercifully, I was acquainted with the Spanish Ambassador in Paris, who acted as go-between for the French, Italian and German Governments, and who was entrusted with the armistice *pourparlers*. He was at Bordeaux. I decided to take the law into my own hands and started off post-haste in my diminutive car for that city. My parents remained in Biarritz, most callous and trivial of French watering places; quantities of *embusqués* from Paris had assembled there, and there was a generous sprinkling of Spanish noblemen who couldn't help remarking that their gloomy prophecies about the war had been amply justified.

Bordeaux. My memories of that opulent city were mostly happy ones. It had its own aristocracy, the sons of the great vintages, laconically referred to as *les fils*, just as in Lyons, the leading *industriels* are known under the designation of *les soyeux*, the silkies. *Les fils* frequently bore English names, Johnstone, Morrison, etc., and were descendants of the English rulers of Bordeaux in the fifteenth century.

Stately, homogeneous, most of the great squares were built in the time of Louis XIV; sculptured satyrs looked down on bearded tritons and plunging dolphins. No, there was certainly nothing tragic about Bordeaux, a trifle pompous, perhaps? Are not securities of being and well-being inseparable?

A sinister parody of social activity possessed the Bordeaux to which I returned. Why, I asked myself, is a bird's eye view of a situation only possible in retrospect, why, if one is not utterly devoid of historical consciousness, is it so difficult to focus the present, to force all these fragmentary impressions into one significant phrase? Would the un-initiated immediately grasp the meaning of all this *brouhaha*, this muttering mob of people, unanimously bent on keeping an appoint-ment on which, seemingly, their life depended? These bloated, dropsi-cal cars, with the invariable mattress on the roof, the ruthless *garde mobile* forcing his way through congested streets, the ministerial limousines, with their muffled occupants, would they spell the word Invasion? But this was hardly the moment to philosophize. My in-quiries as to the whereabouts of M. de Lequerica, the Spanish Am-bassador, met with replies that were not encouraging. "He has received no one for several days, not even his intimate friends. When he is not talking to Mussolini on the telephone, he is talking to Hitler. Your only chance is to waylay him at the Spanish Consulate where he goes once a day, but no one knows beforehand at what time. Anyway, you can do nothing until tomorrow." Tired and disheartened, I set about finding a bed for the night; in the hotels they were sleeping on, and under, billiard tables. I suddenly recollected that the Red Cross had a section in Bordeaux; there, surely, someone would offer me a night's lodging?

A certain confusion reigned in the house taken over by the Red Cross, the general refrain being: "The Germans may arrive tomorrow, if not the day after." A lady flung at me: "If you care to sleep in my house, you can, it's empty; I'm taking my children immediately to Ste.-Foy-la-Grande. *Je ne suis pas folle, moi.*" Another lady remarked: "It's time I got back to Libourne, there might be a raid on Bordeaux to-night. *On ne sait jamais.* The only hotel is packed, we even have a secretary from the Spanish Consulate."

"Spanish Consulate!" I shrieked. "I'm going there."

Libourne is only about sixteen kilometres away, but the blackout was very thorough. The sky was illuminated from time to time by flashes that were either lightning or bombs. It was difficult to tell which. As a matter of fact they were bombs.

At Libourne, it was raining as it only rains in films; I got soaked through in a minute, all to no purpose. The Spanish Secretary was dining in Bordeaux: there was nothing for it but to return there.

As the lady at the Red Cross had truthfully informed me, her house was empty—but for a charming old cook, who was entirely unperturbed and who apologetically gave me some excellent pâté and a bottle of Château Margaux. *"Je me ferai gronder par Madame, mais tant pis!"* The sirens were wailing. She insisted on making up the bed in Monsieur's bureau, which was an attractive little octagonal salon with *camaieu* medallions over the doors. I was very tired and soon fell asleep.

Ernestine brought me my coffee at six-thirty and soon after seven I was at the Hotel Splendide. Most of the potentates were staying there, why not Lequerica? I knew he didn't sleep at the Consulate. The porter was already besieged with inquiries. British and French officers stood about in knots, conversing in sombre undertones, haggard old Ritz girls dozed in armchairs, their jewel cases on their knees; already perspiring messengers dashed down their letters and were off again. "The Spanish Ambassador sleeps in the country," growled the over-worked concierge when I could get near him.

There was nothing for it but to go to the Consulate, and try to discover what time he was expected there. To my dismay, several hundred people, who were shortly to become several thousand, already surrounded the small three-storied house. They were being kept in check by six stubbly-chinned soldiers, who looked the very essence of the *Commune*. No, nobody was allowed in, no, they could not deliver a message. An already remorseless sun beat down on the anxious perspiring faces which were so soon to become panic-stricken.

I pushed, they pushed. They were of all nationalities. Occasionally, the door of the house would open a few inches, and an almost in-variably Spanish name would be shouted. A stampede. The favoured one, surrounded by venomous looks, would fight his way to the door which promptly swallowed him up. Would this ever be my fate? I began to despair. Suddenly a figure appeared on the balcony of the first floor. My pulse quickened. It was the Ambassador's private secretary, whom I had met several times at the Embassy in Paris. His eye raked the crowd, and finally lit on my wildly waving hand.

Significantly, deliberately, he made the gesture of writing. I nodded, and pointed interrogatively in the direction of the soldiers: would they deliver my letter? They would. Galvanized, I withdrew from the crowd, and wrote an S O S on my knee in the *jardin public* nearby; this I affixed to the branch of a lilac tree the length of a small fishing-rod. Then I fought my way back to the Consulate. I was able to hand up my letter over the heads of the crowd to one of the soldiers. He nodded, and disappeared into the house. How long I waited there, I do not know. It is not for nothing that the Spanish national motto is *Mañana*. My legs gave way. I sat in the gutter sucking oranges. After what seemed an eternity Lequerica's chauffeur appeared in the doorway and shouted my name, Spanish-wise, with the accent on the last syllable: TREFUSÈS.

The crowd had considerably swollen. They had not lunched. They had been told that the German army was barely 150 kilometres away, that mechanized units had entered Ste.-Foy-la-Grande.

My name sounded slightly bogus, it did not possess an authentic Spanish ring. If I was to be allowed in, why not they, the Parisians, Belgians, Jews, Dutch, Nordics? Far from facilitating my passage, they did their utmost to bar it. I was pommelled black and blue; for a few terrifying seconds I was forced to my knees, then an order flashed like the lash of a whip. An enormous man appeared in the embrasure of the door, and culled me from the crowd as you would cull a marionette from a puppet show. He carried me bodily in to the Consulate. The door banged in the face of the multitude.

I found myself in a small, stifling waiting-room, surrounded by Spaniards with long, melancholy blue faces which reminded me of Greco's 'Burial of Count Orgaz'. *"Espera Ud,"* wait, I was told; I had long passed the boundaries of impatience. Apathy had set in. I waited. The menacing unnoticed sun was poised like an *espada* over the curtainless room. Patriotic notices, *'Arriba España'*, and old *corrida* posters, adorned the white-washed walls. Franco, in profile, assumed a dictatorial pose above the bureau. The Spanish personnel conversed in guttural undertones. Now and again, a word of their conversation hit me: *'El caudillo'*, *'el viejo Pétain'*, *'gente inferior'*. Flies buzzed, cigarettes were lit, expired.

In the middle of all this, a door opened at the opposite end of the room: the longed-for silhouette of Lequerica appeared. Much to the

[147]

surprise of his satellites, he came towards me, both arms outstretched, embraced me paternally on my excessively grubby cheeks.

"Venez dans mon bureau, nous serons plus tranquils. Quelle joie de voir une femme! Aujourd'hui, ié n'ai causé qu'avec Hitler et Mussolini!"

When I emerged half an hour later, I carried with me visas for myself and for my family, not mere *permis de transit,* but *permis de séjour* for Spain.

Feeling the urgent need of something more sustaining than oranges, I rushed to the Chapon Fin, which I always think is the most sinister-looking restaurant in Europe. It is as though its creators had had a violent altercation, one in favour of something resembling a catacomb, the other, more frivolously, supporting the idea of a rockery. The result, a rocatacomb, in the innumerable fissures of which the dust of generations has accumulated, must have driven many a *femme de ménage* to suicide.

That day, the clientèle was a curious one; of furtive *chefs de cabinet,* discredited ministers, forlorn Rothschilds, fugitive dressmakers from Paris, princelings with the strong international accent of Royalty, writers, painters, prostitutes, bankers, all with but one object; to get out.

Nauseated, I snatched up a bottle of wine and a few sandwiches, and started out on my return journey to Biarritz. I arrived there about 1 a.m.—the roads were jammed—exhausted, filthy, exultant. My mission was incomplete. There remained Portugal.

I knew no one at the Portuguese Consulate in Bayonne, but my fellow fugitive from Paris, who had meanwhile joined us, was, it transpired, a distant connection of the Consul's. We decided to make the most of this relationship. Her first attempt was not encouraging, though less dramatic than my vigil outside the Spanish Consulate in Bordeaux. She was told she must be patient for a few weeks, and that all would be well; the Consul was *débordé,* the Germans might be in Bordeaux, but we were not to be put off like this. She discovered the Consul's private address and we determined to lie in wait for him at his own house. This proved to be a Second Empire villa in the suburbs of Bayonne, full of delightfully prim furniture, milky opaline vases and albums full of photographs of ladies who looked as though they had stepped straight out of an Offenbach comic opera.

Other people who had evidently had the same idea as we, were scattered about the placid salons, waiting for the Consul's return, which, when it occurred, provoked the admiring ejaculations, the effusive gestures, the shrill cries of delight that generally herald the entrance of a prima donna into her *loge* during the entr'acte of a first night. And no wonder! Senhor M—— was geniality itself; his plump, exquisitely dressed person exhaled good humour, he distributed smiles and consolation right and left. To us, he bestowed a wink and a whispered *"Attendez-moi au premier,"* which made us think that perhaps life was worth living after all.

Up we went. Hardly had we seated ourselves on another Bibliothèque Rose sofa, when a delightfully dimpled lady, dressed in purple satin pyjamas, entered, *en coup de vent*, and pressed Gilone to her heart, who, when she had recovered from her astonishment, hazarded: *"Madame Montez, je pense?"*

"Pas Madame Montez, cousine, cousine Bebecita! Je vous ai attendoue toute la iournée, ié dit à Bobby qu'il fallait vous recevoir tout de suite quand ié sou que c'était vous; vous avez l'air fatigué, un pé de champagne vous fera du bien."

She clapped her hands. A gay and impudent young man in a striped waistcoat, who would have made a perfect Figaro, appeared: *"Du champagne pour ces dames, et vivemé!"*

It was too good to be true.

We sat there sipping our champagne and the *si sympathique* Bebecita made inquiries after all Gilone's relations, living and dead, which she punctuated with little stabs of her fan. The fan, the formal sofa, the champagne, struck a chord in my memory. Where had I seen all this before? The answer came pat enough. Cuba. Havana. The presidential ballroom.

My taste for life, which had been dormant for the last twenty-four hours, returned to me. I visualized our sojourn in Portugal, which is a sort of exotic Normandy, semi-tropical and welcoming, the country houses with their 'rètroussé' Chinese roofs, the sensuous Manueline architecture, into which, seemingly, the contents of a cornucopia have been spilt.

Presently, the Consul joined us; he was like a personage out of some Goldoni comedy, voluble, gesticulating, with that extremely penetrating *voix de tête* so frequent in Southern countries. Refreshed in mind and body, we took our departure and triumphantly returned to

Biarritz, brandishing the Portuguese visas. My parents met us on the steps of the villa. "We won't need those now," Papa jubilated. "There is a boat leaving for England to-night. Just time to pack your things!"

My heart sank to zero: my mission had been useless. The knowledge sank into me that I was leaving France, my home, my friends, for a long time, perhaps for ever. Portugal had seemed a respite, less irrevocable.

I shall never forget the horror of the embarkation at Saint Jean de Luz, in the middle of the blackest blackout I have ever seen. Great ropes of rain lashed the quays. I was carrying two small bags, one containing my jewels, and the other such homely essentials as a sponge, a tooth-brush, pyjamas. In my agitation, I gave the bag I thought contained these to what I took to be a porter, who vanished into the blackout and was never seen again. Too late, I realized my mistake, but I was past caring.

Did Mary, Queen of Scots, I wondered, sail from France at night, in the rain?

There was worse to follow. For three mortal days and nights we remained in the harbour of Saint Jean de Luz, not two hundred yards from the spot where the tender had come to fetch us. France was still at hand, attainable, proffered, but we were not allowed to leave the boat, which was by way of sailing 'at any moment'.

In reality we were waiting for several detachments of the Polish army, fugitives from all parts of France, magnificently eager to go on fighting in England.

There was quite an *embarras de richesse* of the things that could happen to us in the meantime: (*a*) bombs from above, (*b*) submarines from below, (*c*) the Gestapo from Bordeaux who were about to occupy all the ports of France. Each had his favourite calamity, mine was the submarine.

At length, after three interminable days of waiting, and the last Pole had either walked, or been carried, on board, the anchor of the ship was lifted.

Our relief was not to be described; anything seemed preferable to this monstrous immobility, and (for me) the agony of almost being able to touch France without being allowed to land.

A German submarine waited outside; two torpedoes were fired at us, and missed. Apart from this incident, the sea was as boring as I have always found it. Our boat (a troopship) was intended to carry some 1500 passengers; there were well over 3000 on board. There was neither comfort nor privacy; sleep was impossible on account of our life-belts; I had exhausted my supply of cigarettes, we had little to eat, and nothing to drink except rather brackish water. As in *Outward Bound*, I felt we were all dead, and knew it not. I had lost my home, my friends, my possessions, and last, but not least, my identity. I was the Woman without a Past. Nothing remained but to turn over a new leaf.

Part Three

ENGLAND

CHAPTER EIGHT

I RETURNED to a seemingly irresponsible, care-free London, where people entertained, played bridge, danced, made jokes.

What I mistook for indifference was the determination to make the best of things; *la pudeur des sentiments*, the cult of the understatement. I became acquainted with that, to me, unfamiliar phenomenon, the stiff upper lip. The silence which prevailed whenever France was mentioned was due to magnanimity, not callousness. It took me a long time to attribute the right motives to misleading outward manifestations, or lack of manifestation. People were very kind; they forbore from questioning me; it was as though I were in mourning for an unmentionable relation.

Fear is an excellent diversion from sorrow. Though terrified, I almost welcomed the first air-raids. They created a diversion. I even became acclimatized to the sick silence of the sky before it began to be nibbled by almost inaudible sound, like a taut curtain against which invisible forms are pressed. My parents and I went to stay with my sister in Hampshire, but my mother rapidly discovered that she 'preferred bombs to boredom'; it was being in the country that bored her, she was essentially an urban character.

I did not share my parents' affection for the Ritz. I have always detested hotels, the Ritz was no exception. I longed for the isolation of the country; on whom dared I inflict my haunted, nostalgic self?

Who would be in sympathy with one, who, though English and proud of it, looked upon England as exile? The only bone of contention between my darling mother and myself was France. She considered we had been let down disgracefully; the subject was taboo. I twisted this way and that, longing for some kind of outlet, someone with whom I would not have to conceal my yearning for France as though it were an unsightly disease.

After days of retrospective searching, a name leapt to my mind: Dorothy, Dorothy Heneage. Although I had not seen her for ten, or perhaps fifteen, years, I knew she would understand, would sympathize; she had a genius for understanding; besides she was alleged to have French blood. I gratefully recalled some of her *petites manies* which seemed to me typically French. Greatly daring, I wrote, telling her everything.

Dorothy Heneage came into my life when I was about seventeen. As regards age, she was midway between my mother and myself. She had been very kind to me as a girl; many were the week-ends I had spent at Coker with the fiancé of the moment.

The reverse of beautiful, Dorothy had a fabled charm, or, more accurately, the charm of a fable. She resembled a furry little animal, an animal out of one of La Fontaine's fables; that is to say, an animal which, while retaining its animal characteristics, could lay claim to every form of feminine sophistication. She was quick as a magpie, cunning as a fox, one of La Fontaine's foxes. Her circle numbered a certain amount of grateful dupes, *maîtres corbeaux*, lured by her flattery into complacency. She was so charming to her victims that they remained her slaves for life.

Of an extreme fastidiousness, her small Boucher-like hands, sheathed in white suède gloves, were seldom allowed to see the light of day. A cup of tea offered by Dorothy was a privilege; a handshake, a promotion. With a sinuous witch-like smile playing about her lips, she would make a middle-aged Blimp into a young Alexander, a groping journalist into a very Coward of success. In short, she was a witch, but a witch turned fairy-godmother. What pumpkin was not the happier for being turned into a coach?

Certain purely animal traits added to her fascination; her secretiveness, for instance: she could not bear to be watched, divined, forestalled. She was at infinite pains to conceal some perfectly innocent displacement; would go to unheard-of lengths to distract attention from a plan which did her nothing but credit; indeed, she went through all the misleading flutterings of a bird, to entice you away from its honourable nest. Secretiveness was the breath of her nostrils. She shared the suspicions of the smaller rodents, suspicion of noise, of unfamiliar food, unfamiliar smell. She was terrified of almost everything, thunderstorms, disease, accidents, travel. Bombs, which, in Somerset, were few and far between, caused her to spend the night under the staircase. The precautions she took to preserve herself from physical contamination were scarcely credible; garglings, disinfectants, additional clothing, temperature-taking, etc.

Every morning, in front of Dorothy's bedroom was stationed a trolley, laden with cotton-wool, Elastoplast, forceps, bandages, Dettol. The first time I saw the thing, I was startled. Had the doctor been hastily summoned? Was a minor operation in progress? Later on in the day, I happened to glance at Dorothy's legs. They were tightly bandaged, like a racehorse's. I could not tear my eyes away. My hypnotized stare was not wasted on her. "You see," she explained, "I was once stung by a mosquito."

*   *   *   *   *

Dorothy's response to my letter surpassed my most sanguine expectations. "Of course. Come at once, and stay as long as you like. You shall have your old room." It was characteristic of her to pick up our friendship where it had left off.

I had not seen Dorothy for perhaps fifteen years. I was not prepared for the change in her appearance. When I had last seen her, she had resembled a nimble fox, with her sly, oblique little eyes, long pointed nose, watchful, graceful body. I could not guess that the fox had turned into Mrs. Tiggy Winkle, Beatrix Potter's irresistible, motherly hedgehog, horizontal and homely; her charm, however, was intact.

To this day, I suspect she did it on purpose, weighing herself each week with a wink and a chuckle, impishly assessing the potentialities of this visa to a quiet life, sated with sighs and scenes, adulation and flattery. At the age of, say, fifty, she must have deliberately given *carte blanche* to encroaching fat, to poaching fat. "Ouf," no doubt was the exclamation suscitated by the comfortable reflection in her looking-glass.

Besides, there was Coker Court which took the place of everything. It became her life work, her *raison d'être*, religion. In its way, it was perfect. It was beautifully situated, on an eminence overlooking two lovely counties, Somerset and Dorset. The house itself was partly Tudor, partly Georgian, partly taciturn, partly gregarious. There was a great hall with a Jacobean screen of a gloomy richness, dark angular furniture, Persian rugs, the colour of bruised peaches. A great bowl of agate, like a round of beef, dominated the room. Set on a kind of pedestal, lit from the inside, it resembled some profane Gargantuan grail.

A turn to the right, and a few steps, brought you into a different world, a world of Georgian green walls, elegant fireplaces, parquet floors, Coromandel screens. The six or seven members of a chubby, delightful Georgian family, who, one felt, still wished for company, were hung about the room; over one was suspended the viol which figured in the portrait.

One of Dorothy's most endearing traits was her incessant, incorrigible, imaginative present-giving. The most casual visitor could scarcely believe his eyes when some charming little object would be pressed into his hand as a souvenir of Coker. There was, apparently, an inexhaustible supply of these, rather like Royalty's tie-pins. Her greatest achievement was perhaps, the muniment room. Here she had assembled all the documents concerning Coker since its purchase by one of her ancestors, in the sixteenth century.

Musty, reticent, the little room behind the arras would submit to the raising of the baize covers which protected each scroll from the dust, revealing the shrivelled crowded characters of missals, written, as it were, in dried blood, the deed-polls, with their elaborate tentacular capitals, the great seals of England, cracked, caracoling and tremendous.

England

I have always loved the English countryside, its drowsy, hypnotic charm. It was a taste I had never been able to indulge in to the full. It was like a cool hand on my brow. I loved the gracious, deliberate rooms through which no one hurried; the only things which were ever changed were the flowers. I loved the smell of pot-pourri, and Floris bath essence that clung to the passages; most of all, I loved the carillon high up in the clock tower; its chilly chimes were like a courtly aerial minuet.

My love of birds, always kept in abeyance—what is the use of loving birds in a country where there aren't any?—reasserted itself. It was shared by Dorothy, who put one in mind of a feminine St. Francis. A tiny mossy nest, recently evacuated, all curling feathers inside, was given the importance of a *bibelot*, placed *bien en évidence*, on a fifteenth-century chest.

First I was given as promised my 'old' room, with a black and gold lacquer fourposter, narrow, mottled Venetian looking-glasses, a dressing table which inspired the following lines:

> "Autumn at her mirror lolls,
> Matching yellow'd laces,
> Negroes holding parasols,
> Shield those portly graces.
> Presently she pouts and frowns,
> Tho' fops do not stint her,
> In the glasses' faded browns,
> She sees, reflected, Winter."

Later, I was moved down to the ground floor, under pretext that my room was cold and isolated. I liked my new room—one of the Georgian suite—even better. A venerable magnolia grew against the wall outside. I had only to put my hand out of the window to touch the lemon-scented petals, of the same texture as a white kid glove. Wagtails strutted on the daisied lawn. I slept on a narrow white enamel bed, which provoked the dreams of my childhood.

One is never cured of one's childhood: too happy, as in my case, it exhales an aroma with which the present cannot compete, too unhappy, it poisons Life at its source. In either case, it is wiser not to look round.

I loved the mushroom-scented dawn, the small shrewd stars so different from the Latin blotches I was accustomed to. Inevitably, the tempo of my life changed. It had been *appassionato*, it became *andante*.

Dorothy and I had many tastes in common: books, muniments, old silver, anything French. The life I led at Coker was a delightful rehearsal of old age, though I was but forty-five. We both made ourselves out to be older than we really were.

At that period of my life, I had a devoted friend, Tancred Borenius, the famous art critic. Of Finnish origin, he did his best to resemble Mr. Pickwick (or Sir John Lavery?), his chubby cheeks encased in what appeared to be false whiskers. Romantic, he dealt in regicides, pretenders, lost causes. Our triangular conversations would not have been displaced at the Court of Weimar. Throughout my five years' stay in England, I, a European loafer, a *cosmopolissonne* if ever there was one, suffered acutely from claustrophobia. Tancred was always there to help me escape; his mind was a turnstile to speculative adventure.

Dorothy had a charming companion, an older lady, who treated Dorothy as though she were a naughty child. Miss Darnell, humorous, tolerant, practical, subscribed to my mental convalescence in no mean measure, part confidante, part nannie, she put one in mind of those slightly ambiguous elderly characters, half poor relation, half housekeeper, who figure in Russian novels under the term *prijivalka*. She was embossed with great cabochon virtues set in tiny seed faults.

Meanwhile the threat of invasion became very real. We received notices enjoining us to remain in our homes, not to encumber the roads, whatever happened. Evacuees arrived from London and were comfortably installed (Dorothy was Charity itself) in the basement, where the most extraordinary Hogarthian scenes would be weekly enacted. It was against my hostess's hygienic principles ever to set foot in a shop (germs, draughts, men rough and rude). Accordingly a young lady from Yeovil (the neighbouring town) would arrive with her tongs once a week. If it so happened that she coincided with an air-raid warning, the séance would be continued in the basement.

The fastidious figure of Dorothy, waving a Vapex-scented handkerchief, on her little island of purity with the hairdresser, and all around a ring of awed but inquisitive Cockney brats, dishevelled mothers, arms akimbo, the muted chorus of "Coos", and "Oo-ers", is a picture not easily forgotten. How would the *drei Nornen* have behaved, I wonder, if the invasion *had* taken place?

It goes without saying that the German Kommandant would have been completely unnerved by Dorothy.

$$* \quad * \quad * \quad * \quad *$$

The village of East Coker must be one of the prettiest in England. Most of the cottages are Tudor, a few are Georgian. These are built of the honey-coloured local sandstone, festooned with wistaria, encircled with lilac. Some of the diminutive back-gardens boast a weeping willow, like part of a ballet set, or a lady washing her hair.

Needless to say, I made friends with the inmates. Mrs. Mayo owned the prettiest cottage of all. The drawing-room was low-ceilinged, pleasantly crowded with miscellaneous objects. I liked the portraits of a Carolean couple, one of those willy-nilly Lelys in frames that looked as though they were made of coarse lace. The man displayed a self-indulgent profile and one fine deprecatory hand; the lady, a face like a melancholy egg, with some button-hook curls glued to her forehead. She had none of the gimlet-eyed ferocity of the Elizabethan women who all faintly resemble Bess of Harwicke. Mrs. Mayo was a hospitable soul; a chronic smell of clever cooking—as opposed to the odourless English anonymity—hung about the house.

Occasionally, Dorothy would honour Mrs. Mayo's tea table (I say honour because the brief bestowal of Dorothy's finger-tips was always considered as such). Although she was the local Lady Bountiful, she seemed more like a fragile, exotic, and essentially migratory, royalty. She made the neighbours behave in a delightfully uncharacteristic fashion. Hard-boiled majors would stammer clumsy compliments, parsons would kiss her hand. I have not yet referred to Dorothy's foreignness. The daughter of a much travelled diplomat and a prominent Edwardian hostess, with her French foxy face, her fastidious feminity, one was constantly reminded of it. Her childhood reminiscences contained such sentences as: "When I was a little girl, I drowned my doll in the Neva. . . ." Only she pronounced it Nièva, *à la russe*. (She even invented Slavonic expressions of glee: "*Tchi! Provka! Provka!*")

Her outbursts of gaiety were irresistible; they gave one the impression of complete, if momentary, recklessness; her wishful thinking was proverbial; if she really wanted anything, it was inconceivable that it should not happen. She was the most stimulating companion I have ever known; but for Dorothy, I would never have recovered my equilibrium.

Meanwhile, another friendship was born and slowly matured. Colonel Batten, a shy giant of six foot four, somehow guessed that I was fundamentally sad and homesick. He had all the nicest qualities of the Englishman: modesty, loyalty, courage, discretion. It was largely due to these two that at long last my longing for France was subdued to a dull intermittent ache. I began to love Somerset, the golden stone, slate roofs, West Country drawl.

In the autumn of 1940, a bombshell exploded, shattering my self-administered anaesthesia. A great friend of mine, Hélène Terré, had contrived to escape from Vichy, where she was working on behalf of the Red Cross, and had arrived in London. She accompanied her chief, who hoped to collect comforts for French children. Before they had been in London four days both women were arrested and clapped into jail.

In order to understand the full horror of her predicament, it is necessary to explain the character and achievements of Hélène Terré. When I first knew her, she had just published the complete works of Paul Valéry, who spoke of her with affection and esteem, (*a*) because she had a first-class brain, (*b*) because of the selfless life she led. The youngest of a bevy of handsome sisters, she came too late to enjoy the easy-going family life destroyed by the First World War. Cheerfully, without resentment, she accepted the fact and went to work. I had never known her other than needy, overworked, and victimized by her numerous and needier friends.

There was always enough for an extra mouth for dinner; always a sofa where any down-and-out could doss down in her tiny flat in the rue de Seine. As she was a devout and practising Catholic, she was regarded with superstitious reverence by all who knew her. It was infinitely shocking that such an impeccable person should be behind the bars of Holloway jail.

The moment war was declared, some ten years younger than I, she joined the Red Cross; she was awarded the Croix de Guerre in the Belgian retreat. I had only seen her at long intervals during the 'phoney' war, when she was always exhausted, never giving a thought to herself, thinking only of how she could best serve her unfortunate country.

Needless to say, I was overjoyed when I heard she had arrived in England, although I could not help asking myself by what means. I rushed up to London having burst my bandages, all my pent-up love of France bleeding like a severed artery. We only spent one day together, during which she told me that St. Loup had, of course, been occupied by the Germans, who had wantonly destroyed a great many valuable things, which, had I been in their place, I should have contented myself with looting. What had been conjecture became reality, crueller far. With painful clarity, I saw the mechanical *korrekt* gestures, heard the rapped-out orders: '*le bruit de bottes et de bottes et de bottes*'. I tried to concentrate on the infinitely greater suffering of others, but, for the moment, it wasn't any use. The following day, I left London to spend the week-end with my uncle Edmonstone, who had rented a small house near Guildford. On the Monday morning, I was rung up by my faithful Borenius, who had met Hélène with me, to tell me she was in prison. Together we sped to Holloway, in the middle of an air-raid. We were shown into a terrible little waiting-room, malevolent, scrubbed, reeking of disinfectant, full of people whose anxieties seemed to protrude like horns from their foreheads. Finally, I was fetched by a large square wardress, aggressively scrubbed, she also. (Is cleanliness really akin to godliness, I wonder?) I found myself in a narrow, even bleaker room, confronted by Hélène Terré, flanked by robot-like wardresses. She was in tears. I instinctively stretched out my arms.

"No nearer, please." We were separated by a large scrubbed table.

It was dreadful. All I could do was to keep on asking her if she needed anything.

"A blanket, a book, perhaps," she murmured brokenly, "though one cannot read in the dark. The lights are out when there is an air-raid." And there was an air-raid every day.

"Very well," I slowly and meaningly said. "I will bring you a blanket, books, and one or two things you are accustomed to."

"Time's up!"

The next day I brought, in addition to the books and blankets, a gold pencil with a diamond stuck in its tip. The wardresses goggled. "Is it reel?" one of them gasped.

"Of course. I want Miss Terré to have something which is not purely utilitarian."

"Well, I never!" The look she exchanged with her colleague spoke volumes. There is no doubt, the gold pencil was the first step towards Hélène's social rehabilitation.

Though I went more than once to the Home Office, it was impossible to discover what Hélène was accused of (later we found out that there had been a mistake). Alas for my newly acquired resignation! What had I done to deserve the relative calm of the country, the nights only occasionally disturbed by gun-fire?

I had horrible visions of the searchlights, like probing fingers seen through the bars of Holloway, the locked-in hysterical women, the inflexible blackout. My mother shared my distress and did everything in her power to help.

It was useless. Once a week I went to see Hélène. The brief self-compassion she had accorded herself was already silenced by the pity she felt for others. Weeks turned into months. Hélène knew by now she was not the only innocent suspect; she was without rancour. Such things were bound to happen in wartime. Then one blissful day, the wardresses, wreathed in smiles, told her she was free. She had been completely cleared of all complicity. Nothing was too good for the prison pet. Hélène subsequently became the head of the French A.T.S. After Armistice Day, when her last 'soldier' was about to be repatriated, she gave a party at her Headquarters in London and very characteristically invited the Governor of Holloway Prison and the Inspector of Scotland Yard. They had become friends.

I was by then installed in the Manor House, West Coker. She spent her first free week-end under my roof. My mother who was staying with me at the time behaved with characteristic *espièglerie*. The day after Hélène's arrival, we had been asked to luncheon in one of the stately homes of Dorset.

"May we bring a French friend?" she artlessly inquired over the telephone.

"By all means, but who is she? I mean, where does she come from?"

"From Holloway jail," my mother announced gleefully; then she rang off.

In the early spring of 1941, I had begun to look for a small house in the neighbourhood, not that the happy routine of Coker Court had in any way palled, but I felt I could not indefinitely take advantage of Dorothy's hospitality.

I had not far to look. I found a house in a village not far from East Coker, less like something out of a musical comedy, less self-conscious, more proletarian. Mentioned in that old gossip column, the Doomsday Book, my Manor, a rich apricot in colour, if outwardly satisfying, was inwardly hideous. It was full of sentimental bric-à-brac, doubtful antiques, souvenirs from Madras, Japan, the Commonwealth, etc. (The house belonged to a family, in Canada for the time being.)

Then began the 'peaceful penetration', Dorothy, waving her handkerchief like a Regency buck, offered to replace all fakes by the genuine article. Soon the bewildered Manor was at pains to recognize itself: where there had been tea-shop tables, saucy cushions, Japoniaiseries, there were now Chippendale chairs, Venetian niggers, Chinese lacquer cabinets. Kind friends had lent me pictures—Borenius, a Titian; Kit Sandeman, a Van Dyck.

My first callers were the clergyman and his wife, George and May Nicholson. So far, I had not had many dealings with the clergy. I was open-minded, slightly on the defensive. The defensive was short-lived. George was a good-looking, rather frail-looking man of about fifty. He faintly reminded me of my Uncle Archie with whom, I presently discovered, he had much in common: sensibility, receptiveness, and an unassuaged, perhaps unconscious, craving for the exotic, the unusual.

In his youth, he had fought in the 1914 war, had been one of the most successful snipers of his regiment. He had only discovered his clerical vocation later in life. A repressed sniper, he no longer had any outlet for moments of intolerance. He might have been many things: a traveller, a diplomat, an eighteenth-century abbé. As it was, he was an excellent gardener, a devoted husband, a sensitive and responsive friend.

His wife was Scottish; she had an anxious, somewhat bird-like profile, a soft articulated Highland voice, dignity, appreciation. I rapidly grew very fond of them. They composed the background on which all sorts of themes came to be embroidered. Colonel Batten and George Nicholson, so different in character and build, were the asymmetrical caryatids of my English country life.

Of course, there were other neighbours, pretty animated Mrs. Gould, solicitous, motherly Mrs. Michel, chic, accomplished Claude

Petter. Above all, and in another sphere, was Mrs. Clark, the cook-housekeeper, who marched with the house. I could write volumes about Mrs. Clark, her melancholy, well-bred face, plaintive voice, fervent, though conflicting, ideologies. When I took her over, so to speak, she herself would be the first to admit that she knew nothing about cooking, the former patrons having been of the species who are content with boiled mutton and 'shape', and who consider sauces immoral (the cruellest thing the French ever said about the English was: '*A partir de* 1940, *les Anglais restèrent seuls avec leur cuisine*').

One of the greatest triumphs of my life was the gradual conversion of Mrs. Clark to French cooking. This did not take place in a day. Unaware that she was the perfect medium, Mrs. Clark began, out of the kindness of her heart, to pander to the whims and caprices of the poor homesick lady who could only eat messed-up food. This pandering brought her in, strange to say, a harvest of compliments from all and sundry. Mrs. Clark began to take pride in her work. She pored over cookery books like Faust over his alembics.

The result was electrifying. After six months' tuition, Mrs. Clark, heralded by the most savoury smells from the kitchen, whispered darkly in my ear: "Come and see." I came and saw. She raised the cover of the saucepan gingerly. "*Moorish*," she hissed. In less than a year, she was a *cordon bleu*. No sauce was too complicated, no dish too far-fetched. Boiled mutton forsooth! "What will you have to begin with? *Promiskis* or *bosh*[1]?" she would suggest in the tone of a *blasé gourmet*.

She was aided and abetted by Mrs. Bastin, a 'daily', who also 'marched' with the house, and who resembled a jolly *tricoteuse*. An elderly arbitrary ladies' maid completed the trio. I nick-named them: Bubble Bubble, Toil, and Trouble. Each was potent in her way. Mrs. Clark usually gave notice on Christmas Eve, but oh! what a honeymoon we had the day after!

I loved the slow progress of spring (in no country is it so prolonged), the transition from snowdrop to crocus, from crocus to daffodil.

In the evening, somnolent, supine, I would listen to the wireless. The news from France was like a handful of gravel flung at the window. All my life I have suffered from claustrophobia. Accustomed to

[1] *Kromeskis* or *bortch*.

[166]

loaf about Europe as the fancy took me, England's exquisite, if stuffy, prettiness was no consolation for the geographical promiscuity which had been my lot. Widowed of Europe, I would look angrily out over the country, neat as a patchwork quilt, which tucked me in on every side. If I walked long enough I would reach the sea. *Et puis après?*

"So you're the famous scoundrel, the escapist, the expatriate?"

We are as so many statues, in Youth, insolently, magnificently intact. Then the mutilations begin, here a chip, there a scratch; it is not long before Life emboldened, *encanaillée*, really gets to work. We stagger under the onslaught of unpredictable blows. The statue becomes a maimed thing, debased, crippled, a torso.

Two well-aimed blows at my tottering effigy were the deaths of my cousin, Colin Davidson, and Napier Alington.

Napier was a childhood friend, one of the most seductive beings I have ever encountered. Human laws did not apply, he was a law unto himself, exotic, immune, he could have taken murder in his graceful stride. He was what we dared not be; bourgeois, pedestrian, we would watch, spellbound, his breath-taking exploits.

All the gods and goddesses were on his side, he was the 'Chéri' of Olympus.

The other blow was my cousin, Colin Davidson, a man of great courage and gaiety ('*la gaîté,*' said Mme de Staël, '*est un courage de plus.*').

Physically superb, an Ombrellino cactus had deprived him of an eye. Running out on to the terrace, he had not seen the thing. The scratch became septic, Colin stoically endured agonies and, finally, the eye had to be removed. But if it at first handicapped his activities, the black patch gave him a romantic piratical air which did but add to his charm. It didn't even act as a deterrent when, on the outbreak of war, he insisted on returning to the Army, in spite of being forty-seven and the father of a family. He was posted to an anti-tank regiment. Subsequently promoted, he was sent overseas in command of his regiment, only to fall, alas! leading his men in battle as did his father and brother before him. A curious mixture of gregariousness and mysticism, the Catholic in Colin had triumphed over many a Graham-Greene-like conflict. Marriage was to bring him the stability he lacked. His wife was the wise and delightful Rachel Howard, eldest daughter of the late Duke of Norfolk. She had the intimacy and repose of a Dutch interior, in which everything contributes its quota of contentment: the purring cat; the dewy vegetables; the quiet canal.

Yet this unpretentious girl had been called upon to take the part of the Queen in the Coronation rehearsal. The ceremony lasted five hours. She did not even have the satisfaction of seeing herself crowned in the film made by the B.B.C. with the object of recording any flaw in the ritual. On a less well-balanced nature this episode might have had curious repercussions, but Rachel took it all as a matter of course.

They spent their honeymoon at St. Loup and would doubtless have lived 'happily ever afterwards', had not Colin succumbed to the temptation of the ineffable sacrifice.

As for me, I seemed singularly useless: too old to join any of the services, I could not even drive a car. I was asked to give my blood. I gave it. The sequel was unexpected. I received a letter of thanks from the Ministry of Health stating that my blood came under the O (not O.K.) category.

Alphabetically, my blood was clearly not all that it should be. I should never, I guiltily suspected, have given it at all. Meanwhile my fellow donors mentioned airily that theirs had been placed, of course, in the A class. Mum's the word, I thought to myself. Subsequently prostrate with a bout of influenza, I cautiously questioned the doctor, relying on professional secrecy. "Oh," he grinned, "why, that's marvellous! If you are in the O class, it means you are a universal donor!"

I joined the salvage group, a step the staff thoroughly disapproved of, as I stank to Heaven. After several nauseating mornings (nauseating for all) I thought it politer to desist. Meanwhile, my sister, six years younger than myself, and sixty times more capable, was commandant of an R.A.F. reception station in Portsmouth. Later, she became County Superintendent of St. John's Ambulance Brigade in Hampshire, which post she still holds.

*　　　*　　　*　　　*　　　*

French friends began to arrive, Palewski, General Catroux, Hervé Alphand. Once again, my equanimity was in tatters. They poured down to Somerset where we evoked the happy past. "*Je ne me suis pas consolé, bien que mon coeur s'en soit allé.*"

General Catroux's arrival never failed to cause a small stir on the local platform. Romantically handsome, he would be dressed as a full General (*Général de Corps d'Armée*) with a kind of *brassière* of ribbons. I used to enjoy lunching with him at Claridges, with two magnificent Spahi sentinels guarding the door. He won all hearts with his elegance, tact, unfailing courtesy, in the most trying circumstances. I had known him when he was Resident in Morocco, which is the French equivalent to being Viceroy of India. Since then, he had been Governor of Indo-China; he had not hesitated to sacrifice his career to his patriotism, and was one of the first to place himself at the disposal of General de Gaulle. All Dorothy's latent Gallicism blossomed on coming into contact with these representative and charming Frenchmen; they would leave Coker Court staggering under the weight of souvenirs.

In connivance with Dorothy, I had persuaded my parents to spend several months at Coker Court, which made me very happy. Papa was quite content to potter in the garden, but Mama had the spirit of a pioneer. In a few days the village was at her feet. She had provided spring-mattresses for the crippled, wireless sets for the lonely, ear-trumpets for the deaf, gossip for all and sundry. East and West Coker united in her praises.

Dorothy's lovely garden, founded more on shrubs than on flowers, must have poignantly reminded my mother of her own garden which she would doubtless never see again; envy was foreign to her nature. She was a born hedonist.

The fishmonger's in Yeovil was my spiritual home. It somehow satisfied my wanderlust to see those fish who had travelled so fast and so far, all resigned, acquiescent on the marble slabs. Besides, they were so pretty, the mackerel a Cézanne blue, the lobsters armed like Samurai. Now and again, a great salmon reminded me of Scotland, and of my childhood. Then there was a curious fish, a John Dory, I think, that was the living image of Lord Beaverbrook. No wonder I enjoyed the fish queue.

One day, Lord Berners, who was my guest, was sharing my favourite occupation of fish-gazing. Suddenly he clutched my arm. "Look! It can't be true!"

"What?"

"The sturgeon, as long as a submarine!"

Sure enough, there it lay, streamlined, covered with knobs, which gave it a topically armoured look, on a bed of parsley. I held my breath. A mute interrogation passed between us. We entered the shop. "Good morning, Mr. Bloater, may we look at your sturgeon?"

"Indeed you may, ma'am. Like you, he's a stranger in these parts, fished in Cornwall, if you please."

With questing fingers we prodded it, turned it over.

"It should be there, in that bulge," Gerald muttered.

"Can I 'elp you, ma'am?"

"Well, er, as a matter of fact, we were wondering if there was any —er—roe?"

"Caviare? Why, bless your heart, there's a whole bag of the stuff!" He pressed the sturgeon's side between finger and thumb. It yielded a spurt of caviare.

Gerald and I dared not look at each other. "Can we buy the—er bag?" I questioned with glistening eye.

"Why, certainly. My customers don't take to the fish somehow."

"If you are counting on me to carry that," Gerald rightly guessed, "you are mistaken. It would be in a disgusting state by the time we got home."

"Why not let me send it?" Mr. Bloater kindly suggested. "We are delivering fish in your neighbourhood this afternoon." With soaring hearts, we left the shop.

"Just think," murmured Gerald ecstatically, "of all that lovely caviare for our dinner! Little did I think that the only place where I would ever eat my fill of caviare would be Somerset!"

In the afternoon we went for a walk, to while away the time. We were just turning in at the gate, when we saw what appeared to be an ambulance drawn up at the door. My fears were further confirmed when I saw two men in white overalls carrying what appeared to be a corpse covered with a sheet into the house.

"Oh dear, an accident!" gasped Gerald, turning pale. One of the stretcher bearers seemed vaguely familiar. On seeing me he touched his forelock.

"Mr. Bloater's assistant, Mum. We was passing in your neighbourhood, so we brought the fish." He indicated the long white casualty. "Mr. Bloater couldn't rightly remember which part you chose, and as no one seemed to fancy the fish, he thought you might like to have the whole hanimal."

"How very kind," I faltered, "but where——"

"It can't possibly get into the frigidaire," said Gerald briskly, "short of cutting it into sections——"

"What about the chaise-longue in the hall? Surely that might do?" It looked ungracious to chop up a present.

The sturgeon was accordingly installed and tucked into the chaise-longue. It looked so *grand-guignolesque,* we pushed it into a dark corner of the hall.

The same evening, a posse of local ladies came to tea. One was very shortsighted. "Oh! I beg your pardon," we heard her murmur, as she tripped over the sturgeon's tail on her way out.

Alas for the sequel! Detaching the 'bag' from the sturgeon, proved a laborious, not to say, nauseating, process. Then we discovered that the glutinous mass was quite uneatable. It had, we suspected, to be treated in some way before it could be assimilated. Mr. Bloater had had no previous experience with sturgeons; we rang up Fortnum's, we rang up Jackson's. The caviare expert, in either case, was absent. Meanwhile, the sturgeon was not quite as fresh as it might have been. It had to be eaten. It takes weeks to eat a sturgeon. The caviare went bad. The greedy are always punished.

Can you bear another fishy story?

A girl in the village was getting married. I offered her the Manor House for the reception, as her own home was too small. The only stipulation I made was that I should be allowed to invite some of my own friends, such as Mrs. Heneage, Colonel Batten, Lord and Lady Ilchester, Mr. Bloater and Miss Winkle, his cashier, a young woman with flaming hair, an ingratiating manner, and a wonderful flair for fish.

My parents were staying at Coker Court. We had a lovely day for the wedding. A few bottles of rare champagne had been set aside for the bridal families; I had requested my parents to go out of their way to be nice to Miss Winkle. She was accordingly ensconced between my mother and myself, when my father appeared, brandishing a bottle of champagne. It turned out to be Miss Winkle's favourite drink. "Ah, well!" she said archly, "you can't have enough of a good thing." After her third glass, her head comfortably resting on Papa's shoulder, she announced, wagging a roguish forefinger: "As long as there are any fish in the sea, Mishish Kettle, they will be for Mishish Toofewfish!"

A pretty Keppel of fish, indeed!

The French influx continued. Colonel, now General Billotte, who had escaped both from the Germans and the Russians, compared the methods of his captors. The Russians, he said, were more dangerous—they might easily shoot you in a fit of high spirits—the Germans, more consistently deadly. On the other hand, the day the Russians became our allies, he was given a banquet, a derelict palace and three servants. Jean-Pierre Giraudoux, Marc de Beauvau, and others, flocked to Somerset.

I now belonged to an organization, known as the Fighting French, over which my friend, Lady Crewe, presided. How to do justice to so subtle a personality? A daughter of the great Lord Rosebery, she is the last person in the world of whom it might be said that all her goods are in the shop-window. On the contrary, they are disposed in such a manner that you are not immediately conscious of their presence. You are allowed to discover them little by little; it is like being in rather a dark room full of rare objects: Tact, Sensibility, Intuition, are, as it were, the three shy statues which set the tone. There are the Curtains of Discretion, the Mirror of Lucidity, the magnificent Buhl writing-table of Organization and Achievement. Dotted about, all over the place, are the Bibelots of Imagination, you breathe the pungent Air of Wit. Neither is this Pope-like allegory entirely irrelevant, for Lady Crewe belongs essentially to the great Whig tradition of the eighteenth century. An imaginative realist, she is without pity for certain traits; your only chance is to be yourself; you are not allowed to get away with hypocrisy or prevarication. Sycophancy and pedantry are remorselessly nipped in the bud.

Years ago, when Lady Crewe was lunching at St. Loup, I was boasting to my guests that the artisans who built Chartres Cathedral were also responsible for the village's church. "One can only assume," came a jocose voice from the opposite side of the table, "that they threw off the Cathedral of Chartres in their spare moments!"

Lord and Lady Crewe were among our most popular representatives in Paris. Here was born a love of France, which manifested itself in the most sensitive and practical manner during the years of occupation. The Fighting French were indeed fortunate to have Lady Crewe on their side.

As balm to my bruised susceptibilities, was *le temps retrouvé* of

Raymond Mortimer and Vita. Irreverent as Marsyas, adventurous as Odysseus, Raymond has an Attic aplomb on which unpractised spirits are all too inclined to skid. *"Les dieux existent; c'est le diable,"* Cocteau once wrote. There is a lot of Cocteau in Raymond, a Cocteau more stabilized, less iridescent, perhaps, a Cocteau with a good solid eighteenth-century background, more humane, less narcissistic. Raymond is a frightening person to those who do not know him, and even more frightening to those who do. Twitching with impatience, he listens to your pedestrian story, on the look-out, nevertheless, for anything which could possibly enliven its tempo, anything worth retaining, or reporting. I know no greater reward than Raymond's laugh, when, for once in a way, you have said something not too stupid.

In spite of his intransigence, he is the kindest, most understanding of men, one to whom I would not hesitate to confess any crime—provided it were not a dull one.

Vita played *andante* to Raymond's *scherzo*: as well compare a bouncing mountain torrent to a deep and melodious lake, off the beaten track, quietly beautiful, if inaccessible. Raymond and Vita are among the tallest feathers in my immodest cap: I am worthy of neither.

In the summer of 1941 I visited lovely Sissinghurst for the first time; was amazed to discover in Sissinghurst a contemporary *pendant* to St. Loup. *Chacun sa tour.*

It was only after the collapse of France that I became acquainted with Leslie Hore-Belisha; he was a frequent visitor to me in Somerset. Dynamic, exuberant, he goes to meet life in a hostessy spirit, convinced that he will not be let down. Whenever it does, it is just too bad, There! There! We hasten to re-assure him. We know you did your best. but Life's like that, you can't really count on anything.

A fellow European, I enjoyed 'travelling backwards' in his company. His second country was, as in my case, France. How hard he had tried to galvanize the reactionary French generals, when he was Minister of War; how desperately he had striven to prolong the fatal Maginot Line, but, no, if I may be forgiven the pun, the French lacked iMaginotion.

Experience, however, has not made him cynical, sophistication has not impaired his confidence in himself, or in others. *Il continue à se laisser épater* like the small boy he persists in being at heart (did I omit to say he was lovable?).

Shall I ever forget taking him to luncheon at the Bishop's Palace at Wells? The party consisted of Leslie, 'Chips' Channon, my mother, and our host, the Bishop. Wells has a certain *air de famille* with Bruges. It is beautiful, contemplative, sunk in its lilied past; it has a clerical atmosphere; not the atmosphere of the Cathedral Close, but something slightly foreign, dissonant.

During the war, it was alleged that the Palace was waited upon by domesticated swans, who answered the bell, went to market with a basket in their beaks. (One pictured the advertisement in the 'wanted' column of the local newspaper: 'Swan, reliable, honest, sober, good with children, no followers.' Would Leda, one wondered, have ranked as a follower?)

"And what, Bishop," inquired my mother, striving to breach a lacuna in the conversation, "are your favourite books?"

"Well," replied His Lordship, "my idea of a perfect afternoon is to relax on that sofa with my favourite Trollope."

Leslie was always deeply interested in religion; one of my more unorthodox memories is taking him to the children's service at Faringdon. We arrived too late, the children were pouring out of church. I wandered off to look at some Jacobean tombs. On emerging I saw, to my astonishment, Leslie sitting in the porch surrounded by a couple of dozen village urchins. And no wonder! On each child who could recite the catechism correctly, he bestowed half a crown. Gerald Berners, whose local church it was, assured me that on the following Sunday, children in luxurious cars converged on Faringdon from four counties, all word-perfect.

Another visitor to Somerset, who had quite a lot in common with Leslie, was Jan Masaryk. He, too, was built on broad, sweeping lines, morally, as well as physically. He, too, loved life, women, wit, good fellowship, but where he differed from Leslie was that he had a Bluebeard's Chamber full of the horrors he had seen and suffered, the persecutions, tortures, ultimatums. At times, I would surprise an expression on his face which he would quickly efface. In a flash, I would see him with his coat collar turned up, unshaven, hugging the walls, at bay; a hunted man. His lucid love for his country shone through everything. I have not the slightest doubt that, rather than submit to coercion, he killed himself. Defenestration was but a convenient local alibi.

My nights were as tormented as my mornings were peaceful. In winter, a robin on the window-sill would let fall a few desultory drops of song. An alert smell of frost would make me sit bolt upright in bed, full of curiosity for the day to come. From my window I could see bunches of mistletoe stuck in the trees like flies in a spider's web. The Jacobean fireplace with its involved and pompous scrolls would remind me that I was in a country where it is easier to live in the past than in the present. A morning's shopping in Yeovil would bring me back to the present with a jolt. The posters, queues in front of the butcher's, the fishmonger's, where the course of the war would be treated with jocular optimism, were like a layer of compulsory make-up.

Yeovil, itself, had an unquenchable vitality, a Hogarthian swarming, which was the reverse of depressing. One night it was bombed. The next morning, I went in, as usual, to do my shopping. The main stores had been gutted; in the only vertical part, the usual languid young lady, quite unperturbed, was fluffing up her hair.

Me, idiotically: "What a terrible night you must have had!"

Y.L.: "Pardon?"

I said: "You *have* been badly knocked about!"

"Oh, definitely."

"Anybody killed?"

Y.L., stifling a yawn: "Pardon?"

I persevered: "Anybody killed on the premises?"

Y.L.: "Oh, definitely!"

Le flegme britannique could go no further.

In 1941 I had published a book of reminiscences; from time to time a short story of mine appeared in *Horizon*. I found I could not give my mind to a novel; I could not work regularly; I had lost the rhythm.

In France, I wrote every morning on waking, for two or three hours; as the day progresses, my brain grows woollier. I missed the implacable avidity of my French circle: "*Qu'est ce que vous préparez? C'est pour quand?*"

It was really necessary to keep up to the mark. A writer must write, a conversationalist must dazzle, a beauty must renew herself. In France everything tends to become professional, in England everythings tends to become amateurish. Take even Sport, once a British monopoly: the Latin races now practise it with desperate concentration and a startling degree of success—'relaxation' is a foreign word which is admired *en passant, mais on ne voudrait pas l'avoir chez soi.*

I am always struck by the difference between an English and a French audience, the unanimous guffaws, the facile tears of the Anglo-Saxon, the reserve, the economical smiles of the French. Yet we are supposed to be 'cold', and the French are supposed to be 'demonstrative'! Which drives me to draw the following conclusion: the French have nearly all the attributes we credit ourselves with, and vice-versa. The French are reticent, formal, conventional, fundamentally austere (or, at any rate, abstemious), whereas we are communicative, free and easy, self-indulgent, incurably frivolous.

My English friends would not like me any the less if I gave up writing (for some, it would be, if anything, rather a relief); I was not expected to have read the latest book, seen the latest play.

Now, I am naturally indolent; had I lived all my life in England, not France, it is very doubtful whether I would have published anything; Anglo-Saxon modesty would have seen to that. "Well, you know, I don't want to add to all these literary outpourings which lead nowhere, I prefer to keep my scribblings to myself."

The most popular qualities in England are the most unpopular in France; modesty, discretion, understatement, chaff, or ferocious family fun. It has taken a Nancy Mitford to put this across. Before her advent, jokes about one's family, or, worse still, indiscretions, were not considered in the best of taste. One did not trifle with one's mother, still less with one's grandmother. One wrote depressingly profound studies of family idiosyncrasies, transposed, disguised as novels, but these were never *funny*! The most incomprehensible form of humour to a French mentality would be Cautionary Tales for Children:

> "Godolphin Horne was Nobly Born,
> He held the Human Race in scorn
> And lived with all his sisters where
> His father lived, in Berkeley Square."

In Nancy Mitford's novels, I like to think I recognize all the characters out of Cautionary Tales, grown up. Even genealogies:

> "He married Fifi, only child
> Of Bunyan, first Lord Aberfylde."

[176]

has a topical ring. Fifi, you see, was also a 'Hon.' Fanny and Fifi, two all-British products, have reached France at last: it just shows how much the French have evolved since the war.

Since then, Nancy has had the courage to break with the familiar paraphernalia, the décor, family jokes, even the vocabulary, Fanny fans were entitled to expect. She has, so to speak, 'gone over' to the French of whom she writes with the slightly myopic ardour of the convert. Her last book,[1] founded on a love-affair (with Paris), is indubitably her best. She has looked, she has listened, she has retained. She is the best kind of propaganda; France's wittiest conquest.

Sometimes, however, I cannot help wishing that my compatriots were less excessive, less *entiers*, as the French would say, in their beatitudes: down, down, below the exchange of ideas, below the responsiveness, the flattery, acquired habits, loyalty, colouring, is a strong, an unmistakable streak of fanaticism, virginal, puritanical, dedicated (shades of Florence Nightingale, Hester Stanhope), the pioneer puritanical core which insists on pinning its faith to something deemed infallible. *Fetichised* in spite of itself, the country shrugs fatalistic shoulders. *"Vous l'avez voulu, Georges Dandin!"*

This might easily have happened to me, had France not caught me so young that I was able to take for granted what a more mature Columbus would have dramatized. Things that distress an adult are easily assimilated by a child. One loves the gardener *because*, not in spite of, his wart, the teddybear *because* it only has one ear. One loves without illusion, therefore without limit. And that is how I love France.

To return to Somerset: two of the finest houses in England were but a few miles away. Montacute like a huge glass coach, without any magic, squatted squarely in a French-looking park; it is curious that the conjunction of Lord Curzon and Elinor Glyn, whose abode it was for some time, should have failed to produce a more suggestive atmosphere.

There was another, perhaps less stately, but more endearing, home in the vicinity, Brympton d'Evercy, belonging to a lady who could not have been other than English. Mrs. Clive, muddy, irascible and magnificent, was the owner. The slave of her garden, she digs, hoes, clips, unaided. The loveliest flowers, the rarest shrubs, spring into

[1] *The Blessing.*

being at her bidding. A house half Tudor, half William and Mary, its lofty tranquil rooms suggest a retreat for Bishop Burnet.

A trespassing tripper, greatly daring, once picked a lupin which had strayed beyond the garden's precincts. He was immediately confronted by the enraged châtelaine.

"I thought they were wild!" he stammered.

"*They're* not, *I* am!" came the terrifying rejoinder.

I once took a distinguished Frenchwoman to Brympton. Rather on the principle that all people living in the country are oafs, she exclaimed, recognizing the product of a French eighteenth-century *ébéniste*, "*En France, nous appelons cela une console Régence.*"

"*Nous aussi, Madame!*" rapped the châtelaine of Brympton.

The French, it must be borne in mind, detest the country: it is, at best, a *pis-aller*, where one goes to economize, to placate one's mother-in-law (*Jean-Pierre ferait mieux de s'occuper de ses terres*) or to consult one's *notaire*. The Frenchman settles down there with a sigh of resignation from, say, July the 13th to December the 10th, that is to say, if there is any shooting. His château (if any) is largely filled with members of his own family. Guests are rather the exception than the rule, unless, of course, you have the good fortune to own a house within motoring distance of Paris, where *le week-end* (in its most condensed form) has become almost a social obligation.

An exception, however, must be made in favour of the French who live over five hours from Paris, and who are consequently less discontented, inasmuch as they are not in the position to make constant comparisons. Some large provincial towns, such as Lyons, Bordeaux, Toulouse, are self-sufficing, even gay. The local landowners come only occasionally to Paris to attend, say, the Concours Hippique, or the Grand Prix.

One of the many reasons why French châteaux have never achieved the popularity of their English counterparts is that their owners lived at Court, and could only be torn from Versailles and Fontainebleau when in disgrace. They visited the King, the King seldom returned their visit.

If you happen to be a Franco-Englishwoman, such as I, endless confusion arises over two entirely different conceptions of the week-end. The British arrive firmly on Friday evening, leaving, preferably, by the midday train on Monday. The French, on the other hand, arrive a

shade regretfully in time for dinner Saturday evening; they are inclined to get restive about seven o'clock on Sunday evening. In winter,
the greatest proof of affection you are ever likely to get from a Frenchman is if he consents to spend an integral week-end in the country.
If you can achieve this, you can achieve anything.

I have yet to speak of another valued friendship that I owe to my
five years' sojourn in Somerset. Betty Richards[1] owned a charming
little house just over the Dorset border. It had all the attributes of the
nursery rhyme, chubbiness, cosiness, a certain primness: *parva sed
apta*. Most suitably, Betty collected china, rustic Bow, ornate Chelsea;
the small stylized groups further emphasized the primness of the house;
its desire to act as an object lesson to unruly guests.

Betty herself would follow you about with an ash tray, a duster, a
feather broom. It was nerve-racking. The only incongruous object in
the house was Betty herself. Just under six foot tall, blonde, decorative,
muscular, the *belle* in the china shop.

Nobody was funnier than she, her farce was her fortune. The
possessor of a magnificent, not unpedantic, vocabulary, the tiny
house resounded with the rich roll of her rhetoric, jokes as *cocasse* as
they were penetrating, tumbling over each other in baroque profusion.

"I'm having Violet to lunch to-morrow, just we three," a mutual
friend once telephoned; "there are eggs, and a duck, that should be
sufficient?"

"Surely you realize that Violet is a *one* duck woman?" was Betty's
only comment.

Her husband was killed in his plane over Germany in 1942. Their
little girl took after her father; she had inherited his beautiful, pale,
shut face; she was curiously reserved and dignified for so small a child.

Occasionally, I would be taken to Exeter, where Betty, as a farmer,
had business connections. I loved its boisterous Elizabethan swagger,
shops full of treasures and trash. The part that had been bombed
achieved beauty in record time, tufts of valerian gushed from the
pink ruined walls, the red earth showed like a healthy body through
a torn shirt. It might almost have been one of the purlieus of Pompei.

In the flower market, the golden plumes of mimosa, camellias,
round as a Tudor rose, gave the lie to winter, only a few miles away.

[1] Since writing the above, my two charming friends, Betty Richards and Bill
Batten have had the sense to get married; I am sure life will do its best to accom-
modate this heroic size couple.

CHAPTER NINE

DURING the war, London was international, inspired: it could even boast a kind of reckless gaiety. Let us eat, drink, be merry, for tomorrow we die. Even the journey up from Yeovil was exciting. The early morning train, cold and clammy, with its stale reek of 'Players', would be crowded with young men in every conceivable uniform, with, perhaps, one or two brand-new ribbons which I, always a medal-snob, would try to identify; elderly local ladies, up for the day, scanning their shopping list; haggard, sleepless girls in the Forces, who started conversations which shared dangers rendered quickly intimate. Then the arrival at Waterloo where, more often than not, we would be greeted by the wail of sirens.

I arrived one evening when the doodlebugs were having it all their own way. Always absent-minded, and, on this occasion, panic-stricken into the bargain, I left most of my luggage on the platform, and dashed for shelter.

I was dining that evening with Lady Cunard at the Dorchester. Somebody was sent, in all haste, from the Ritz to try to retrieve my suitcases; the night porter had to lend me his torch; a wretched *chasseur* scoured London for a taxi. When I returned, after midnight, I over-heard the following dialogue between the night porter and his col-league: "Well, we've 'ad V.1., we've 'ad V.2., we've 'eard of V.D., but in my opinion, V.T. is the worst of the lot!"

Emerald Cunard was, in those days, one of the last representatives of a world she had not been born in. Her toughness and gallantry were remarkable in a septuagenarian American, whom nothing compelled to leave America, where she had spent, very unwillingly, the first two years of the war. She lived on one of the higher floors in the Dorchester, where, night after night, impervious alike to bomb or doodlebug, she entertained the most interesting men and women of the hour. There would always be a much-discussed politician, the latest musical dis-covery, a distinguished writer, or a diplomat, a *brochette* of beautiful women. Never was war so snubbed. It played little or no part in the conversation. I could almost hear Emerald say: 'O, but dear, war is so *vulgar!*" True, she was always a brilliant hostess, indeed she was one of the few women in London who had anything approaching a *salon*. Still, entertaining in peace-time is a very different matter.

Now she was handicapped by insomnia, old age, rationing, every kind of restriction. *"On va à ses diners comme au spectacle,"* a grate-ful Frenchman was heard to murmur. For two or three hours, she made it possible to forget the war and its horrors. More often than not, the evening would end in Lord Queensberry or Hore-Belisha reciting one of Shakespeare's sonnets; quotation would be capped by quotation. Then out into the ragged belaboured night, still a little drunk with the fumes of a gracious past.

She mastered her sleepless nights with books, and the telephone. Long Proustian dialogues which began at 1 a.m., and which continued until the other party fell asleep.

Tony Gandarillas was her favourite confidant (also mine). Small, dapper, international, he had the prestige and power of a Figaro— Figaro *ci*! Figaro *là*! He was in the 'wings' of every intrigue, in the prompter's box of every social dilemma. Neither the mighty or the flighty could dispense with his advice. Mischievous, inventive, he would speed from one to the other, bringing a delectable eighteenth-century element into the dullest lives, suggesting screens where there were doors, masks where there were spectacles. No woman in her senses would ever be without him. Neither was I.

You began to look upon Emerald's sitting-room at the Dorchester as one of the last outposts of civilization. You longed to touch Emerald's brittle arm as you touch wood: if *she* can resist, good gracious, what about me?

What did she look like? She was tiny, exquisite, with a sudden imperiousness in nose and chin, '*un canari de proie*', as I once described her. How amusing she was! She had the merciless logic of an Alice in Wonderland. Her assaults were as unexpected as they were audacious: the only thing she feared was boredom, which, in her presence, was impossible.

One of the pretty daughters of the Argentine Ambassador got married. The war was nearing its end. Chips Channon, a mutual friend, escorted us to the reception at the Argentine Embassy. Glancing round the room, he remarked, a trifle sententiously: "Look, Emerald! All these elegant people, the scions of the oldest families in England, these well-groomed men, beautiful, unperturbed women, that is our reward for having won the war!"

There was a dart, a blue flash.

"O, but dear, they can't *all* be Poles!"

If Emerald can be described as '*la cigale*,' another woman, also a *salonnarde*, of outstanding merit, if not brilliance, was Sibyl Colefax. Where Emerald sang, Sibyl toiled. I'm afraid you could hear the wheels go round, but she was, perhaps, equally successful in getting together the people 'who were worth while'. If Emerald was a talker, Sibyl was a listener, sympathetic, retentive, a Martha to Emerald's Mary. Poor, industrious, ailing, she was obliged to give herself twice as much trouble. Accident upon accident failed to daunt her spirit; those precise invitations in that chaotic, Napoleonic handwriting, continued to pursue their quarry. I admired and respected Sibyl, I admired and was dazzled by Emerald.

My mother was very different from both these ladies, she neither appeared to take trouble, nor gave herself trouble. People came, or they didn't come. She had had everything, what more could she aspire to? She was great; they were successful. An amused and benevolent spectator, she dispensed advice and encouragement. When Emerald announced her intention of changing her name from Maud to Emerald, my mother merely remarked: "Oh, but why Emerald, dear? there is nothing *green* about you." They were always the best of friends.

If Emerald pretended not to notice the war, my mother was completely indifferent to danger. One evening at the Ritz, when bombs were raining round the hotel (one fell only a few yards away, in Green Park) an elderly Jewess burst into hysterical tears in the lounge. My mother rose, crossed over to where she was sitting, tapped her lightly on the shoulder. "Madam," she rebuked her, "this is not the Wailing Wall."

Ever since they had left Italy, my parents had had no news of their Villa. Not unnaturally, they imagined that their home had been gutted. They refrained from all speculation, never complaining, never repining, silently offering it up as their sacrifice to the war.

In 1944, the Allies landed at Naples, in August they occupied Rome. A few months later, a sunburnt, travel-stained young man burst into my mother's bedroom at the Ritz, in the early hours of the morning.

He was Major Hamish Erskine, M.C., just arrived from Florence.

"Mrs. Keppel, Mrs. Keppel," he exulted, "I can't wait to tell you that the Villa is safe, everything is intact, even the Chinese pagodas!"

This was altogether too much. My mother disliked being taken by surprise; besides, by then, my parents, by mutual consent, had 'buried' the Villa. It was exactly as though they had decently mourned a relation for years, only to be told now that the relation was alive and kicking.

"Those, my dear Hamish," my mother returned with *hauteur*, "those were the *common pagodas!*"

Hamish and I both subsequently agreed that no term of opprobrium could be more effective; threateningly ambiguous, it gave one furiously to think: "She was nothing but a common pagoda! O you common pagoda, you!"

Of course, as soon as this wonderful piece of news had been properly assimilated, they were overcome with joy. The curtain we had thought drawn for ever, parted: Florence, a terrace overlooking the town, orange and lemon trees in tubs, the air vibrates with a jangle-tangle of bells. . . .

*   *   *   *   *

[183]

The war was drawing to an end. My mother was with me when the wireless announced the liberation of Paris. Andromeda, *la débrouillarde*, had freed herself without the aid of Perseus. We sobbed in unison.

Later, much later, I learnt the truth: the monster had fallen in love with Andromeda, in other words, General von Choltitz had been instructed to mine the capital, and to blow it up when circumstances should dictate. Paris was duly mined, but the order to blow it up was never given. Von Choltitz, an imaginative and impressionable Austrian, deliberately misinterpreted the more and more pressing orders he received from Berlin—anything to gain time. Sometimes, the messages were truncated, sometimes, apparently, they never got through. It could not be long before the conjunction between the Americans and the French was effected.

The night before the Liberation started, Paris was heavily bombed. Choltitz, it is said, was driven to take shelter in an underground *abri* where several of the Resistance Chiefs had assembled. Mutual chivalry forbade them to recognize each other. Von Choltitz might have been the prototype of the German officer in *Le Silence de la Mer*.

Ever since the days of Frederick the Great, the Germans have felt an attraction for France, akin to the one we British experience for Italy: as it were, a biological attraction for a country of a different sex (for Italy is also a feminine country), a different tempo, different orientation. According to this theory, an Entente Cordiale between Britain and Germany is a biological impossibility, like a marriage between pederasts.

Comparable to the rich parvenu who longs for an elegant mistress to advertise his wealth, Germany, fluctuating between threats and cajolery had, for the last two hundred years, paid tribute to the aloof and disdainful Marianne. The books Germany has written about France abound in fulsome praise, in undisguised covetousness: in, for example, Curtius's famous *Essay on France*, Sieburg's *Dieu est-il Français?*

Now and again, a German of mixed stock, with, say, an Austrian mother, or a Polish grandmother, falls irremediably in love with France, which seems to him the incarnation of all he can never hope to be, learned, yet light, elegant yet unpretentious, logical, yet imaginative.

Turning from the Superfluous, the Superlative, the Supernatural, those three distended *rocococottes*, the Teuton marvels to discover the accessible, the everyday, the humdrum, charm of France. A cock, not an eagle, governs the French landscape; washing, rather than flags, flutters in the breeze, the bugle is replaced by a concertina. '*Et dire que la vie est là, simple et tranquille. . . .*'

Poor von Choltitz, how Paris must have worn him down!

One can picture his arrival, as Military Governor. From the word 'go', it must have been demoralizing; instead of in a square impersonal Government dwelling, a Ministère full of red tape, with sentinels guarding it day and night, he was lodged in the Hotel Meurice, just an ordinary hotel, with a curtained coquettish old lift, which contrives to resemble both a gondola and a sedan-chair. It overlooked the intoxicating rue de Rivoli, that most Gallic of all Parisian streets, with its Offenbach lighting and frisky *fanfreluches*.

His family, entourage? Let us assume, as this version is based on wishful, wasteful thinking, that he was married to a Prussian *hochwohlgeboren*, good looking, with pale eyes like aquamarines, hair like Baltic amber, and every inch a Nazi. There is, I like to think, a son and a daughter; the son takes after his mother, the daughter after her father. They adore each other, these two. Mitzi, who is eighteen and vulnerable, has always longed to visit Paris. Together they sight-see, museums are thrown open at unofficial hours, guides mumble their resentful piece.

"Papachen, it is such a bore, why must they always know who we are, can't we go anywhere incognito?"

Papachen sighs. He was a student in Paris. Little did he dream in those far distant days that he would be given power of life and death over the lovely city.

Months, a year, pass. The first seeds of the Resistance are sown. Reports come in of trains derailed, German officers shot at night on their way to their billet. Something must be done.

Hostages! The thing is clear (I suppose): there must be hostages.

Mitzi bursts into her father's study, brandishing a newspaper.

"Papachen! It can't be true! Twenty people shot in one village. But why? *Wie grausam!*"

Papachen shifts uneasily in his chair.

"Discipline, my dear, we must teach them a lesson."

"But so many, in exchange for one? *Ich verstehe nicht. . . .*"

And so it goes on. No longer do they go sight-seeing, no longer do they stroll, carefree, along the quais, father and daughter.

Frau von Choltitz is always urging him to greater repression: "*Aber schwach bish Du.*" "You are not energetic enough!"

Late one night von Choltitz is sitting alone in his study. The day has been a terrible one; there has been a recrudescence of derailments, an important German officer has been stabbed in the Bois de Boulogne, a British aviator has dropped the tricolour flag on the Arc de Triomphe.

He sits there with his head in his hands. A shrill whistling is heard just under the window. Another whistle, more distant, responds. Did he but know it, it is the song of the Liberation, which serves as a password between resistant and resistant.

Poor von Choltitz!

Every month, the sabotage became more extensive, the hostages more numerous, *les occupants* more hated, the Allies more successful.

Then the supreme order was given: blow up Paris. Destroy Paris. Exult in the hideous glory of having destroyed the most beautiful capital in the world. It came too late. Von Scholtitz was in love with Paris: the sacrifice of his career, his prestige, perhaps even his life, was willingly, almost joyously, accepted.

*   *   *   *   *

My birthday is on the 6th of June. On the morning of June 6th, 1944, my old maid burst into my bedroom: "Madam! It's started! They've landed!" At last! Great joy is as annihilating as great pain. Knocked out, inarticulate, beyond tears, beyond speech, I lay flooded, drunk with gratitude that pulsed through my brain like the reverberating chords of a mighty organ. So this was the culmination, this, the reward of 'blood, sweat and tears'! For four years this sorely tried country had never flinched, never faltered, its inner eye filled by the great Design. Not for nothing were the skies scrawled with aeroplanes, the lanes choked with tanks.

France! '*Mes voix ne m'avaient pas trompée.*' God was good. An assortment of disconnected objects suddenly appeared before my eyes, in surrealist juxtaposition, the blue letter boxes of Paris, the undulating Art Nouveau lettering of the Métro stations, the thick blue cups of the P.L.M., the black alpaca sleeves of the *employées des Postes*, the blue blouses of the porters, the little girls with gold rings in their prematurely pierced ears, the concierge's crocheted shawl, her fat sated cat; '*Cordon s.v.p.*'! I heard the clang of the *porte-cochère*, the imprecations and hootings of the taxi chauffeurs, the shuffling of small black larvae carrying other people's dresses in the *maisons de couture*. It was too good to be true. I was back in France.

★   ★   ★   ★   ★

A year was to elapse before I returned there in the flesh; a year of preparation, readjustment.

I now broadcast to France at the B.B.C., I spoke on literary subjects; it was both tricky and stimulating. The charms of Somerset began to pall; I was half gone, feathery poplars were apt to substitute themselves for trees almost opaque; the low 'Tudor' sky gave place to one of Gothic loftiness.

I knew I would miss Somerset, its cosiness, security; my comfortable circle of friends. (What has Paris got that London hasn't got? First a sense of proportion: more go-ahead than London, less up-to-date than New York, architectural harmony, resulting from homogeneity; the stimulus of danger, always latent, the threat of Revolution, of Invasion. It is therefore necessary to keep on your toes, the precariousness of life gives it more pith, there are seventy per cent chances of your being run over in the course of the day, for one thing! You live for *le vierge, le vivace, et le bel aujourd'hui*. Then there is the daily challenge of renewed inspiration, you have only to glance at the shop-windows in order to realize this. Nothing is allowed to remain static. Nothing is definite, or irrevocable. When I was a child, I thought of Paris as a goddess crowned with laurel; London, as an old granny nodding over her teacups.)

I had the privilege of lunching with Palewski the day after he had returned from the landing in Normandy; Anthony Hill sent me a squashed and cherished camembert, Philippe de Rothschild some faded flowers which had been thrown to him in a French village. Hélène Terré, now a V.I.P. (she was head of *les Femmes Voluntaires Françaises*, with two mansions at her disposal, not to mention a car and an aeroplane), was one of the first 'Free French' to enter Paris with her General. From her I received a bottle of scent and a powder puff! "Blissikins," as Nancy Mitford would say.

Madame Massigli, whose husband had just been sent as French

Ambassador to London, came to stay with me in Somerset. Never shall I forget her clothes. I realized I had been clothed, but not dressed, during the last four years. There was simply no connection between her clothes and mine. I might as well be in fancy dress, indeed, I realized that in Paris I would indeed look as though I *were* in fancy dress.

She was practically mobbed by the local ladies. Good-naturedly she allowed them to finger stuffs and gadgets. Now, as then, I look upon her as one of the six best-dressed women in France. In the autumn of '44, Duff Cooper took up his post in Paris. Duff's courage, integrity, erudition, well-known love of France, made him ideally suited to the part. As for Diana, she was the radiant incarnation of all the French had been deprived of during four long years: blondeur, candour, humour, loyalty, hospitality, even a certain Tudor toughness. No wonder the French were subjugated.

Part Four

PARIS RECONQUERED

CHAPTER TEN

AT last I got permission to return to France. I have no hesitation in saying it was the happiest day of my life. The never-to-be-forgotten thrill of taking the boat train from Victoria, that maimed, that amputated station, which for five years had only led to the coast and no further, the knowledge that a French colleague was waiting to take over on the other side of the Channel, the shared emotion of my fellow travellers, these were the things I had unconsciously lived for ever since 1940. All that had been taken away was given back in full measure, pressed down, and running over.

The crossing to Dieppe took six hours instead of the customary four. I treasured every minute of it. When, at long last, the lightly stencilled, undramatic coastline of France appeared, I caught my breath in an agony of gratitude. At last the boat grated against the jetty. The nannie-like stewards, optimistic chintzes in the cabins, officious cups of tea, faded into the background. A raucous rabble swarmed on board, blue-bloused porters hoisted trunks as defenceless as the Sabine torsos; all was vituperation, triumph, injustice.

I was home at last. A high fence of wire netting separated the train from the hoarding. Its purpose was soon explained; it was to prevent half-starved children from importuning the travellers; undaunted, the wretched urchins endeavoured to swarm up it, tearing their hands in the process. With tears in our eyes, I and my fellow travellers pelted them with chocolate, sandwiches, anything we could lay hands on.

It was a long time before the train emitted the prolonged hiss, prelude to departure. The earth on either side of the train was pock-marked with craters of varying size and depth. Elegant, aristocratic Dieppe had been terribly mauled. The landscape I had been starving for, flowed into view, spacious, lofty, curiously abstract. France is essentially a blonde country. Skies, trees, even houses, are faintly, delicately coloured; it has none of the vehemence of Spain, the pictur-esqueness of Italy.

The Gare du Nord with its inky post-office smell was just as I remembered it; only there were no travel posters, as, until quite recently, there had been no travel. A few visibly anxious people, who had no doubt come to meet friends or relatives from whom they had been long parted, hung about the platform. Among them, to my delight, was Hélène Terré. A car had been mercifully sent for me by the British Embassy. Of course, there were no taxis. We drove to my friends', the d'Harcourts', house in the rue de Verneuil, where I was to stay. They were only returning the following day, Hélène informed me, not having received my telegram in time. The only person living in the house at present was the concierge. Sight by sight, sound by sound, the Past was returning; it was really like a reincarnation. My stubborn memory triumphed at every turn of the street. Why do we imagine places have changed because we have left them? The same moon I had known in Somerset, looked indifferently down. 'Too late came, carelessly, Serenity.'

At length, we drew up in the narrow silent street; a few minutes later, the *porte-cochère* clanged. After Hélène had left me, I was too excited to go to bed. Paris, I was back in Paris! I went from table to chair, from chair to console, touching everything to make sure it was real. On the mantelpiece was a clock, which had once belonged to me, and which I assumed François d'Harcourt had hidden from the 'occupants'. I opened the window, looked down on the street, where, not a year ago, Germans had paced. What had it witnessed. what unexplained arrests, what threatened people, holding their breath, had crouched in the *porte-cochères*?

*   *   *   *   *

I was awakened by a tray being dumped on my bed. My breakfast consisted of ersatz coffee, rusks, as dry as dust, a little jam. I was lucky to get it; in those days you only tasted butter if you were sent it from the country, or if you received it in a *colis* from America. Anything would have seemed nectar to me, for was I not back in Paris? Presently, I was brought a small jug of hot water. A hot bath was a thing of the past. As to the *Figaro*, it had been reduced to a single smudgy sheet.

Hélène came to fetch me in a borrowed car. We drove round a miraculously intact Paris, more beautiful even than I remembered it. A great many of the houses were pitted with bullet holes. In the façade of the Ministère de la Marine a few balusters were missing, negligible, almost coquettish damage, like scratches received in a duel.

We decided to lunch at the Ritz. It seemed strange to see nothing but military cars drawn up outside. Inside, the place looked normal enough, save that there were no carpets or curtains. I shocked an old lady, who had never been a friend of mine, by kissing her on both cheeks, because I had known her before the war.

Diana Cooper had asked me to come to the Embassy that evening. A surprise awaited me. She had taken the trouble to collect all the people she knew to have been my friends before the war, and who happened to be in Paris at the time. Bébé Berard, who could not resist making people think they were irresistible, Jacques Février, who is as vital as he is gifted, lovely Daisy de Cabrol, Louise de Vilmorin, who would be left bankrupt if there were a tax on charm, Minou de Montgomery, so Anglophile that I rechristened her Mrs. Minniver! There they waited as the hosts of the departed await the arrival of Charon's boat. The world I came from practically amounted to a previous existence.

It was extremely moving to see Diana presiding over this gathering. There was something mythological about her appearance, she could so easily have burst into flower, or into leaf; her moth-like, myth-like pallor stamped her as a being apart. Only goddesses have the right to be so pale.

As soon as I got back to the rue de Verneuil, I was told my host and hostess had returned from Normandy. I braced myself for a shock. I knew the Germans had put Antoinette in prison. (She was one of the organizers of the dangerous and laborious interzone service, indeed, the first who, in 1940 with Mme de la Nove and Hélène Terré, under cover of the Red Cross, made the necessary contacts between Occupied and Unoccupied France.) But I was unprepared for an entirely different Antoinette, not so much that she looked older, though her lovely sherry-coloured hair had turned grey, but it was as though a different being looked out of the window of her face. Where there had been confidence, credulity, there was now sternness, mistrust; her face had been re-cast in a different substance; it had been of terracotta, it was now of stone; for three dreadful months she had been in solitary confinement, I learned. Her main preoccupation was her two little boys left in Normandy. "Are they alive?" she went on asking her jailors. "O yes, they are alive," came the fiendish reply, "but perhaps it would be better for them if they were dead!"

She had nearly lost her reason.

No wonder her face had turned to stone.

The following day, she took her sons, who, by the way, had never been in German hands, for a holiday, the first for five years, in the South of France.

Francois suggested I should occupy his wife's bedroom, as it was the only one where the telephone functioned properly. I hadn't been in it for five minutes before I realized that something was the matter with the room: what, I couldn't tell, but I wished I had not been moved.

I suppose it was about two o'clock in the morning when I awoke with pounding heart, and straining ear. Of course, there was someone pacing the street below, up and down, up and down, in front of the house. I sprang out of bed, rushed to the balconied window. Not a soul to be seen. Terrified and sweating, I got back into bed, turned on all the lights, waited. Silence. At length I fell asleep, only to awake as abruptly as though a hand had been laid on my shoulder. Up and down, up and down, the steps rang out. Again I rushed to the window, looked down into the deserted street. This time I kept the light on. It seemed hours before I dozed off again. When the concierge brought me my breakfast, I awoke with a shriek.

She looked at me with interest, but without surprise. "What happened in this room?" I demanded point-blank.

"This is the room where Madame la Duchesse was arrested. For weeks beforehand, *un type de la Gestapo* paced up and down outside the window."

★　　　★　　　★　　　★　　　★

The last time I had seen Jean Cocteau was, of course, before the war. He is endowed with the prescience of a medium, the sensitiveness of an insect; indeed, he has much in common with an insect, its lightness, iridescence, fragility. He is winged, he has a sting. Moth-like, he makes straight for every lighted candle. Termite-like, his depredations are secret and devastating. He has the industry of the ant, the long narrow face of the praying mantis.

No wonder I was anxious to note the effect of the war (which I had not yet learnt to refer to as *l'Occupation*) on this extraordinarily elusive person; we lunched at La Mediterranée, his favourite restaurant, Place de l'Odéon. At four o'clock of the afternoon, we were still lunching. "How," I questioned, "did our friends react to the occupation?"

"*Une volière au milieu d'un incendie,*" he flashed.

The Germans, I realized, could have no power over him, he was always a street ahead, a sky higher, flittermouse, how could they follow? Because Cocteau is aerial, people fail to realize he is profound. He cannot forget that Nemesis is on our track, that however much we struggle, we cannot escape the preordained design, the beckoning road, the fatal encounter.

Nobody has made Death seem more enviable. It is always the majestic, redeeming climax. Death by violence, unimpeded by the tiresome formalities of dying. His heroes do not die, they are killed magnificently, appropriately, struck down with the clean finality of lightning. The insignificant are promoted to beauty by an accident.

'*Un grand mystère y devient limpide: ce n'était ni pour sa fortune, ni pour sa force, ni pour son élégance qu'Elizabeth l'avait épousé. Elle l'avait épousé pour sa mort.*'

He knows dangerously much. The intuitions of his childhood have not deserted him, neither have the privileges of that state. To him, the Inanimate is still articulate; he knows that objects possess a personality, good or bad. Jocasta's scarf, Oedipus's brooch, always had designs on the lives of their owners. We are probably intimate with

[195]

the stair which will break our neck, that honest Iago of a lamp that intends to set fire to the house.

The same day that I lunched with Cocteau, I dined with the Charles de Chambruns. This genial couple had played an outstanding part in the life of their country. Charles had gone as French Ambassador from Ankara to Rome, where even the intractable Mussolini had succumbed to his charm. If Charles represented France, his wife represented Paris.

Part *gavroche*, part *grande dame*, if she disconcerted by her impudence, she impressed by her simplicity. The princely shadow of the magnificent Rohans weighed ever so slightly on her sunny, noisy apartment, overlooking the Esplanade des Invalides. The duc de Rohan, leader of the Calvinistic Party under Louis XIII, frowned down on us from his elaborately chiselled frame; le Chevalier de Rohan, Grand Veneur de France, under Louis XIV, debonair, in spite of his towering marble periwig, looked as though he would like to join in the conversation; last, but not least, the superb Cardinal in his watered silk robe, painted against a background of Versailles, shot a glance of ineffable scorn at the full-length portrait of Joachim Murat, King of Naples, my hostess's great-grandfather by her first husband, Lucien Murat.

Marie's own jaunty paintings wound in and out of these solemnities; I never tired of studying her funny unconventional Clouet face; or was it Corneille de Lyon? I visualized her against one of the duck's egg green backgrounds, a ruff round her neck, toying with one of the small sinister jewels of the period. She would have been a friend of the gay Margot; together, they would have made fun of Catherine de Medici's Italian accent, Jeanne d'Albret's provincial economies.

Marie would have got on better with Henry IV than Margot; his rustic improprieties would not have offended one who always delighted to mix with the people; Margot was more fastidious.

Down the vistas of History tripped a hereditary, an ever recurrent Marie, an *enfant terrible*, the pride and tribulation of her family, one who snapped her fingers in the face of Etiquette, but who respected Tradition, one who was haughty with princes, and familiar with inferiors: '*Roi ne puis, prince ne daigne, Rohan suis!*'

She brought her waggish sense of humour to contract and christening, her brave philosophy to sick bed and funeral, but, like Colette, she had a horror of *le morbide*, and was swift to turn the page. (I cannot bear to dwell on her present condition. She had a stroke nearly two years ago, and is now completely paralysed. She can neither move nor speak, though her entourage miserably suspect that her brain is still active.)

They gave me a wonderful welcome. I had been without news of them since 1940: Charles and his brother, the Senator, had refused to recognize the Vichy régime. Charles, pointing to his gay tie, giggled: "During the occupation, I always wore a black one."

If Marie was popular, Charles impressed. He was large, eloquent, aristocratic, and an admirable raconteur. They were a devoted couple these two; *être deux contre la vie*, had always been the *leit-motiv* of her existence. To be his companion, guide, his own familiar friend, was always her purpose and her pretext.

Why, it may be questioned, had I let forty-eight hours elapse before returning to St. Loup? Surely my first impulse should have been to hurl myself into the train for Longueville? As a matter of fact I was waiting for Hélène Terré to motor me there. The train service was detestable, the trains all started at five in the morning and the journey instead of taking just over an hour was apt to take four hours.

On the third day after my return, Hélène came to fetch me. I sat beside her, feeling hushed and small. *A la recherche du temps perdu,* what would I find at the other end? Nothing is more unpleasant than the knowledge that one's home has been occupied by the enemy; what I did not know was that their favourite occupation consisted in dressing-up in my underclothes in which they strutted up and down the dining-room table. A monocled Colonel applauded this ravishing bevy of young homosexuals.

The familiar road, with unfamiliar landmarks, such as a camouflaged battery, a burnt-out tank, came to meet me. A ball of apprehension rose in my throat. At last came the dreaded, longed-for dip in the road; the village of St. Loup, miraculously unchanged, lay scattered like a box of bricks, in the bloomy valley beneath. We drove up through the tangled little wood. With dramatic suddenness the Tower confronted us.

My old couple, who had never left the place, Germans or no Germans, ran to greet me. I could not trust myself to speak. They led me to the dining-room, which had been practically cleared of all its furniture, but which was of a scrubbed and bone-like cleanliness. A bunch of huge scarlet zinnias had annexed the long refectory table, too large to loot. They had prepared some kind of meal. My tears, I am ashamed to say, splashed into the soup.

After it had been cleared away, Gustave, the butler, said: "I hope Madame will have no objection, but we have been sleeping in the Louis XIV bedroom; we moved in there because it was in a better strategical position. Besides, we had hidden many things behind the bed."

I braced myself to ask to see the house. A curious little ritual was enacted on leaving the dining-room. Gustave effaced himself in front of his wife, gracefully waving her out of the room: "*Passez, ma mie.*" "*Je n'en ferai rien.*" Had I heard aright? This was not the language of the twentieth century. Moreover, a married couple of the lower classes invariably 'tutoyer' each other.

The so-called *chambre Louis XIV* owed its appellation to the fact that it boasted a fourposter of the period, some high-backed tapestry chairs, a Buhl writing table. Little had been displaced, but my eyes nearly popped out of my head when I saw on the *table de nuit de Monsieur, La Princesse de Clèves*, and on the *table de nuit de Madame*, a copy of *Les Liaisons Dangereuses*.

Later, the kitchen door remaining ajar, I could not help overhearing the following dialogue:

Gustave: "*Evidemment, elle est un peu commune . . .*"

Marie: "*Mais elle a si bon coeur, il faut la garder . . .*"

They had turned into Louis XIV and Madame de Maintenon.

Before the war, I had been interested in a blind young man in the village, a wicker chair-mender by profession. The day after my arrival I felt an imperious need to know if he was still alive. Down the village street I walked, unable to recall which house he lived in. Suddenly I saw him squatting on the steps of his cottage, his head in his hands. As I approached, he said, without raising his head: "*C'est Madame Trefusis, n'est ce pas? Je vous ai si souvent entendue passer.*"

This might almost constitute a pendant to the authentic and well-known story of the Scottish lady, who, in a recurrent dream, saw always the same mediaeval castle, every feature of which grew to be so familiar that when, one day, in the course of a country walk, she suddenly came face to face with the castle of her dreams, she nearly fainted. It took her several minutes to summon up enough courage to ring the bell. An old and forbidding manservant opened the door. "Please," she faltered, "can you tell me who lives here?"

"No-one, Madame. The house is haunted" (a pause, while he looked her up and down), "but you ought to know that better than anyone, for *you* are the ghost!"

In the course of the day, an ancient man who had once been our gardener asked me if I had seen my *phoenixes*? Before the war, I had owned three pheasants, one golden, one silver, and a third, '*couleur de temps*', like the princess's dress in the fairy tale. When the Germans were seen approaching, the pheasants had been released. They had fled to the woods, where, apparently, they had mated with the local breed. The result of this *mésalliance* was a dazzling creature, all the colours of the rainbow, with a tail like a comet—*les phoenix*, in fact.

To come down to earth again, perhaps it would be of interest if I were to tell you how people lived in French villages, a year after the war was over. Thanks to the Black Market, one section of society was supposed to be glutted; the other starving. Neither is quite true. Though one could buy anything at a price, it was not always available; nor did the people starve in the country. It was more a case of fasts, followed by feasts, as the rationing, at any rate in *my* village, was irregular.

Those who did not own a farm, seldom, if ever, saw butter, or milk, except in Paris. As for the bread, it was disgusting, scarcely eatable, a brittle grey concoction tasting of saw-dust and smelling of mice. The coffee was worse; most repulsive of all was the home-made soap, inchoate yellow lumps which stank to Heaven.

On the other hand, *charcuterie* was not rationed, wine was good, but expensive. I had brought provisions of dried egg and spam from England. I was shocked to see Marie pouring the dried egg down the drain and distributing spam to the hens. People seemed to prefer to go practically without food for days and then have a blow-out.

The Germans had removed, among other things, the village church bell. It was not long before a committee was formed, under the auspices of the Communist *maire*, to replace the bell. Each donor had the right to have his, or her, name inscribed on the rim. The bell rejoiced in the names of Gustave, Henry, Jules, Raymond, Marie-Louise, Violette, Gabrielle.

"And what arrangements, *chère Madame*," inquired the *maire*, "have you made about the *toilette de la cloche*?"

"*Sa toilette?*" I stammered, completely at sea.

"*Son baptême*," he patiently explained. "What dressmaker do you propose to call in? There is Madame Grossac of Provins and Mademoiselle Tirelire of Nangis. Either would be suitable."

I was determined not to betray my ignorance.

"Madame Grossac, I am sure, will do very well, if she is in the habit of dressing—er—bells."

"It is perhaps advisable that you should see both ladies?"

I agreed to this.

It was evident from the start that Madame Grossac and Mademoiselle Tirelire were life-long rivals. They eyed the bell, assessing its possibilities, as though it were a débutante. Madame Grossac was for pink, Mlle Tirelire favoured blue.

"As the bell, '*la cloche*', is feminine, I personally should have thought that pink was indicated, but as you have never had any children, you cannot be expected to know," said Madame Grossac, with a compassion that rankled. But Mlle Tirelire had her answer ready: "I find it so natural," she cooed, with feigned commiseration, "that you should advocate pink, after having put all those charming daughters into the world. It must have been so disappointing to be unable to produce a son!"

"Supposing," I hastened to appease, "that the bell had a pink petticoat *and* a blue one?"

The cloud lifted, claws were sheathed. "Why not, indeed?" both ladies beamed.

So the bell was endowed with 'undies' that would have been the envy of any can-can dancer. After the inauguration ceremony, at which the Bishop of Sens assisted, the bell was undressed like a bride, and hoisted naked, into the belfry.

*   *   *   *   *

Let it not be supposed that my home had escaped unscathed. Most of the remaining furniture was crippled, half my very valuable books had disappeared (Gilone de Chimay had hidden the other half), cherished *bibelots* were missing, German inscriptions were scrawled all over the walls, they had kicked in my Chirico and my Dufy. Curtains and carpets were in rags. Nevertheless the place gave the impression of vitality increased, rather than diminished.

That summer was torrid. Brilliant, almost tropical, butterflies

[200]

palpitated on vampire zinnias, that looked as though they had sucked up all the blood on the earth. Buzzards—before the war, a rarity—hung poised over the parched woods.

St. Loup was revealed in all its latent ferocity.

"*Nouvelles ont couru en France*
Par mains lieux, que j'estoye mort;
Dont avoient peu de desplaisance
Aucuns en ont eu desconfort,
Qui m'ayment de loyal vouloir,
Comme mes bons et vrais amis.
Si fait à toutes gens scavoir
Qu'encore est vive la souris.

Je n'ay eu mal ne grevance,
Dieu mercy, mais suis sain et fort;
Et passe temps en esperance
Que Paix, qui trop longuement dort
S'esveillera et par accort
A tous fera liesse avoir.
Pour ce, de Dieu soient maudis
Ceulx qui sont dolents de veoir
Qu'encore elle est vive la souris.

Jeunesse sur moi a puissance;
Mais Vieillesse fait son esfort
De m'avoir en sa gouvernance,
A present faillira son sort;
Je suis assez loin de son port.
De plourir vueil garder mon hoir
Loué soit Dieu de paradis
Qi m'a donné force et povoir
Qu'encore est vive la souris.

ENVOI
Nul ne porte pour moy le noir,
On vent meillieur marché drap gris;
Or tiengne chascun, pour tout voir,
Qu'encore est vive la souris."

My £75 allowance could not last for ever. I returned to England two months later, proposing to return to France for good as soon as my French account had been stabilized. This took several months.

I spent Christmas of 1945 at the Ritz in London with my parents. I had jaundice at the time; my only distraction was watching my face turn from ochre to citron, from a rich Etruscan to 'old gold'. My mother and I made lovely plans for the future; we were all to return to Italy the following summer; she could visit St. Loup on her way back.

It never occurred to me to look upon my mother as an old lady, or that, perhaps, she would not live very much longer. One of the things I most regret is that I never would go for walks with her, though she would often ask me to, I was the cat that walked by itself, and have had this pathological 'thing' about shopping with others since my childhood. This, and other pieces of selfishness, will not pass my customs; they remain there, unwieldy, incriminating, a lesson to people who refuse to realize that their parents are not eternal.

CHAPTER ELEVEN

THE following March I returned to Paris.

1946 was my last year of unadulterated happiness. France had been restored to me, my parents were alive and well, my former friends had rallied round me; Paris was brilliantly convalescent after a nearly mortal illness; it knew a zest for living comparable to the frenzied festivities of the Directoire.

Parties, defiant, triumphant, based on the Black Market, which began as a virtue, and ended as a vice, vied with each other in culinary daring: *la Haute Couture* threw off the carnival-like exaggerations which it had used to make fun of the Germans; hats subsided, pockets returned to normal, wooden soles lost inches overnight.

The British Embassy was the centre of attraction; an invitation from the Coopers, spelt, of course, social rehabilitation. It must have been difficult for them, at first, to disentangle the *collabos* from the patriots, the former being naturally far the most *empressés*.

[203]

St. Loup, patched and repainted, began to recall its worldly past. Trees were planted, grass, more difficult to grow with me than orchids, sown. The gardener was allowed to indulge to the full in his passion for gravel, a feature which certainly outweighs the importance of flowers in the mind of any right-thinking French gardener; indeed, some appear to regard flowers as vermin! I began to replace the books that were missing; the Germans had stolen a magnificent morocco-bound eighteenth-century edition of *Les Roses de Redouté*, which fetched over a million francs in a recent sale. I did not realize at the time that had I put in a claim, they might have been restored to me. I thought this only applied to pictures, not books. My silver had been hidden in a château in the neighbourhood of Toulouse, by my friends, the d'Harcourts. What condition would it be in, after five years' interment, I wondered?

The journey was most exciting. The full-blooded Southern spring was at the height of its deafening exuberance. I had forgotten the meridional cult of noise (never be content with a klaxon if a siren is obtainable), the shuffle of nocturnal feet, the beautiful cacophony of bells, donkeys, street cries, cutters-out. Toulouse is rich in vitamins, half Spanish, half French, it has neither the opulence of Bordeaux nor the *canaillerie* of Marseilles. It is gay, pink, noisy, young.

The drive to the Château de L—— was a hilarious affair, in a taxi reminiscent of a picador's horse, with a garrulous little chauffeur whose hands were seldom on the steering-wheel.

Madame de L——, Antoinette's aunt, had hidden my silver in the cellars, so that, far from being corroded by the damp, as I had feared, it revealed itself, when unpacked, to be in mint condition. We packed it up again in numerous cardboard boxes, preparatory to taking it back to Paris. The packing was neither aesthetic nor secure. When I boarded the train, the conductor informed me, with a twinkle in his eye, that I was sharing my compartment with a monsieur who was getting in at Cahors. Would it not be possible, I expostulated, for the monsieur to be put with another monsieur? No, all the sleepers were taken, it was out of the question. Besides, he added with a leer, "*Sait-on jamais, ce monsieur sera peut-être charmant?*" I cast an apprehensive look at my bulging boxes. Perhaps le monsieur, not content with being *charmant*, would also be an amateur of old silver?

However, there was nothing to be done about it. The conductor was clearly a passionate reader of *romans feuilletons*, and hoped for the worst. There was no concealing the cardboard boxes, or their contents. A Queen Anne teaspoon was already peeping out of one of them. In despair, I concealed them as best I could.

Then I had a brain-wave. I whisked out my lip-stick, and rubbed it all over my face and hands, lay down, and composed myself for sleep. Some two hours later, the train stopped. The door of my compartment opened, the light was switched on, a stifled shriek, a panic-stricken bang. I was left alone with my silver.

$$\star \qquad \star \qquad \star \qquad \star \qquad \star$$

In August, my mother had planned to go to Aix-les-Bains for a cure, preparatory to returning to Italy. She had not been abroad since the war. I surprised her by meeting her at Dover and escorting her to Paris. It was the last time we were to be in Paris together. The implacable series of 'last times' had started.

She had always loved the French capital, which had taken her to its heart when she was young and lovely. Paris was associated with some of the happiest days in her life. Despite her Britishness, she had many qualities that appealed to the French; was she not witty, wise, gay, logical, practical, urban, elegant?

In any case, her advent in Paris was always the signal for a kind of Keppel festival, with me as a rather breathless lady-in-waiting. On this, her last visit, there were no mondainités, save a luncheon party given for her by the Coopers, and a flying visit to Groussay.[1] The Season was over, most of the Parisians had left the capital, there were, on the other hand, two magnificent exhibitions, one at the Orangerie, of the pictures and furniture which had been looted by the Germans, and the other, at the Musée du Trocadero, of the superb Cluny tapestries, which included the famous *Dame à la Licorne*.

My mother could not tear herself away. She adored beauty, openly preferring the works of man to the chaos of nature—another French trait. She must have been one of the first women of her generation to break with the fashion of plaster cherubbish and scratchy silverware.

Afterwards, we went to sit on a bench in the Tuileries; opposite the

---

[1] Monsieur de Beistegui's château near Paris.

Chevaux de Marly, that prancing prelude to the Arc de Triomphe apotheosis. I was acutely conscious of being in the place I loved most with the person I loved best.

'Time's wingèd chariot hurrying near' was for the moment noiseless. She left for Aix the next day. I was to join her a fortnight later, meanwhile I went to stay with some friends at St. Tropez.

I have always disliked the banal, ostentatious Côte d'Azur; the musical comedy sea, the monotonous and perfect blue of the sky which overwhelms the eye with repose. St. Tropez is less sophisticated; there were two attractive fellow guests; a girl, tall, distinguished, rather shy, with elaborately beautiful manners—she treated me as though I were a centenarian—and her impetuous, freckled, infatuated fiancé, whom I discovered later, rather to my surprise, to have been one of the Maquis leaders; he seemed so young and guileless.

I had not been there for more than twenty-four hours, when my hostess, rather beating about the bush, asked if I would care to visit the villa of a (retired) brothel-keeper. "I thought it might interest you to see their interior; a novelist ought to see everything. . . . Don't you agree?" she prattled. "Besides, they have been decorated for their conduct, during the Occupation; they will be thrilled to meet an Englishwoman, they have always been Anglophile—even before the war."

Accordingly off we set, one scorching afternoon. I was not surprised when the car drew up in front of a villa that looked exactly like a French conception of something on Sunset Boulevard. It boasted wrought-iron gates, a Spanish patio, a Florentine loggia, a 'byzantine' swimming pool. "Their *établissement* was one of the most important in Paris," whispered my hostess snobbishly.

A small bustling man, dressed in beige alpaca with the most elaborately 'tooled' brown and white shoes I have ever seen, rushed to meet us, apologizing for his lack of English. "My wife, she tek lessons, eet 'as always been vairee useful," he assured us. On being told I spoke French he gratefully relapsed into his native tongue. "*Mélanie s'excuse*, she has just had her sea bath, she will be with us in a minute."

We sat on the terrace; a table with an incredible variety of drinks was brought in. It was not long before we were joined by Madame, who looked every inch a—well—what she was. To my utter surprise, the distinguished and aloof Mlle de L—— kissed her hostess on both cheeks, who, with what I couldn't help feeling was professional solicitude, ran her hands up and down the girl's arms. *"Trop maigre, mon petit poulet, va falloir se remplumer!"*

Mlle de L—— beamed. It was clear she regarded Mme Mélanie with the utmost affection. Quite frankly, I was shocked. What were these people thinking of? How could this girl have ever come in contact with such a person, worse still, how could her fiancé look on complacently while his future wife's anatomy was being assessed by this all-too-competent judge? I suddenly recalled my hostess's words. "They were decorated for their conduct during the Occupation." Perhaps this was the key to the mystery?

Meanwhile, I had absentmindedly accepted a drink which proved to be whisky, neat. "No doubt, your English friend would like to visit the *fumoir*, the smoking-room, where we have a fine collection of Pickwick (sic) prints. We know what a great part sport must play in your life, Madame!" she added reverently. Not for worlds would I have disillusioned her. Feeling national prestige was at stake, I followed my hostess into a room which was so dark that it was difficult to distinguish anything, let alone the 'Pickwick' prints.

I vaguely discerned the form of a billiard table, stumbled over a huge leather armchair. "This must remind you of that so-well-known club, le Turf, in London. No? We have had many English cl— friends, who were members of le Turf."

Here Madame's spouse broke in. "It may be English, but it is not gay," he rebuked her. "She has not come here to be reminded of her London club. Mélanie, let us rather show her some of the new bedroom suites; they are really successful."

Looking back, I am sure they were. The suspicion grazed me that in spite of their 'retirement', it was just possible that the bedroom suites, in which mirrors played a prominent part, might, exceptionally, be had *à l'heure ou à la journée.*

I couldn't wait to question my hostess about this and other matters, as soon as we got home. . . .

The occasion arose after dinner. The engaged couple were encouraged to go for a walk—they didn't need much encouragement—I turned to Mme R——. *"Et alors, dites, dites!"*

"Vous voulez tout savoir?"

"Je suis tout ouïe!"

"*Eh bien, voilà!*"

This is the incredible story she unfolded. In 1940, after the Armistice, Jacqueline, who was in Paris, was peremptorily recalled by her parents who had a *château en zone libre*. Her beloved brother, Guy, had been reported missing; once Jacqueline was in the family fastness, she might as well give up hope of ever hearing of him again. She accordingly refused to budge, more especially as she had just made the acquaintance of the boy she was now about to marry. After several ultimatums, the parents gave up. Jacqueline remained in Paris, where she did some vague nursing with my friend Mme R——, who, since the beginning of the war, had worked for the Red Cross. Of course, they were all predestined to become members of La Résistance. "*Nous étions*," said Mme R—— with pardonable pride, "*parmi les membres fondateurs, si j'ose ainsi m'exprimer.*"

Jacqueline's brother contrived to escape from the Germans; he, Gaston, Mme R——, all belonged to the same *réseau*. Jacqueline's own particular line was slipping leaflets into German cars, German post boxes, overcoats, etc. It was a tricky task. In the end she was denounced. Every concierge in the quartier was her friend. Her hiding places were as varied as they were malodorous.

Mme R—— realized with dismay that it was only a question of days before they caught her. Where to hide a girl, so conspicuous for her height and breeding? She sent for an old friend, le comte de Y——, an elderly man of resource and cunning.

"*Laissez-moi le temps de me retourner. Je vous apporterai ma réponse demain.*" The following day, he returned, triumphant, but a shade embarrassed. "*Je crois que j'ai trouvé*, but your first reflex, I warn you, will be one of horror."

"Beggars can't be choosers," muttered Mme R——, or words to that effect.

"*Eh bien, voilà*," he disclosed his scheme, keeping a wary eye on his notoriously peppery old friend. He had been to consult a lady who ran one of the most successful—er—*bordels*, in Paris; he had known her for twenty years. "*C'est une très brave personne.*" Well, this Mme Mélanie was willing to take the risk of harbouring Jacqueline, of passing her off as one of her pensionnaires.

"She wouldn't have to do any 'work'," he quickly added as he saw Mme R——'s hand beginning to twitch, and no one in this world.

German or otherwise, would ever dream of looking for Mlle de L——,
daughter of le Général Comte de L——, in such a place: she would be
perfectly safe for all time.

"What makes you think she would be safe from the clientèle?"
inquired Mme R—— sweetly.

"Er, well, Mélanie would see to that. I mean, she could always
say the girl was ill, or something."

"I see, you haven't gone into that. Neither has it occurred to you
that once the war is over, and le Général Comte de L—— discovers
where we have been hiding his only daughter, why, the tortures
devised by the S.S. would be simply nowhere compared to those he
would think up for us!"

"My dear Simone, I am quite aware there are risks. Of course, if
you had rather the girl were caught and deported, where she would be
for German 'consummation' only, that is your affair."

"I will see the woman. Men are so *niais*. I will make it worth her
while to see that nothing happens to Jacqueline."

And so it came about that Jacqueline entered Mme Mélanie's
select establishment.

She had to be explained to her colleagues.

"*Mes petites*, you must all be kind to my little niece, Anne Marie,
who has had a nervous breakdown, *et qui n'a pas toute sa tête*. Of course,
we hope that in time, she will recover. . . ."

It was easy to see that Jacqueline was not quite as other girls. '*Les
petites*' experienced no difficulty whatever in believing that she had had
a nervous breakdown. She hardly ever uttered, and never entered
into any of their pranks. In fact, socially, she was a flop, and had they
not all been so fond of *la patronne* they would have certainly made her
into a scapegoat.

Life pursued its course. Madame Mélanie hated the 'occupants' in
her heart of hearts, but of course, she couldn't keep them out. One fine
day, a rather overdressed gentleman, who, despite his civilian clothes
and fluent French was quite unmistakably of Teutonic extraction,
entered the establishment. It was obvious that 'pleasure' was not his
main preoccupation. With false nonchalance, he asked to be shown
a few 'specimens' of Madame's taste and discrimination. It was her
prudent custom never to conceal Jacqueline, who would sit, looking
particularly idiotic, either reading or knitting, in a corner, while her

'colleagues' were brought up for inspection. That afternoon, as ill luck would have it, she was not knitting, but reading, significantly enough, Maupassant's *Boule de suif.* The visitor barely glanced at the appetizing morsels proposed by Mme Mélanie.

"*Cette demoiselle,* over there, *tenez,* is much more in my style," he said, nodding in the direction of Jacqueline. Instantly Madame was all commiseration, eyes and shoulders were raised to Heaven in comic protest.

"*Mais vous ne voudriez pas, mon pauvre monsieur, la pauvre Anne Marie* is my niece," she tapped her forehead significantly, "*elle n'a pas toute sa tête, je l'ai recueillie par pitié.*"

"*Peut-être, qu'elle n'a pas toute sa tête,*" conceded the visitor, "but she has arms and legs, and, as far as I can judge, an exceptionally good figure," and he fixed an eye like an X-ray on the unfortunate Jacqueline, who hadn't missed a word of this conversation.

"*Venez ici, ma'moiselle,*" he patted the couch on which he was sitting; Jacqueline had to be told twice.

"She is slow, poor child," confided Madame, contriving a lightning nod to Jacqueline, who clumsily rose and slouched over to where they were sitting. "What is that you are reading, *petite?*"

"That, oh, an old book I found in the *grenier*——"

The man snatched it from her. "Maupassant! Not so slow, it would appear?"

"*Oh, elle fait semblant de lire,*" Madame shrugged, "she cannot really take it in."

The man slid an arm of steel about the girl's thin shoulders. "Well, I have made my choice. This one, and no other!"

"*Mais, mais*"—how to keep the panic out of her voice?—"she is not, not well, poor child. She is undergoing treatment. The doctor comes to give her *piqûres* once a week. Yes, alas! once; *brutalisée,* violated. She was so frightened she has never been the same since. I should not say all this in front of her. See, how she has turned pale, poor pigeon. *Si encore,*" she whispered rapidly in his ear, "*si encore il avait été sain. . . .*"

The man looked his victim up and down. "I wonder . . . I wonder. When is the doctor's next visit due?"

Poor Mélanie lost her head: "Friday, Friday, we are expecting him. Friday at six."

"Very well, I will interview this doctor. Today is Tuesday, Friday at six, I will be here." He rose to go. "But no nonsense, mind. You will rue the day. I could make things very unpleasant for you and *ces demoiselles.*"

"I leave you to imagine," Madame R——— resumed, "what a state they were in."

"My poor husband," Mélanie whimpered. "*Un homme si bien,* there had never been a breath of scandal."

The house was obviously watched. It was impossible to smuggle Jacqueline away. Drugs, artificial fever? They would not last for ever. The poor child was beside herself.

"Rather than submit to that man, I . . ."

The night before the ordeal, she went to Mélanie. "My mind is made up," she sobbed, "I will go through with it, rather than see you all deported. *Pour la France.*"

Melanie was in despair. "*J'ai charge d'âme,*" she moaned. "I love her as though she were my own child. If only we could communicate with Guy or Gaston. . . ."

But it was out of the question.

The hideous day dawned at last. Mélanie put every sedative she could lay hands on in the girl's coffee. There they sat, hand in hand, hour after hour. Five struck at the church nearby. Half past five, six. Their heartbeats became almost audible. Still, no steps were heard on the stairs. Six-thirty, seven. Something must have happened. Hope struggled for expression. Suddenly there came a ring, peremptory, strident. Mélanie rushed to the door. A red-haired urchin, grinning from ear to ear, stood on the landing.

"I was told to give Mlle Jacqueline this." He held a few bedraggled flowers in a piece of filthy paper. There was a letter attached.

The gallant gentleman meant to bring these himself. He has been unavoidably detained. In fact he will never send anyone flowers again.
                                                                          Presto.

Presto was Guy's *sobriquet* in the Resistance. The donor of the flowers had been bumped off in the Bois, by Guy and Gaston.

This was but the first step in the heroic career of Mélanie and her husband. So stimulated were they by this episode of Mlle de L———

that they turned their *établissement* into a wonderfully successful 'school for spies'. The *pensionnaires* were coached in the art of extracting confidences from German clients in their cups, all of which was faithfully transmitted to Resistance headquarters. They knew the German plans almost as soon as they knew them themselves. The place became so popular that the Mélanies, incidentally, made a not inconsiderable fortune.

I was sorry to leave St. Tropez.

* * * * *

Theoretically, one must be attracted by mountains, it is part of an honourable tradition, which included waterfalls, grottoes, lakes and sunsets. Nature for beginners. We all begin on mountains, but some of us grow out of them. Some of us turn to swamps, viaducts, Betjeman churches, bombarded sites, and other abominations. A mountain is always respectable. Especially the Alps, on their Swiss façade. The Italian side is distinctly more rakish. One would never think that the same God had designed them both. The higher the mountain, the more boring. Mountains are terribly like old watch-dogs; comatose, *routiniers*, with an inescapable sense of duty (unfortunately one cannot take them for a run). ·

The mountains of Savoy are tolerable inasmuch as they are not too high, too above themselves, so to speak. Besides, frolicsome woods scamper up them, they do not go in much for haloes, they are human, or better still, dionysiac, like the mountains in Poussin's pictures. The lake of Annecy, though pleasing, is genteel.

When I arrived at Aix-les-Bains, Mama, as usual, was waiting in the hall for me, long before I was due. We were very happy. It was, did I but know it, the last time we were to be alone together.

My mother never tried to influence me; the result was that, in point of fact, she was the only person who did. She took people as she found them, did not attempt to modify or retouch; unlike her daughter, she was not tempted to tamper with people's characters; she made the best of what she found; she did not, as the French say, 'seek for midday at fourteen o'clock'.

One of the things which must have most exasperated her in me was my incurable absentmindedness. To one of her letters, she once added a postscriptum: "Your father, whom you *may* remember, sends his love." That, and my extravagance, acquisitiveness, carried to lengths unjustified by my means. On one occasion she arrived in St. Loup earlier than she was expected. I had intended to hide my more outrageous purchases. On the dining-room table was a magnificent James II Montieth. "Oh, darling," she exclaimed on seeing it, "you *are* lucky! I was never rich enough to buy that!"

Another day, in disgruntled mood, I announced my intention of leaving my reprehensible silver to Dorothy Heneage.

"But what a good idea," she approved with a chuckle. "I intend to leave Dorothy *everything*!"

The cure at Aix, far too strenuous for a woman of my mother's age, proved a mistake; it tired her out, did not even locate the real source of her trouble which was sclerosis of the liver, not rheumatism.

Being unable to secure a sleeper for the same day as my mother, while she went on in advance to Italy with the maid who had been with her for twenty-five years, I remained another week at Aix. The only people I knew in the hotel were the Duke and Duchess of Windsor.

I enjoyed every minute of the laborious journey, half the bridges were down, there were interminable waits at Milan and Bologna. The first thing that struck me after over six years' absence was the ineradicable beauty of the population. They seemed, in spite of privations, as healthy as young animals, lustrous of hair, dazzling of tooth. There wasn't a paunch or a bald patch among them: they appeared to be in mint condition, needing neither repair nor readjustment. Where were the dentures and straggly moustaches of the British working-man; the pear-shaped body of the French *rond-de-cuir*? *O sole mio*, was this all thine own work? Then I recalled their frugality, all the greater (*per forza*) since the war. What propaganda for an almost exclusively vegetarian diet!

Despite the war, despite the blown bridges (a further confirmation of Teutonic bad taste: to have spared the Ponte Vecchio, which might have been designed by Walt Disney and to have destroyed the incomparable Santa Trinità), despite the fantastic cost of living, despite everything, life was good, love was round the corner, the Italian vocation for happiness had the last word.

In the Villa, nothing was lacking, not even the common pagodas.

[213]

It entailed a considerable amount of mental readjustment. Instead of a smoking ruin, a house sophisticated and beautiful beyond belief!

Alas, my mother's return to her home was marred by fatigue and suffering, resultant from an unsuitable and exhausting cure. Her condition, had we but known it, was a kind of warning rehearsal of the illness which was to prove fatal less than a year later.

Italians are not content to be beautiful; charm is also theirs, *gentilezza*, derived from a favourable prejudice. Unlike the French, they *expect* us to be amiable, forthcoming, handsome. We are apt to become so. In Giraudoux's last play, *L'Apollon de Marsac*, a young girl, devoid of social assets, consults a wise old man as to the shortest cut to success. "*C'est simple, mon petit,*" is his reply, "you have only to gaze at a man, or for that matter *anything*, with those great eyes of yours, then with a sigh as though it escaped you unawares, you must exclaim: '*Que vous êtes beau!*' It is infallible," and so it turns out to be. The girl practises with a butterfly; it settles on her shoulder: with a hideous Henry II chandelier: it becomes illuminated. Finally, she tries this technique on her fellow men. They are subjugated.

A fortnight after her arrival, my mother's health began to improve. The punctual sun, the neglected garden, her dear Dindo, all contributed to put her on her feet again. Knowing her recuperative powers, I left much, if not entirely, reassured.

On my return to Paris, I stayed with the Duff Coopers at our Embassy. Every day a dazzled Paris paid tribute to the beauty and verve of my hostess. She slept in the crimson and gold bedroom of Pauline Borghese, her *petit lever* was in the eighteenth-century manner, a pampered pug on her pillow, an admiring and attentive friend at her bedside, waiting to record the first sally of the day.

Diana is an inimitable *raconteuse*: endowed with an excellent visual memory, plus the gift of mimicry, her rendering of a scene, brusque and burlesque, gives one the feeling of a delighted surprise one experiences in looking over the shoulder of a caricaturist. Envy is not one of my shortcomings, yet it was impossible not to envy this woman, who was not only the most beautiful of her generation, but also the funniest.

I have known many ambassadresses, conscientious, inspired, arbitrary, timid, apposite, tactless, protocolaire, freakish—unfortunately my tongue is tied, for what an amusing book I could write.

One of my ancestors, the second Lord Albemarle, to whom Queen Anne stood sponsor in person, was accredited to the Court of Versailles. It is recorded that the then Lady Albemarle seldom, if ever, presided over the Ambassadorial table. Her place was taken by Mademoiselle Chonchon, or Chouchou *de l'Opéra*. *"Cette demoiselle,"* writes Casanova in Volume II of his Memoirs, *"était passée des bras de sa mère à ceux du noble lord à l'age de 13 ans, et sa conduite fut toujours respectable."*

I have always enjoyed autumn, autumn in Paris; the last of the tourists has departed, Paris has escorted him to the door, bowed him out. Quickly, however, the door is shut and bolted. The first wood-fire, resinous and rich, leaps in the chimney. A not yet adult wind mews through the keyhole. With a sigh of pleasure and relief, Paris turns back into the room.

"Enfin seuls," it breathes into my ear, *"enfin seuls!"*

In winter, one is more conscious of the past, forgotten epochs creep nearer, warm themselves at the fire, the wind carries centuries in its mane. In winter, the stained glass windows of Chartres burn with a deeper flame, the great forests which surround Paris seem to draw closer, in summer, opaque as tapestry, in winter, a threadbare curtain, through which we glimpse the russet of startled deer. I love Winter, silent, discreet, black and white as a confidential abbé. 'Winter draws what Summer paints': it has an elegance which Summer, the green prey of the tourist and the holiday-maker, might well envy.

In Paris, it is the season of 'premières', little dinners, literary prizes, reconciliations. The friendships and love affairs, wrecked or disintegrated by the heat of July, have a tendency to resuscitate in December.

"My dear, forgive me, if you remember, that day it was 40 in the shade, really, one was not responsible!"

The winter of 1946 was the first I had spent in Paris after the war. I had elected to spend Christmas in London, and the *Jour de l'An* in Paris, as being, in France, a day of greater rejoicing.

The *réveillon* was to take place in Jean de Gaigneron's ravishing apartment, overlooking the Quai Voltaire. The heating system of Paris was not yet functioning properly, there was little or no coal, we had to rely on stoves which gave out a concentrated breath of oppressive fug, while the outer circle was immune. Like the coachman in

Petrouchka, we paced up and down, beating our forearms with our hands, in order to bring back the circulation. Numerous libations of vodka strengthened the analogy.

At nine the guests began to arrive: Guido Sommi (a beloved Italian friend I had not seen since the war), Palewski, Duff and Diana, Dolly Radziwill and her husband, Nancy Rodd, Jacqueline de Contades. The dinner, at any rate, was excellent, culminating in the traditional *buche*—a kind of imaginative Swiss roll.

When I look back, that evening seemed to be the climax of all our aspirations.

★   ★   ★   ★   ★

In the early spring of '47, I was at last able to return to La Caboussie which in the lives of so many people had represented what Barrès calls '*un lieu significatif pour l'âme*'. It belonged to my friend, Gilone de Chimay, with whom, it may be remembered, I made my escape from Paris in 1940. Born in a Renaissance Palace, of a family so ancient, so illustrious, that under the portrait of one of her ancestresses is the casual mention: '*Aïeule de la Maison d'Autriche*', she lives in a small apricot-coloured Directoire house, like a tiny Doric temple, in the midst of vines and tobacco plants.

For one accustomed to the splendours of Carrouges, for one whose ten times great-uncle designed the Field of the Cloth of Gold, there could be no *juste milieu*: Carrouges, the palace, or La Caboussie, the cottage. Symbolically speaking, for in reality it is more like la Maison Carrée of Nimes, in miniature.

Here with a sapience worthy of Colette (or Candide) she cultivates her garden, she rears her chickens, she devises dishes so delicious, that she should add the three asterisks of the Guide Michelin to her address.

Her life was not always so peaceful. She was one of the heads of the South-Western section of the Resistance during the Occupation. I was regaled with stories of local valour.

One of Gilone's friends was sitting in the kitchen with her son on a winter's evening of 1942. Suddenly there came a knock at the outer door. They exchanged glances. Any knock in 1942 was suspect. After a moment's hesitation she got up and opened it. A very tall, very fair young man stood on the threshold.

[216]

"Good evening," he said pleasantly in English. "I was told you spoke my language?" Madame X was staggered. For the last two years she had only heard English spoken on the wireless, to which she clandestinely listened, and here was this young man, indubitably Anglo-Saxon, speaking the forbidden tongue as if it were the most natural thing in the world. As for her son, he stood as though rooted to the ground. "Y-e-es," she stammered, "but how did you know?"

"We make it our business to know these things. May I sit down? I did not land as gracefully as I could have wished." An amazing, intoxicating possibility caused the woman to catch her breath.

"You, you mean to say, you were *dropped* here?"

He held out a packet of *'gauloises'*.

"Mind if I smoke? Yes, indeed I was, the first swallow, you know. I'm one of a large family."

She caught at his sleeve. It was too good to be true. "Invasion, you mean you are going to invade, to land in great numbers?"

"Not just yet. Ultimately, of course."

It was too much. She burst into tears. "You do not know, you cannot know what it means, what you have just said."

He patted her paternally on the shoulder. "Cheer up! You have got to be patient, and very, very careful. I can see you are going to be useful to us."

"Useful, *moi*!" Galvanized, she sprang to her feet. "How can I be useful. I'll do anything—anything."

He smiled. "When I knocked at your door, I was not at all sure what kind of reception I should get. I needn't have worried."

And so this is how it came about that Mme X became one of the most useful members of the Maquis. The 'clients' she hid on the premises became more and more intrepid, less and less easy to camouflage.

One young Britisher, so British that he looked a music-hall caricature of an *Angliche*, filled her with impotent fury. "Ah, *non*, this is too much! *Vous exagérez*, you mock yourself of me, I might as well dress you in a Union Jack; you might as well sing 'God Save the King' every time you meet a German!"

"I say," cried the boy, slapping his thigh, "that's an idea of genius! All we need is a Union Jack—don't you see? I'm your poor zany nephew"—he tapped his forehead—"who lives under the illusion he's an Englishman, pipe, plus-fours, and all. As a matter of fact, I speak

French like a Frenchman, but it won't be necessary. This appeals to me more than the original programme, and I could make my contacts just the same."

Mother and son contrived some very plausible Union Jack knicker-bockers out of odds and ends, he grew a long '*du Maurier*' moustache. He was a *succès fou* with the Germans, who never tired of offering him drinks; in fact, no really smart party was complete without him.

Sometimes they would be English, sometimes they would be French. One day, she had to hide a French boy at a moment's notice. The Germans, she was warned, were on their way to her house, to make an investigation. There would be an exhaustive search in every room. She pushed the boy into the bathroom. "*Déshabillez-vous*," she commanded, turning on the hot water, "undress as quick as you can, *faites mousser le savon*, the room must be full of steam."

When the Germans arrived she flung open one door after another. They came to the bathroom, here she paused, hand on the door-knob. "A young lady is in there, having a bath. If you must . . ." The Germans thrust past her, could scarcely see for steam. A curly blonde head was, however, clearly discernible.

"Oh, *Verzeihung, gnädiges Fräulein*," muttered the abashed Germans.

At last came the long-awaited message over the wireless, '*la fée a la sourire*' which, being interpreted, meant that the invasion had started.

$$\star \quad \star \quad \star \quad \star \quad \star$$

The South-Western part of France comprising the departments of Dordogne, Corrèze, Tarn, Lot, Aveyron, Arriège has always had a powerful appeal for me. It is a virile, muscular territory, rich in expletives and phosphates. The Gascons, who had for their *chef-lieu* the curse-like syllable of '*Auch*', were no sissies; the symbolical Cyrano is to the Sud-Ouest what Tartarin is to the Sud-Est, but as Spain is nearer than Italy they are more truculent, bigoted, heroic, less amorous, and more superb. (It was disappointing, however, to discover that the famous Cyrano had nothing to do with Bergerac; the little town so richly flavoured with garlic and red peppers, could lay no claim to the famous Cyrano, who, as a matter of fact, was born in the rarefied atmosphere of Bergerac, Seine et Oise.)

Dordogne, Corrèze, Tarn, Lot et Garonne! They sound like musketeers. No wonder they put up such a brave show during the Occupation. No wonder the Germans were always asking to be moved to a more tractable locality.

This little-exploited province abounds in Romanesque churches, truffles, prehistoric murals, seventeenth-century morals, officially extinct, but nevertheless flourishing, fauna. (As no one takes any interest in birds or wild animals they can multiply for ever, happily incognito.)

I would like to say a word in passing about the famous Bête du Gévaudan (pendant to our Loch Ness monster) which devastated the population of La Margaride in the year 1765. It is presumed that in reality it was nothing but an outsize wolf, but personally, I am inclined to believe that it was a small aurochs. Last year I was offered *pâté d'ours* at an inn in Brive la Gaillarde. It was excellent; but so ingrained is the art of good cooking in France, that I am convinced that the prehistoric *pâté de mastodonte* was just as good. I would not care to spend the night in the Cromagnon caves of Les Eyzies or Lascaux. One is never quite certain as to what is extinct, and what isn't. Les Eyzies's frescoes are fascinating enough on account of their *gauche* antiquity, like the drawings of a precocious child, but in the caves of Lascaux you realize with a thrill that you are in the presence of a master, or perhaps several masters. These drawings are extremely beautiful; they worried me at first because they reminded me of something I had seen already. Where could it have been? Of course, the Scythian jewels in Leningrad, streamlined, stylized panthers, stags. The Cromagnons, I was told, mixed manganese with their paints; this corroded the rock's surface giving a slight 'relief' to the drawings, and rendering them indelible.

"*Trop mignons, ces Cromagnons*," I heard a fellow tourist murmur.

Now I was back at La Caboussie, in the little house which had so successfully stood up to the Germans. It was impossible to look less tragic.

One day, my hostess took me to call on an elderly heiress, '*tout à fait un personnage de Balzac*', who kept house for her two old bachelor brothers in a kind of overgrown peasant's house, near Sarlat. The heiress turned out to be a tall commanding woman with a *white* wig, tightly pressed down on coarse black hair. Was this to emphasize her authority, like a barrister's wig, or did she consider white hair more becoming? She received us in the kitchen, where there were two long dresser-tables; one, she informed us, for herself and her brothers, the other for the '*métayers*'. Two forbidding-looking dogs lay *couchant* on either side of the fireplace like the supporters of a coat of arms.

Our hostess conversed in a racy contralto. Would we care to visit the salon, the *chênaie*, the fishpond? Could we begin by the salon, please?

Nearly all the furniture was covered in home-made *gros point*; there was a certain amount of solid Second Empire furniture, and, in front of the fireplace, a large stuffed wolf. Noticing our hypnotized expressions, Mlle Z—— waved at it airily. "You are admiring my wolf? One of my brothers killed it in the *chênaie*, the last of its race, let us hope!"

On closer inspection, the wolf proved to have a distinctly cowed expression; it looked as though it had been hounded from pillar to post. Our gaze instinctively erred from the wolf to our hostess, her predatory black eye, pointed white teeth, bristly black hair, protruding from the white and woolly wig.

"*Le plus loup des deux,*" whispered Gilone, as our hostess ushered us out, "*n'est pas celui qu'on pense!*"

*   *   *   *   *

In France, there is no such thing as 'common' decency, nor can we rely on what we comfortably call 'team-spirit'. Decency exists, but it is a purely fortuitous growth, not by any means a seedling culled from a catalogue. Nothing can be taken for granted. 'Decency' will spring in enthusiastic clusters out of the most unpromising soil; 'team-spirit' will wanton over an arid wilderness.

That is why, after the Liberation, the English couldn't believe their ears when they discovered that in a family where father and mother entertained the Germans with gusto, the son would be one of the most intrepid leaders of the Maquis, and the daughter die of ill-treatment in Ravensbrück.

In France, the sublime and the abject are often seen arm in arm. Not long ago I was staying in a house in the country which caught fire; some neighbours worked all the night with supreme disregard for danger, others, nearer ones, simply did not dream of getting out of their beds.

People do as they feel inclined, not because it is *done*. The same applies to French manners, which are eighteenth-century or non-existent. Any attempt at communal life is bound to be a failure. An officer of the Paris Salvation Army once told me that they had 'down-and-outers' of all types and nationality, but that the French were a minority, because they loathe communal meals, communal bedrooms; communal life, in a word. Their instinct was to wrap up their portion of the communal meal, and go and eat it on a bench in the street. As for communal singing, or games, they could not be persuaded to take part in either. In short, they were non-co-operative; a problem.

It would be an exaggeration to say that club life plays a large part in the life of an average Frenchman. A cross between a boudoir (literally, a place where one goes to sulk) and an alibi, the idea of unmitigated masculinity holds little or no charm for our French friends.

Half the reason for the relative popularity of the Jockey Club is that you may invite your girl friends there. The other half is that it constitutes a *brevet de noblesse* which is equivalent to a *dot* (*Comment! Elle n'a pas voulu de lui! Mais il est du Jockey!*). It is a diverting thought, by the way, that double-barrelled names, so suspect in England, belong almost exclusively to ducal families in France, Talleyrand-Périgord, Clermont-Tonnerre, Audiffret-Pasquier, Lévis-Mirepoix, etc.

Lingering in the dining-room with other men when the ladies have departed is looked upon as a barbarous practice, on a par with smoking during meals, or putting a woman on your left in a car or in a restaurant. An invitation to a 'stag' or 'hen' party is not considered enviable. I once went to a tentative hen-party, the first and last of its kind; the collective thought for the day was: What a waste of a good luncheon.

As for women's clubs, they are simply unthinkable. Women do not enjoy each other's company as much as they appear to do in England; friendship between women is less confidential, more formal; you can go on calling people Madame or *chère amie* for years. Dropping in for meals is a practice which would be strongly discouraged, (*a*) because the Frenchwoman only likes to be seen at her best, (*b*) because it would disorganize the menu. Pot luck, literally *à la fortune du pot*, exists as a formula which no one would be ill-mannered enough to take advantage of. It is all very well for French women of my generation to sigh over their grand-daughters and say how emancipated they have become, but I have never heard of any of them having a flat of her own, or sharing a flat with a friend; they still bob to me as though I were Royalty, and confine themselves strictly to *bals blancs*. How difficult it is for us to understand the French! We were brought up to respect all that they were brought up to make fun of, and vice-versa.

But this digression on *moeurs* and manners has lasted long enough; the topic of Bergerac is by no means exhausted. Apart from the heiress, there were other neighbours no less unexpected: a small and jaunty *officier de carrière* who on being introduced to me stressed the fact that he was a colonel. *"Et s'il n'y avait pas eu cette maudite guerre,"* he added resentfully, *"je serais général!"*

Then there was Titi (short for Ouistiti) de Corbiac, a tiny black ant of a woman, with a talent for whistling which emphasized her affinity with an insect. I was reminded of the singing cricket, brought up in a sable sleeve, which my mother had smuggled out of China.

Titi, as stringy as a stick of vanilla, had the vitality of a gipsy brat, its irreverence, acrobatics. In the grape-black eyes beat a tempo that was not of France; like 'noises off', it disconcerted. "Would you, by chance, have any Spanish blood, Madame?" I dared question.

The irresponsible eyes danced. "Most people have a drop of Spanish blood in these parts," was all I got. Her physique was, however, belied by her house, tidy but jocose. Caricatures of her husband, whose magnificent nose entitled him to be portrayed as Cyrano, English sporting prints, ten-course menu cards, adorned the walls, covered with faded *toile de Jouy*. The hall had a charming local feature; it was paved with smooth round pebbles.

Despite all this, the Spanish note persisted, muted, if you like, but obsessive, like a *zapateado* danced in the next room. When its mistress was not whistling, she was humming; once I asked her the words of her song.

> *"Dame la mano, y danzeremos,*
> *Dame la mano, y mi amaras,*
> *Como una sola flor saremos,*
> *Como una flor, y nada mas.*

[222]

Paris Reconquered

Il mismo verso cantaremos,
El mismo paso baileras
Como una espiga endularemos
Como una espiga, y nada mas.

Te Ilaras Rosa, y yo Esperanza
Pero tu nombre olvideras,
Porque saremos una danza
En la colina, y nada mas."

★   ★   ★   ★   ★

In Provence, one of the most popular sports is cow-baiting. It is a gay parody, a kind of comic opera version of the real thing. Plump and bouncing 'cow-teasers' are to the lean cigar-coloured matadors what the principal boy in the pantomime is to, say, Laurence Olivier. The cow-teasers wear 'berets', roguish boleros, espadrilles. The thing is to snatch a rosette from between the horns of the crafty cow, who, in intuition and strategy, is more of a match than any bull. She is, however, rendered practically harmless by being kept on a long lead, so that whenever the poor thing becomes too exasperated, her head is jerked down and her assailant gracefully culls the rosette from between her horns, to the rapture of the lemonade-drinking, facetious public.

A very different spectacle is to be seen in Camargue, where the local *jeunesse bronzée* wrestles with two-year-old bulls, with a view to branding them. Shades of the Minotaur! Blended and hostile, bestial and godlike, the young strong couple of an equal beauty, an equal resolution, stagger this way and that against a burnt-up background of classical aridity.

This stimulating sight goes hand in hand with the gipsy festival, the sacred and profane rites of *les Saintes Maries de la Mer*, where, once a year, gipsies from all parts of Europe assemble.

Here it was that, 1906 years ago, a boat without sail, without mast, landed on the coast of Camargue. Seventy-two people were on board, who, since, have nearly all been canonized. Every year, on the 24th of May, this landing of seventy-two saints is celebrated with great pomp in the little village which has taken the name of Stes. Maries de la Mer.

Mary Magdalene and her sister Martha, the blind man whose sight

[223]

was restored by Christ, Lazarus, Mary Jacobé, Mary Salome, their little Egyptian maid, Sara, who was to become the gipsies' patron saint, were all crowded into the boat, whose compass, wrote Mistral, was God.

Their luggage consisted mainly of relics, the decapitated heads of three saints including that of St. John the Baptist, and the Holy Grail. They had come all the way from Jerusalem. Identified as the disciples of Christ, the Jews had condemned them to die of hunger in the open sea, having stripped the boat of sails, mast, rudder.

But they did not perish. Protected by the Almighty, after weeks of drifting solitude, they came in sight of a coast where fishermen were casting their nets, which the strange apparition of a rudderless boat caused them to forsake. Safe at last! But the rapacious fishermen claimed a payment for their help and the future saints were destitute. Sara, the Egyptian, was a girl of resource; standing well in evidence at the prow of the boat, she proceeded to undress, exposing her beautiful body to the dazzled Provençaux, who, relates the legend, considered this ample reward for their exertions.

As soon as they landed, the Christians built an altar near by; a miraculous spring gushed from the droughty earth. On this site was built the church of les Saintes Maries, which exists to this day.

It was not long before the Camarguais deserted their pagan temples dedicated to the cult of Mithra, and drenched with the blood of bulls, for the gentler doctrines of Christ. The saints became dispersed. Trophime dedicated himself to the Arlésiens whose first Bishop he became. Lazarus, Mary Magdalene and Maxim set sail for Marseilles; the only ones who remained in Camargue were Mary Jacobé (the Virgin Mary's sister), Mary Salome, and Sara. Martha, more adventurous, set out alone to explore the Rhône valley, presently she came to a little town which was terrorized by a monster which was locally known as 'La Tarasque'. In order to appease it, the inhabitants had rechristened their town Tarascon. This tribute, however, failed to touch the heartless (if unsnobbish) monster, who, undeterred, went on devouring the inhabitants. Surprised by Martha in the middle of one of these solitary 'snacks', it cowered in terror at the sight of the cross which she produced from the folds of her dress. She had not the slightest difficulty in slipping her girdle round the monster's neck, which, now mild as a lap-dog, allowed itself to be led into Tarascon where it was promptly put to death by the jubilant population.

This was but the first step to the conversion of Tarascon, where, at length, the Saint peacefully died.

After a long and exemplary life in Camargue, Mary Jacobé and Mary Salome, conscious that the hour of death was approaching, had themselves carried to the seashore, where they died the same day, one at dawn, the other at dusk.

Sara was not long to survive them. Buried in the holy oratory, her tomb has become the rallying point for the unstable tribes, who, for reasons best known to themselves, have selected her for their patron saint.

*   *   *   *   *

It is always interesting to compare the Italian primitives with their French contemporaries. More intimate, less spiritual, French masters envisage the Holy Virgin more as a *confidante d'élite*, neighbourly, compassionate, infinitely accessible, than the ineffable Mother of God. I own a little statuette of the fifteenth-century French Madonna. There is nothing we could not tell her, or that she would not understand. Attentive, a trifle anxious, she inclines her round and charming head towards you, to make it easier. *Allons, mon enfant! Un peu de courage!*

This parochial, slightly rustic, conception of the Holy Virgin, is even more emphasized in the Midi, where she is credited with every human virtue, rather to the detriment of aloof celestial ones.

When the Curé of Sembras (Dordogne) came to the conclusion that the Holy Sacrament was bored with the routine of death-beds, prayers, complaints and supplications, he set out to organize picnics, processions, 'surprise parties' (*sic*), as a welcome diversion. The Divine Sacrament was to be met with, carried by the Curé, protected from the sun by its dais, and surrounded by scampering choir-boys who substituted fireworks for 'O Salutaris'.

Protestants are often shocked by the *laisser aller* of Roman Catholic churches, but I am never quite convinced that God does not prefer to be treated like a club, intimately associated with the life of each member.

CHAPTER TWELVE

RELIGION, for many years, had played a ubiquitous, if curtained, part in my mother's life. She had, if I may so explain myself, succeeded in establishing a kind of clandestine intimacy with God, undertaking nothing without asking herself if it would be agreeable to Him, incognito, performing acts of charity no one guessed, carrying comfort to people whose names were never disclosed. Now and again, I would stumble on some piece of unselfishness humbly camouflaged as indifference, as disinclination. (But I really did not need it, darling. What can one do with two fur coats? I could only get two seats for the play. I'm sure Papa would rather take one of his friends.)

Few people realized her humility, her extraordinary readiness to say she was sorry, even if she was in the right. When she lost her home and her possessions, as she thought for ever, she scarcely ever mentioned them, secretly convinced that it was a just punishment for having cared too much for earthly treasure, which moths corrupt, and thieves break in and steal.

My mother's unselfishness to those she loved knew no bounds. When I became a widow, I know she longed for me to make my home with her. But no. My singular preference for a foreign country came first. To France, she said, effacing herself, "*Après vous, Madame.*" It was all the more meritorious, as she herself did not understand this obsessive love of France. Apart from her love for her own country, she was, like most English people, more drawn towards Italy.

She was responsible for my education, which, though it roughly conformed to the standards of those days, encouraged and sustained any vestige of talent, however slight. If I speak four languages fairly fluently it is thanks to my mother; if I know anything about pictures, furniture, *bibelots*, it is again thanks to her. If I enjoy travel, conversation, good company—but there is no limit to my debt.

Years ago, she was introduced to the sociable, saintly Abbé Mugnier, confessor of *chanoinesse* and courtesan, a man who was as profound as he was effervescent. He glanced from my mother to me. "*La source,*" he murmured, taking both her hands in both of his, "*la source!*"

In 1946, her wonderful health began to fail, sending out small signals of distress which the doctors chose to misinterpret, sending her to Aix-les-Bains, when she should have been sent to Vichy. There came a day when it was no longer possible to 'snub' the encroaching illness. She was about to return to Italy, she divined that this was the beginning of the end, that this time she would not recover. In all her life, she had never missed an appointment; let anyone down.

Uncle Archie and I were to join her in Florence, my father was longing to return to his Memoirs and his documentation. She accordingly forced her aching body, her poor swollen legs, to take the train, to mount the boat. She knew she would never see her beloved country again.

Meanwhile, entirely ignorant of all this, her letters merely referred to a passing *malaise*—I was staying with an Italian friend, on approval. He thought I might conceivably suit him as a wife. Guido owned a magnificent castle near Cremona. We had agreed to give it a trial. It was understood that we should live *en tête-à-tête* for a fortnight: no breath of the outside world was to be allowed to impinge on our intimacy.

We had much in common: a far-fetched, sometimes ferocious, sense of humour; a paradoxical, rococo imagination; an immediate response to beauty in any form. In fun, we would call one another Klingsor and Kundry. He had a fanatical love for his home, I for mine. True, he was no modern character. "You remind me of that sanguinary, superb, pious, depraved, lyrical *condottiere*, Sigismondo Malatesta," I would tease him.

"*Il y a un fond de vrai*," he would smilingly agree. Of mixed blood, his mother had been a Troubetskoi, he had, coupled with a dilettante Renaissance temperament, just that soupçon of Slav perversity I had grown to dread in anyone who interested me. Perhaps one of the most attractive things about him was his imaginative, constructive courage, the courage of a poet and a patron.

The Germans had occupied his home during the war. Unbeknownst to anyone, Guido had contrived to put himself at the head of the local partisans.

In his castle was a theatre, in which for two hundred years the châtelain of T—— had entertained himself and his friends with what is known as private theatricals. Guido was no exception to the rule. Many were the playlets he composed himself and acted in for the delectation of his guests. What resource, what camouflage!

The theatre was accordingly revived, the properties got out and dusted. Once a month the unsuspecting Germans clapped themselves silly over a 'sketch' in the course of which Guido had conveyed to his fellow players (partisans all) the design, in code, for future activities. Of course, he was denounced in the end. A friendly doctor hid him in a lunatic asylum for six months. It was not long before he found himself in a Pirandellian maze. Was he mad, or were the lunatics sane? Everything was open to doubt; the truth, like Janus, had two faces.

The war came to an end just in time. No one so impressionable, so vulnerable, as he could have withstood such a prolonged mental juxtaposition. As it was, he had a nervous breakdown which lasted months.

Ever since, he had been on honeymoon terms with his beautiful melodramatic house, which he treated as a mannequin, draping it to suit his moods, a pin here, a pin there. Castle Trilby.

I was full of admiration, and, yes, fear. The place frightened me. It was ostentatiously possessed, like a bride. How could it fail to be jealous of its owner? Clearly, it would never consent to be shared with anyone.

I am aware that this sounds nonsense, but I really have antennae about places. I get their meaning, they tell me their secrets. I was at T—— under sufferance. It couldn't wait to be rid of me. At night, I would be startled out of my sleep by whisperings in my bedroom; in the daytime, whenever I entered the room alone, it was like interrupting a conversation.

I could not, of course, bring myself to tell Guido this. In his house, I would never be anything but the foreigner, *la straniera*. Whenever he said: "This will be your sitting-room, this your writing-table," the house winced—visibly. I realized I would never dare displace an ashtray, let alone move a piece of furniture.

Would my St. Loup have the same reactions to him? Conceivably, but here Guido cut into my speculation. "Of course, *cara*, we will spend six months of the year here."

"I would never be allowed to," I muttered.

"Allowed? By whom?"

"I was joking," I hedged. "Couldn't we go to Mantua this afternoon?"

His mobile face darkened. "So soon bored? I thought we wanted to be together!"

"But we would be together, even in Mantua."

"I wanted to show you the top floor. We can go to Mantua any time!"

Mantua cropped up again; when it wasn't Mantua, it was Cremona. "I never knew you had such a passion for sight-seeing. You have the fidgets, my dear."

A new note, suspicious, susceptible, crept into our relationship. As I was devoted to him, it became more and more difficult to explain. "You are no longer happy here," he complained. "What has come between us?"

"Your house," I dared reply at last. He looked bewildered, spread out impotent, Gilles-like hands.

"But I thought you loved my home."

"I do, but it doesn't love me."

"How can you talk such nonsense! Why, you are made for one another."

"That's what *you* think, but, I assure you, it resents my being here. I could never relax, feel at home."

It was as though lightning flickered across his face. "If it's like that, there is, of course, no more to be said. You must please yourself—after all, this is but an experiment."

"Oh please"—I realized how deeply I had hurt him—"Oh please try to understand, your house has always had you to itself, naturally it resents the presence of a stranger—a foreigner, at that."

"My dear, why not admit you are bored here? You are always wanting to 'go places'. *Tu ne tiens pas en place.* I might have guessed! You are too *mondaine* for me. Well, we can forget about this unsuccessful test!"

The last days of my stay were overcast and troubled, precariously posed between the past and the future. The hulk of the love that had sunk lay at the bottom of the harbour and wrecked the resumed traffic of our friendship. "You are monopolized by France," was the refrain, "Italy would never have been anything but a *pis-aller.*" I thought it would perhaps be better if we did not meet for a few months, in order to give our friendship time to recover. I was by then in a fever to get to Florence, as in her last letter my mother had hinted that she was far from well. Her legs, she said, were swollen, her back ached terribly. I felt she was keeping something from me.

I was due to arrive in Florence the day after my parents. I took the swaying, stifling *rapido* from Milan. When I arrived at the station I was met by my father's Italian servant. In response to my anxious inquiries, he said my mother was *poco bene* which may mean anything in Italian from a cold to double pneumonia.

When I reached the Villa, my father was waiting for me in the hall. His eyes were full of tears. "She is very ill," he said, "the specialist will be here at any moment." Something comparable to a landslide took place in me. Things just toppled over and collapsed without a sound. Where there had been plans and perspectives, monuments and temples and terraces, there was nothing now but an aching void, full of surprise.

I was not allowed to see her that day. The following morning, long before I was really awake, I was conscious of an odious presence in my room, in my brain. It had come to stay.

The specialist had diagnosed sclerosis of the liver. It had been coming on for a long time and now it seemed unlikely she would recover. She might live for weeks, for months. "Is she in pain?" I questioned with anguish.

"Not for the present. The pain will come later."

O God, I had always prayed, fell me with one blow of Your axe.

The terrible routine of illness set in. As the spring waxed, she waned. Day after day, she lay patiently waiting to be read to, or told small stories about the day's happenings. The contrast between the spring and her hushed room was almost unbearable. Whenever we came into her room she contrived a smile, sometimes a joke. She missed England, her friends; the beauty of her surroundings did not atone for the smoky cosiness of her beloved London. "Look, darling, at the view from your window," I would try to comfort. "Surely you love nature?"

"Yes, the nature of the Ritz," she managed to tease. The state of tension in which I lived, was conducive to many things, including boils. An enormous one appeared on my nose. "Look," Mama pointed to it, "Pierpont Morgan without the money!"

My poor father, who had a weak heart, was never off the stairs. Rejuvenated by his selfless devotion, he was more like a desolate fiancé than an aged husband.

As when a tree is condemned to be cut down, the branches are lopped off first. The mainstays of her magnificent health were amputated one by one. She had no illusions, her nurses told me. And no fear. Her only preoccupation was that those she loved should realize she was dying.

A month before the end, her face from which all lines, all swelling had mysteriously disappeared, acquired a serenity which impressed all those who saw her. She will even make a success of her death, was my involuntary thought. The words of the psalmist seemed supremely apt: 'But ye shall die like men, and fall like one of the princes.'

On the day that was to be her last, in the afternoon, the young gardener next door sang a desultory love song full of frustrated passion. My mother was asked if he should be told to stop. She shook her head. The love song accompanied her almost to the end. All day she had neither eaten nor drunk. "Is there nothing you want?" I bent over her despairingly.

"You," came the whisper, "You."

Yet, I wasn't with her when she died. It was all over in a minute.

When I came in, her head, with its blunt white curls, was buried like a child's in her pillow. 'For so He giveth His beloved sleep.'

*   *   *   *   *

Two months later, my father died also. He did not wish to survive her. Always the most courteous of men, it was as though he were loth to keep her waiting.

Puzzled and homeless, he was like a man in a foreign town without an interpreter. It would have been uncharitable to wish to prolong his life. He went willingly to a secret assignation.

Realization comes slowly with me. Despair, a persevering pianist, began to decipher the tune that was most likely to drive me insane. At first there were pauses, wrong notes, then it came, pat, never to cease again.

Even now, after more than three years, it continues, muted, *piano, piano*, just loud enough for me to hear when I am alone. *Je dis ton nom tout doucement, comme on souffle une chandelle. Nul ne m'entend!* In losing my mother, I lost everything. She was my youth, I was her old age.

What has happened to me since is but a postscriptum. It really doesn't count. Any little success I may have had is dedicated to her. Success is a cul-de-sac, it leads to no lasting satisfaction, it is the smart substitute for happiness.

I can do what I like, go where I wish, there is no one to say me nay. I have what is called 'every facility', all the visas. Trespassers will *not* be prosecuted. Fatuous perspectives open up on every side, every house is for sale.

Assent means absence. (Ascent also means absence.) The unwanted licence of loneliness. Oh, to be hemmed in by frowning family obstacles!

Let us assume that at fifty, old age is still in its infancy; it takes several years to get into its stride, so to speak. With many a sigh and a backward glance, we move on; whether we are willing or not, like diplomats, we are inexorably shifted.

Our new home, hum! A smaller house, not much view. A smaller garden. We should concentrate on the garden, on herbs, perhaps, rather than flowers? Flowers are fleshy, herbs are ascetic, more in keeping. We must learn to be humble, a trifle bent, remembering that we shall be asked for advice, not kisses.

By craning a little, I can see into the sixties.

They are of different kinds; sleek, fat sixties, rich and blue of hair, hostessy, successful; secretly obscene sixties, still lusting after the fresh young girl, shy young student; less successful sixties, hiding their revelatory passports like a crime, not rich enough to allow their hair to go undyed. "Nobody will engage a grey-haired woman nowadays." Haggard, hunted sixties, terrified of missing something, rubbing themselves superstitiously against the topical, the fashionable, men and women of the day, and here and there, in this sad crowd, the sensible sixties, the paunchy, but philosophical sixties, rich in experience and indulgence, unobtrusively cultivating their allotment.

Of these I hope to be, though, indeed, old age has to be exceptional (as in my parents' case) to be palatable.

Extreme old age is as lonely as God. It has no one to talk to. Remains the ultimate snobbishness: to become a centenarian. First you must reach sixty; long before then, most of your friends will have died like flies. The seventies are tricky; Death has not yet learnt to lay off the Grand Old Man, Grand Old Woman. Once you have reached eighty, you can relax; the worst is over. A new form of snobbishness sets in, to make ourselves out to be older than we really are. At a hundred, we can still say, wagging a roguish forefinger at the other centenarian: "As a matter of fact, I'm getting on for 102!"

Survival is the ultimate satisfaction. The only excuse for the old, who are no longer beautiful, is that they can still create beauty, bestow happiness. "*Chaque année devrait apporter un soin de plus, un défaut de moins,*" as my old friend Marie de Chambrun was wont to say. Time and Truth are friends, though they have known many a set-back.

All my life I have suffered from lack of sleep. Sometimes, when travelling, in an anonymous strange hotel, sleep visits all impartially, and I get included by mistake. Sometimes; not often. I try to persuade myself that chronic insomnia gives me a kind of advantage over other people, as though it were an exemption, privilege. The hunchback, no doubt, succeeds in convincing himself that it is *chic* to be different. Technically, it means leading a double life, only the night life demands more careful organization. No subversive reading, certain thoughts are taboo; pressed down by paper-weights. Above all, do not give the impression that sleep is your object, a casual whistling is recommended to those who do not object to shocking the night.

The hours limp by. . . . The clock strikes two. . . . You are on the *qui-vive* for the first incoherence. Round about three, you salute an authentic yawn with rapture. . . . Your thoughts become a trifle slovenly, not as spruce as they were. . . . Then gradually, consciously, blissfully, you feel you are being relieved of your hump. No, it is *not chic* to be different.

God knows I have much to be thankful for, yet I hope I do not cling inordinately to life. I have sojourned, never resided. Doubtless, my lease is nearly up?

'She withdrew', would, I think, be a graceful epitaph.

INDEX

Index